Citizenship

OXFORD STUDIES IN MIGRATION AND CITIZENSHIP SERIES

Migration and Citizenship Politics, edited by
Justin Gest, George Mason University
Sara Wallace Goodman, University of California, Irvine
Willem Maas, York University

Citizenship

The Third Revolution

DAVID JACOBSON AND MANLIO CINALLI

OXFORD
UNIVERSITY PRESS

Oxford University Press is a department of the University of Oxford. It furthers
the University's objective of excellence in research, scholarship, and education
by publishing worldwide. Oxford is a registered trade mark of Oxford University
Press in the UK and certain other countries.

Published in the United States of America by Oxford University Press
198 Madison Avenue, New York, NY 10016, United States of America.

© Oxford University Press 2023

All rights reserved. No part of this publication may be reproduced, stored in
a retrieval system, or transmitted, in any form or by any means, without the
prior permission in writing of Oxford University Press, or as expressly permitted
by law, by license, or under terms agreed with the appropriate reproduction
rights organization. Inquiries concerning reproduction outside the scope of the
above should be sent to the Rights Department, Oxford University Press, at the
address above.

You must not circulate this work in any other form
and you must impose this same condition on any acquirer.

Library of Congress Cataloging-in-Publication Data
Names: Jacobson, David, 1959– author | Cinalli, Manlio, author.
Title: Citizenship : the third revolution / David Jacobson, Manlio Cinalli.
Other titles: 3rd revolution
Description: New York : Oxford University Press, [2023] |
Includes bibliographical references.
Identifiers: LCCN 2023017831 (print) | LCCN 2023017832 (ebook) |
ISBN 9780197669150 (hardback) | ISBN 9780197669174 (epub)
Subjects: LCSH: Citizenship.
Classification: LCC JF801 .C4817 2023 (print) | LCC JF801 (ebook) |
DDC 323.6—dc23/eng/20230603
LC record available at https://lccn.loc.gov/2023017831
LC ebook record available at https://lccn.loc.gov/2023017832

DOI: 10.1093/oso/9780197669150.001.0001

Printed by Integrated Books International, United States of America

To Jamie Goodwin-White
From David Jacobson

and

A Luigi
From Manlio Cinalli

Contents

Acknowledgments	ix

1. Introduction: Who Rules? Who Belongs? Two Questions,
Three Revolutions, Six Propositions ... 1
   The Paradox ... 1
   Two Questions ... 3
   Three Revolutions ... 4
   Six Propositions ... 6

2. The First Revolution: The Ancient and Classical Periods ... 24
   Roots of Citizenship ... 25
   From Kinship to Citizenship: The Ancient Near East, Greece,
   and Rome ... 26
   Greeks and Romans ... 34

3. The Second Revolution: The Medieval Roots of
Modern Citizenship ... 41
   Civic Developments after the First Millennium ... 45
   The European Guilds ... 48
   Republics and Guilds: Florence and Venice ... 50
   Rome and Greece's Influence on Italian Cities ... 52
   The Guild and the Civic Habit ... 55
   The Chinese Guilds ... 56
   The Promise, and the Cautionary Tale, of Medieval and
   Early Modern Guilds ... 61

4. Practices of Citizenship: From the Enlightenment to
the Nation-State ... 64
   The Enlightenment's Conservative Revolution:
   "The Laws of Nature and of Nature's God" ... 66
   "Constitutional Patriotism" or Nationalism? ... 71
   Privileging Membership ... 73
   France's Republicanism ... 75
   A Germanic Response ... 78
   The Winding Road of American Republicanism ... 83

5. The Turn to Human Rights and Its Vulnerabilities ... 87
   Human Rights and the Turn toward Postnational Citizenship ... 93
   Postnational Citizenship and Its Sources ... 96

viii   CONTENTS

The Cascade of Judicial Rights	99
From *Zoon Politikon* to *Homo Legalis*	101
Human Rights and Identity Politics	104

6. Interests and Identities: Citizenship and the Problem of Collective Action — 109

The Leitmotifs of Interest and Identity: Historical and Theoretical Foundations	111
What of Identity?	116
Democracy and the Entanglement of Interest and Identity	118
Borders and Boundaries	120
Creating Just Civil Societies: The Limits of Rawls and Habermas	123
An Ever-Changing Community	126

7. From Borders to Seams — 129

Borders, Boundaries, and Citizenship	130
Seams	132
Citizenship as a Relational Act	134
Multivalent Ties and Seams	138
Transnational Ties: From International Borders to Global Seams	141
The Civic Project	143

8. A Twenty-First Century Guild — 150

The Corporate Nexus	155
ESG and the "Second Wave" of Human Rights	157
The Google Case Study	161
A New Approach: Juridical Democracy	166
The Guild and Juridical Democracy	171
Guilds as a Response to the Digital Economy and AI	172
The Structure of the Twenty-First Century Guild	174
A Role for Universities	179
The Role of the State	180

9. Completing the Third Revolution? A Conclusion — 185

The Civic Nation	187
Citizenship as Collective Identity	189
The Civic Polity	191
Ius Civitas	193
Getting Buy-In	194

Bibliography	197
Index	235

Acknowledgments

Writing a book on this large a canvas demands the help of a wide range of scholars, specialists, students, and librarians. It also demands the support of one's family and closest friends for many years of work. We are grateful, indeed, to every one of them.

We owe a particular debt to James Cook, our editor at Oxford University Press, for his thoughtful and discerning guidance throughout the process of writing this book. We are grateful to Katharine Pratt, our project editor, and the editorial and design team for their wonderful work on the book's production. All these engagements were a joy.

We are honored to be part of the Oxford Studies on Migration and Citizenship series. For that we must give thanks for the support of the extraordinary scholars who are the series editors, Justin Gest, Sara Wallace Goodman, and Willem Maas.

Catherine Withol de Wenden, Espen Daniel Hagen Olsen, and Hwaji Shin read different versions of the manuscript in painstaking detail. Their invaluable advice and insights have made this a better book.

Our exchanges with Maurizio Ambrosini, Adrian Favell, Zacharias Pieri, Ayelet Schahar, Margaret Somers, Yasemin Soysal, Peter Spiro, and Paul Starr were rich indeed and we trust they will note the fruit of those exchanges at different points in the text itself. We had repeated and extensive conversations with, respectively, Eva von Dassow and Steven Grosby on societies of the Ancient Near East.

While working on this book we also benefited from comments at numerous presentations. In particular, we would like to mention engagements at the European University Institute; Sciences Po—at CERI, CEVIPOF, and Menton, respectively; the Sorbonne; the University of Milan; OsloMet; the University of Oslo; LUMSA; l'École française de Rome; University of Miami School of Law; and at different disciplinary conferences in Lisbon, New York, Chicago, and Reykjavik. We are particularly grateful for the detailed comments we received in exchanges with Rainer Bauböck and the subsequent conversations with Rainer together with Maarten Vink, Jelena Džankić, Bronwen Manby, and their colleagues and students in Florence.

X ACKNOWLEDGMENTS

We have been fortunate to intensively engage with one another over a period of years, meeting across different countries, on this book. In addition to working closely together, we had extensive individual engagements. We would like to acknowledge with appreciation some of those engagements.

From David Jacobson

I am deeply grateful for the numerous, wonderfully stimulating conversations that helped inform the book—in cases a respite during the period of the infernal COVID-19 virus, although, alas, online during that time. Dear friends of many years and intellectual comrades-in-arms Bernardo Arévalo, Torkel Brekke, and Subhro Guhathakurta were always ready for countless conversions on topics of the book. To Jamie Goodwin-White, Daniel Levy, John Meyer, Charlie Tafoya, John Torpey, Ning Wang, and Paul Zolan, our respective conversations feel like one unbroken intellectual thread. I owe a special thanks to my colleagues in Florida, Jamie Sommer, Andrew Hargrove, Michele Aquino, and Georgi Georgiev for our joint collaborative study on the corporate engagement of ESG. I had lengthy exchanges with Herman Lebovics and Darcie Fontaine on French history; Celia Rabinowitz and Thomas Williams on Church history; Aakash Singh Rathore on the politics and philosophy of rights; Alison Taylor, Michele Aquino, and Steve Currall on ESG; Charlie Stanish on pre-state societies and emerging social complexity; Stefan Schindler on German history; and Nathan Schneider on cooperatives—all of them a feast for the mind. I also benefited from email exchanges with Maarten Prak on the history of guilds. I will not forget their generosity with their time.

Thank you also to my colleagues and friends Gil Ben-Herut, James Cavendish, and Simone Maddanu for their reading of chapters and their thoughtful commentary. Librarians Cynthia Brown and Natalie Polson and staff members Fransheska Andaluz and Bianca Johnson were tirelessly helpful. It is really a privilege of our profession to be able to advise talented students who enrich our thinking—and here I must mention Shahd Sara Alasaly, Murilo Cambruzzi, Angela El-Faisel, Shumaila Fatima, Margherita Ferri, Georgi Georgiev, and Alphonse Opaku. They are a joy to advise, but much more than that, I have learned so much from them.

I spent a marvelous year as a Fulbright Research Fellow at the Peace Research Institute Oslo (PRIO) while researching this book. At PRIO, I had the pleasure of many engagements but I must mention Kristian Berg Harpviken, Jørgen Carling, Kristofer Lidén, Nicholas Marsh, Henrik Syse, and Henrik Urdal for their support and thoughts on the work.

Most of all, I am so grateful to Sharon, Adam, Maya, and Noam for their sweet, lovely, joyful, encouraging, warm, and much needed constant presence at my side.

From Manlio Cinalli

My contribution in this book centers on relational citizenship, an area I have pursued passionately over two decades of research and publication. I have elicited the deep roots of relational citizenship, stemming from fundamental principles of societal and political organization seen in early political philosophy as well as in experiences in ancient history. My exploration of relational citizenship also considers the intricate interplay between interests and identities, which drive both the social and political dimensions of citizenship. By examining these dimensions and their interconnectedness, I establish a solid foundation for a broader understanding of citizenship beyond conflict-centric approaches.

This research has developed in part through exchanges with an exceptional group of scholars and students. It is a pleasure to note those debts here. I am grateful to Klaus Armingeon, Didier Chabanet, Marco Giugni, Adrian Guelke, Robert Kloosterman, Klaus Larres, Foued Nasri, Ian O'Flynn, Janine Pelabay, Pascal Perrineau, Donatella Della Porta, Andrea Ruggeri, Réjane Sénac, and Thierry Vedel for our conversations. Each of them provided me with vital intellectual support, helping to shape the evolution of my overall research. I also would like to acknowledge my colleagues and students at the University of Milan and in the Global Politics and Society program that I coordinate. I thank those who have attended the GPS International Seminars Series and the Summer School on Citizenship. These include Gabriele Ballarino, Paolo Barbieri, Enzo Colombo, Senyo Dotsey, Elena Fontanari, Alessandra Lang, Marco Maraffi, Giulia Mezzetti, Massimo Pallini, Francesca Pasquali, Orsola Razzolini, Paola Rebughini, and Nicola Riva.

xii ACKNOWLEDGMENTS

I am in debt to my wife, family, and loved ones in Italy, Ireland, and the United Kingdom. There is no greater debt, however, than the one I owe to Luigi, my father, and to Luigi, my son, with whom I have been engaging in endless conversations that are still going on at the time of publication. I dedicate this book to them.

1

Introduction

Who Rules? Who Belongs? Two Questions, Three Revolutions, Six Propositions

The Paradox

For the vast extent of human history, almost all three hundred thousand years of it, kinship and blood ties have been the dominant basis for organizing human association. Questions of who ruled and who belonged in a community were determined overwhelmingly by birth. From hunter-gatherers to tribes, answers to the boundaries of community and the basis of rule came "naturally"—presumed and unquestioned.

And then, from about 2500 BCE, ideas of citizenship were introduced in different ways in societies from the Ancient Near East and, later, in India, China, Ancient Greece, Rome, and Ancient Israel.[1] Even if fragmentary in concept and in practice, this development represented a remarkable expansion in the scope of human consciousness regarding social and political life. This was a hinge moment in the understanding of how humans could associate with one another and of radically new ways of organizing the relationship between the governors and the governed.[2]

Citizenship presumed some degree of human autonomy even then, if only for select individuals and groups. Citizenship did not augur a definitive swing away from subjectship based on birth. But citizenship opened newly imagined forms of community on abstracted scales well beyond face-to-face modes of engagement. Simultaneously, the idea (and practice) of bounded territoriality became a means of marking more expansive communities. Citizenship did not so much transcend kinship as it complemented the ways in which a community could be represented.

Citizenship brought to the fore questions of "who belongs?" and "who rules?" in nascent civil societies. These questions of belonging and rule could now, in principle, be answered in myriad ways, such that every future

Citizenship. David Jacobson and Manlio Cinalli, Oxford University Press. © Oxford University Press 2023.
DOI: 10.1093/oso/9780197669150.003.0001

2 CITIZENSHIP

political community could now always be questioned. Among these early steps, those of Ancient Greece, Rome, and Ancient Israel would be the most influential on Western developments in citizenship.[3] However, the emerging concepts of citizenship, including its origins, went well beyond the West.[4]

Citizenship challenged basic assumptions of the human condition. If humans had thought that the bases of their relationships—from family to gender, from clan to tribe, from chieftain to peasant—were primordial and beyond history, citizenship was a radical break. From the belief in the autonomous individual, territorial identities, and historical agency, societies suddenly became more malleable in the imagination of those able to grasp citizenship's implications. That malleability extended to the individual citizen. If kinship-based societies proffered largely unchanging and fixed attributes of family, tribe, and status based on sex and age, now the seed was planted for more labile individual roles. Citizenship opened a pathway to a new manner of "being in the world" (Koselleck 2002).

Yet a paradox, key to this book, underlies the developments around citizenship. It is a paradox that has not left humanity from the first inklings of citizenship until now. Purportedly primordial categories, such as sex and race, have constrained the emergence of a truly civic polity ever since. More subtly, ideas of "nature" in the construction of nationhood and rights from the Enlightenment have played a similar constraining role. Even modern citizenship's understandings of the nation-state are based on "birth"—on the soil (*ius soli*) and of blood descent (*ius sanguinis*). Both principles are ascriptive means of attributing citizenship. Racism remains an abiding problem that scars the civic project.[5] Understanding this paradox—the introduction of the revolutionary idea of humankind to shape its own destiny, yet unable to shed the harness of kinship and "primordialism"—is key to understanding struggles within democracies to this day.

This book analyzes how democratic practice has diverged from citizenship principles. Approaching citizenship in this vein, we argue, is critical if democracies are to re-stitch a torn civic fabric and re-instill popular faith in its institutions. We treat democracy as the mechanism and apparatus by which understandings of citizenship are realized—or fail to be realized. Citizenship addresses the bases of the relationship between the governors and the governed, and the civic relationships that make up a community (from the local to the national to the transnational). When democracy is threatened, it is a sign that the underlying citizenship principles are compromised.

INTRODUCTION 3

Lest it even need be said, the challenges concerning democracy and citizenship in our present moment are severe. The signs are multifold in almost every democracy: declining trust in governing institutions and elites, declining faith in the future, reduced faith in democracy as a political system, declining party membership, more demands for direct democracy (such as plebiscites), and less trust in experts. The youth can be even less optimistic than the population as a whole (Mounk 2018; Pew Research 2020). Populist parties and politicians of, especially, the far Right (and, to a lesser extent, the far Left) have been generally gaining strength from election to election. To use the word "crisis" regarding the health of democracy is, in this case, not overstated.

These tribulations of democracies reflect underlying challenges of citizenship, namely that citizenship has been in decline and has less value domestically (it has minimal purchase over other legal statuses). Citizenship less defines "who we are," and it no longer promises a modicum of economic equity. Privileged citizenships are now instrumentalized for the advantages of their passports, leading to schemes for buying citizenships (Jacobson 1996; Spiro 2017, 2019; Joppke 2019). Of late, citizenship has been attacked as a feudal-like privilege and akin to Apartheid (Kochenov 2019).

One other matter on defining citizenship: we seek less to define citizenship as such, because definitions have the effect of rarefying the concept. Take the common notion that citizenship is defined by a panoply of rights. But, as we will argue further, rights are a tool of citizenship and rights do not always serve civic goals. Rather, by setting up citizenship as a set of questions (notably on issues of rule and membership), we are also able to capture contingency, process, and change—and the civic shortfalls of actual practice. We share Maarten Prak's (2018, 300) view that in defining citizenship, we should not be tied down by formal definitions (or legal statuses) and instead consider the ways citizenship is engaged and practiced.

Two Questions

The book asks two questions, or better said, two sets of questions.

First, we seek to reveal the underlying grammar and logic of citizenship. What would citizenship look like without being, as has hitherto been the case, braided with kinship and primordialist strands? Here we seek the intrinsic logic of citizenship and its social and political basis. We can speak

4 CITIZENSHIP

of a grammar of citizenship because, in part, parallel patterns emerge in disparate cultural and geographic contexts, from the Ancient Near East to Classical India.

Second, from this step we think prescriptively, building on what we have learned. How can we move forward to revive citizenship and democracy? Rather than addressing symptomatic issues like polarization, we engage in how the practice of democracy has become decoupled from the underlying principles of citizenship.

Three Revolutions

To arrive at a new understanding of citizenship, we need to comprehend how the roots of its practice were historically formed. In so doing, we can begin to transcend culturally and politically habituated concepts of how it "should" work, and the ways the flowering of citizenship has been constrained— principally by the enduring stickiness of kinship-like and primordialist practices.

The First Citizenship Revolution: The Hinge of History

Civilizations in the Ancient Near East—geographically roughly the modern Middle East—introduce incipient, characteristic elements of citizenship. Among the most familiar of these civilizations are the Babylonian and the Assyrian. These characteristics of citizenship relate to the basis of both political authority and of social life. Similarly, bounded territory becomes a way of identifying a community of people beyond strict blood ties. This "hinge" period in human history starts from approximately 2500 BCE. The evidence from this period reveals the foundations of political liberty and citizenship, in practice as well as principle, in the Ancient Near East. Most people in the civilizations of the Ancient Near East were free, and not enslaved.

From the classical period (from about 500 BCE), the Greeks, Romans, and Ancient Israelites have had a particular influence on the development of citizenship. Greek citizenship was revolutionary for subsequent civic discourse because the Greeks put the issues of rule, of "ruling and being ruled," in the polis as the purpose of citizenship. Rome's formative contribution lay in the attention to rights and obligations as a basis to unite citizens within the broader political community, and from the development of jurisprudence radiating from a legally grounded citizenship (Nicolet 1980; Vishnia 2012). This is at the root of the observation that Rome's model citizenship is a matter of "suing and being sued" (Pocock 1993). Ancient Israel imparted a model of territorial nationhood, influencing concepts of national citizenship following the Protestant Reformation (Grosby 2002; Levinson 2002).

The Second Citizenship Revolution: Guilds, Communes, and City Republics from 1000 CE

In the mid-eleventh century, the Church, under Pope Gregory VII, sanctioned the "corporation"—a body based on civic principles rather than blood ties (Berman 1983). This is a keyhole moment in what was an otherwise overwhelmingly kinship-based, feudal society in which birth determined social status and political rule. New civic corporate bodies, notably guilds, communes, and the Italian city republics, eased the transition from the close, personal bonds of the clan. "As a small face-to-face group, the guild perpetuated some of the characteristics of . . . tribal human association," wrote the historian Antony Black (2003, xxiii), and, as such, corporate associations provided the pathway to "dispersed and impersonal relationships of modern society and the state."

Crucially, the guilds merged economic interests in the trades and crafts together with mutual aid, shared identity, and a broader political vision in their towns and cities. The corporation as a basis of association that transcended kinship was the seed of pivotal and long-term institutional developments. Examples include religious associations that became, ironically, a basis for Protestant dissenters, business corporations such as the Dutch East India Company, voluntary associations, and the nation-state itself.

The "Unfinished" Third Revolution: The Promise of Human Rights and Citizenship

Under the auspices of expanding post-World War II human rights treaties, the individual has certain rights and protections irrespective of their citizenship. The right to request asylum under certain conditions is a case in point. Individuals, not just states, became objects of international law. A gradual

6 CITIZENSHIP

turn in the democratic world takes place from the 1970s toward what has been called "postnational citizenship." The turn was uneven but clear (Soysal 1994; Jacobson 1996). Postnational citizenship contributed to, *inter alia*, growing rights for noncitizen residents, the partial "decoupling" of nationality from the state, and to dual citizenship. The state remains critical in this turn, as it is through the state that human rights may be advanced. Human rights legally do not make a frontal challenge to state border control, for example, but on the criteria of regulation.

This postnational turn held the promise of pivoting toward a more civic political system, less driven by the primordialist elements of nation-states. But key vulnerabilities have meant that this turn makes for an "unfinished revolution." Human rights have been driven, primarily, judicially. This "judicialization of politics" went together with a partial shift from the "politics of consent" to the "politics of rights." The growing role of judicial and administrative officials making decisions for the public, outside of democratic accountability, gave sustenance to charges of a democratic deficit. These developments gave ballast to populist movements that frequently threaten civic politics, as we now witness across democracies.

Six Propositions

In this book, we proffer six propositions, which we ground in different ways:

One: Citizenship, unencumbered by primordialist attributions, has an underlying grammar.

Two: A paradox underlies rights. Rights are a tool of citizenship, not citizenship itself. The paradox of rights is that rights can both serve citizenship or lead to its devaluation.

Three: The two principal approaches to effecting collective action have been based respectively on ideas of "interest" and "identity." Both approaches put forward arguments regarding the basis of social cohesion. Interest and identity correspond to the distinction, respectively, between *demos* and *ethnos* in models of citizenship.

Four: The effective functioning of citizenship depends on its social embeddedness.

Five: Seams provide a better description of present trends, and promise better prescriptive purchase, than concepts of sharply delineated geographic borders and social boundaries.

INTRODUCTION 7

Six: The empirical foundations for prescribing a "twenty-first century guild" are increasingly evident. Such a guild can address to a significant degree what ails citizenship and democratic practice today.

Let us briefly consider these propositions in turn.

Citizenship, Unencumbered by Primordial Attributions, Has an Underlying Grammar

By pivoting the organizing principle of social and political relations from a kinship-like or primordialist basis, social and political relations must be, necessarily, voluntary and constructed. They must be *relational*—in such a scenario there are no *a priori*, essentialized social categories for automatic "sorting." The frequently essentialized notions on which we base citizenship today—the ethnic group, the interest group, and the nation—obscure the underlying anthropological (relational) foundations of citizenship. The root meaning of "primordial" is "from the beginning (of time)," unchanging, predetermined, and immemorial. The intertwining of civic and kinship-like threads through the history of citizenship has blunted (but not completely compromised) the underlying relational process of citizenship.

Being relational, citizenship is logically associated with the "making" (not just the objectives) of a civic community. Citizenship is, as such, looking at the question of "where are we going" rather than the *ex-ante* basis of attributions of "where do we come from." The *ex-post* (rather than *ex-ante*) character of citizenship makes it a *civic project*. In this light, "process" rather than "structure" (or models) becomes the better lens to comprehend civic life. In Norbert Elias and John Scotson's (1994) words: "[the] reduction of processes to static conditions obscures the understanding of the human webs in permanent transformation . . . It is against such hypostatic character of [such description] . . . that one needs to be on guard."

Consider cultural, primordialist, and essentialist approaches to social and political engagements, notably in the case of nationalism. In nationalism, "where we come from" is the *sine qua non* of identity. While nationalist narratives can be the basis of unifying "a people"—say, the Italians in 1871—clashing claims of "where we have come from" have been the basis of countless bloody conflicts. In contrast, citizenship, in its principled, grammatical sense, involves the production and reproduction of the civic fabric.

8 CITIZENSHIP

Citizenship, and its underlying logic, creates a basis for a new form of social connectivity based on a shared civic project. As such, human relationships can connect across the usual ways we divide humanity (race, nation, gender, tribe, religion, and origins). This has implications for how we think of geographic borders—and the metaphorical boundaries that organize and delineate communities. When the human connection is genuinely civic, "the lifeblood of social solidarity in civil society and political communities," writes the sociologist Margaret Somers (2008, 69), is "comprised of noncontractual membership rights, relationships, and reciprocal responsibilities."

Citizenship is more than the individual citizen and their rights and conduct; it is about civically engaged sets of ongoing acts. It does so by linking civic and political dimensions of citizenship, engendering shared membership, common purpose, and mutual engagement between citizens *across* different cultural, social, and economic cleavages. Citizenship enables a fluent interaction between rights and participation in civic and political life.

What we are proposing here is a fundamentally new way of framing citizenship. We move from the nation-state lens to that of a civic polity. When we assume citizenship *reflects* attributes and their interests—for example, when social movements and actors of different kinds mobilize singularly against or in favor of groups based on race, religion, or gender—citizenship is instrumentalized rather than the armature in which a civic political community is induced and practiced. Democratic institutions have tended to become proceduralist, a mechanism for counting and arbitrating (at best) different interests and finding ways to resolve conflict. But by doing so, democracy also reinforces a particular mode of politics and organizing.

By reducing people to a demographic category—such as migrant, White, working-class, or Hispanic—human complexity, identities, and interests are flattened. The multivalent ways people can connect and disconnect, and the multifarious ways that can evolve over time, are short-circuited. In the way nation-states patrol their borders so, analogously, demographic boundaries are patrolled through institutional, social, and elite practices. This in turn narrows the verdant possibilities and varieties of human exchange and association. Interests and identities are aggregated, stated in essentialist ways and, in the process, those interests and identities become sedimented. This "demographic reductionism" is reflected in the way citizenship has been reduced to "membership" and belonging, both in neo-nationalism and in the politics of identity.

Eliciting the grammar of citizenship is a significant consideration because it allows us to consider citizenship in a distinct light. For one, citizenship is not rooted in any one cultural context. Citizenship was not a product solely of the West (or even something that originated in the West), even if Europe had a particular impact on citizenship in the contemporary world. Modern citizenship is a story of (selective and gradual) progress since the Enlightenment—indeed going back to the Gregorian reforms in the eleventh century—but it also involved mixing bluntly primordialist practices around religion, race, and gender into practices regarding citizenship. Those practices led to severe forms of exclusion and discrimination, from antisemitism to racism, to gendered oppressions, to nationalism. The grammatical, principled basis of citizenship, however, can be extricated from much of its (mistakenly) assumed Western moorings.

Furthermore, by eliciting a grammar of citizenship, we can elicit practices that are "citizenship-like," even if not formally called citizenship as such. A case in point is resident noncitizens who have integrated into communities as civic participants. The citizenship of ancient societies can equally be discerned even if they did not use the terms citizenship, or at least the linguistic terminology is a matter of interpretation and discovery. Moreover, by gaining such knowledge of the underlying grammar of citizenship, we can think prescriptively, to move forward to a fuller citizenship, to arrive at a more civic polity.

The Paradox of Rights: Rights Can Both Serve Citizenship or Lead to Its Devaluation

Scholars and activists have uniformly viewed a plenitude of rights as the path to perfecting citizenship and democracy. But, ironically, rights both qualitatively and quantitatively can also generate voids and vulnerabilities. The extension of rights can aid the dynamic formation of a civic community on any geographic scale, and indeed are essential for such. But rights can disrupt, too, insofar as they do not build upon social and political embeddedness. For example, if rights reinforce what are felt to be *a priori*, primordial-like attributes, they can be a source of fractionalization and competitive bidding.

Rights are a tool of citizenship, not, as frequently argued, tantamount to citizenship itself. Take the definition of citizenship widely used by scholars, that citizenship is the "right to claim rights" (Isin 2012).[6] The definition, as it

10 CITIZENSHIP

has been employed by scholars, makes no distinction between the kinds of rights or their individual impact on the body politic. By implication, rights may be infinitely expansive and of any character. Curiously unnoticed is the underlying paradox of rights which is that they can both serve citizenship or lead to its erosion. Rights are not simply of an invariant quality that may expand in the number of rights, types of rights, and populations that enjoy rights, and which will invariably lead to a corresponding improvement in citizenship. The extent and character of rights have qualitative and differentiated effects.

It is in this regard we speak of rights as a tool, not the institution of citizenship per se, in whole or part. The key test in terms of citizenship, in its grammatical and principled sense, is to ask if rights (and the institutions that enforce rights) represent interests of discrete, essentialized groups—that is, the rights are *per se*; or do rights facilitate and effect relational, cross-cutting forms of human association and civic engagement—that is, the rights are *inter se*.

The allocation of rights does not *as such* resolve problems of social connectivity and embeddedness—they can facilitate it and make it possible. Institutions must be developed to effect civic projects, such as the guilds. But rights, depending how they are defined and institutionally configured, can dilute social connectivity insofar as rights are linked to *a priori* attributes. Rights, to support civic society and politics, must be mutually reinforcing. The formalistic and legalistic approach to rights, which frequently seeks to arbitrate between different "interests," rather than a substantive approach in which rights are embedded in evolving social relations, can generate an environment of competitive rights bidding. We have, unfortunately, arrived at such a point in many democracies. Such circumstances become polarizing, tear the civic fabric, and indeed increasingly risk civil violence. Rights, to nurture *civic* ties, must be seamed and relational, and not bounded and transactional.

Rights can be deleterious in two primary, intersecting ways: (1) when a sector of society is largely protected from democratic accountability, notably in the case of the market; and (2) when governing institutions themselves, notably judicial, administrative, and technocratic bodies, make decisions either genuinely or ostensibly in the public interest, but also with limited democratic accountability. When rights do not facilitate civic and relational ties, they tend to be used (intentionally or unintentionally) to close off institutions to democratic rule. Market institutions and state bodies become "sovereign islands," legally near-impervious to civic and democratic accountability.

In the first case, the market has been treated as if it operates best when largely autonomous from government or, for that matter, from civic engagement (such as in cooperatives and guilds). This extensive autonomy (although to varied extents across democracies) has been presented since the Enlightenment as rooted in natural law. The market was presented as a "natural" phenomenon of barter and exchange, reflecting biological human drives. Those assumptions remain, if articulated in different words (see discussion in Chapter 4). The market, as such, became largely immune from civic and democratic accountability. In fact, markets have never been "autonomous" but have been dependent on elaborate legal rights, protections, and institutional support (see Polanyi 2001; Block and Somers 2014; Somers 2021).

Thomas Piketty (2014) points out how the claims of "merit" have been used to justify vast economic inequalities on the basis that the disparities reflect what people "naturally" bring to the market—as if this is a democratic outcome. In fact, the legal and institutional support of the market provide capital an exquisite, rarefied, and almost sovereign isolation. It is as close as we get to Marx's otherwise flawed notion of a superstructure of democratic legitimacy, blinding us to substructure inequities—although now the substructure inequities are glaringly evident. When rights are distributed unequally and differentially, people are "valued" differently; that, in turn, contributes to the commodification and instrumentalization of citizenship.

In the second case, legal rights have expanded dramatically in democracies in recent decades—in numbers of codified rights, of those claiming rights, and in the cascading of rights into the operations of corporate and public organizations. This has been a process driven mostly judicially and administratively; this process of "judicialization" significantly shifted the *habitus* of rights from its republican moorings. The density of rights, and the related lattice of institutional and organizational rules, helped effect a partial shift cognitively in how rights-bearers (citizens and others) think about politics and engage (or do not engage) politically. The individual experience of citizens and other denizens has become, over time, increasingly one of implicit and explicit rights claims and less about civic engagement. The courts and other administrative agencies also have been perceived as being detached from democratic accountability—a major factor feeding into populist protest.

12   CITIZENSHIP

Neoliberal policies have, since the 1980s, benefited from both market protections and judicial developments, both of which limit civic and democratic accountability. The toleration of severe inequities stemmed partly from the flow of political power away from legislatures and toward regional organizations, like the European Union, and to international organizations, like the World Trade Organization, that help set rules for the global economy. Globalization and judicialization in important respects went together (see Jacobson 2003). The point is not whether the judiciary and administrative and technocratic agencies bring benefits—they unambiguously do—but rather how the perceived deficits regarding their civic accountability contributes to the present crisis of democracies.

The anti-democratic challenges of the market have been chiefly a concern on the Left; the administrative and judicial state has been a concern on the Right, and more recently on the Left in terms of the United States Supreme Court. But, from the perspective of citizenship, the problem is profound and goes well beyond the maneuvers of this or that party or this or that political movement. Countering these developments can be an opportunity for civic engagement across sectional differences of all kinds.

In sum, we argue rights cannot work in the way they are intended if they are not embedded—civically, politically, and relationally. Citizenship, in its substance, demands a communicative mediation between rights and participation (directly or through representatives) in political decision making.

What job are rights expected to perform? The answers we come up with are critical for the formation of citizenship and for the kind of citizenship that emerges.

Interests and Identity, *Demos* and *Ethnos*, and the Problem of Collective Action

Citizenship creates a problem of collective action. In rejecting, in principle, kinship-like criteria as the basis for rule and membership, citizenship raises the question: In the absence of such criteria, on what basis can "society" be shaped as a shared collectivity? The challenge is fundamental if we are to have a civic democracy at all.

The Enlightenment is a key moment in setting the foundations of the concepts of "interest" and "identity" as the organizing principles of collective agency in the modern era. Interest provided a contractual grounding for linking individuals into a social whole. Identity, alternatively, pointed to cognitive and emotional foundations for anchoring the individual as an expression of the social whole.

The framing of interest and identity, respectively, has had extraordinary influence in shaping institutions of government, the market, law, and society at large. But the Enlightenment thinkers, in rooting their theories in natural law and making humans of nature, implanted primordial and naturalized categories of the individual, race, sex, and nation at the center of society, politics, and economics. Such purportedly primordial attributes were concomitantly linked to preferences, which is to say that interest and identity were juxtaposed together in ways that fundamentally held back the civic project. Democratic political systems and constitutions came to be based on the premise of inherently self-interested actors—both individual and corporate—and, as such, demanded systems of governance that mediated opposing interests. Those interests could be based on individual or sectional identarian goals. Contemporary identity politics of both the Left and the Right are permeated with such primordialist associations. The Enlightenment origins were a step forward, in terms of advancing rights and liberties, but it was also a step backward in creating an environment of hardbound actors—individual, corporate, institutional, social, and national—driven by transactional, rather than civic and relational, premises.

In this environment, the civic could not become the basis of an overarching collective identity; rather, it was superseded by nationalism. In this light, the concepts of interest and identity mirror in curious yet significant ways the organizational framings of, respectively, *demos* and *ethnos*, political and cultural states, and what has been referred to as the German ethnic versus the French republican understandings of nationhood. The distinctions between *demos* and *ethnos* in delineating national differences have tended to be overstated, or at least not as stable as until recently assumed.[7] In fact, there is an interactive dimension to *demos* and *ethnos*. As Ivor Jennings (1963) put it, the "people cannot decide until somebody decides who are the people."[8]

The sense of collectively felt identity is generally captured in the cultural affiliation of sectional or national identities. Many people perceive themselves to be, for example, Black, Jewish, or Japanese not as generally a thought-out act. Such identities are *felt*; they are experienced "intuitively"—not because they are inherent but because identity is a deeply ontological and social experience formed over years. The identity of being something, of an emotional commitment rather than a contextual calculation, is an ontological matter.

14 CITIZENSHIP

In the nation-state, nationalism has been the basis of collective identity. In so doing, nationalism has complemented the *demos*. Consequently, while citizenship has served the role of defining rights and membership, its transformative role in making the individual part of a collective civic identity is less evident at the national level. Citizenship, as such, has not been the basis for a particular "people to seek agreement with any one group of individuals rather than another," in Yack's (1999) words. Citizenship has not invoked the sense of a shared, felt, intuitive identity. This contrasts with the hitherto, at least, compelling felt identity of nationhood in democracies. The historical power of the *ethnos* should give those who argue for building civic societies on a fundamentally contractual basis—such as Habermas' civic constitutionalism—pause. In isolation, that seems to have little traction.

Our argument doesn't suggest interests, and self-interest, do not exist. But, in moving to more genuinely civic approaches, interests need to be structured as more multi-faceted, cross-cutting, more fluid, and less anchored in singular identities. In that context, interest is not identified with some supposedly singular attribute like class, gender, or race.

Primordialist understandings of identity, and its fusion with interest, have become intertwined with democracy, its legal frameworks, and its notions of rights and institutions. As such, citizenship *practices* have inverted the grammatical basis—the principles—of citizenship. Democracy has thus been harmed. Not only ethnonationalist ideologies, but republican experiments have been far from free of this provocation and share culpability for this turn of events.

Arriving at a "collectively felt" civic identity is, as we will argue, increasingly important for repairing democracies. What kind of "political emotion" do we need for the civic to be felt rather than experienced as cold, legal principles, such that it can be a substitute for felt ideologies such as nationalism? What kind of institutions are necessary to approach that objective?

The Effective Functioning of Citizenship Depends on Its Social Embeddedness

What do we mean by social embeddedness? Citizenship, in its relational logic, recognizes the fundamental ontology of the individual as a *social* being and not as, foremost, an ego. The "social," the foundations on which we can speak of a "society" or a "community," is made up of mutually constitutive relationships—friends, teacher and student, mother and child, and so on. The social emanates from foundational human connections that are relational and non-contractual, not transactional. Individuals engaging one another is one aspect of this but, equally, individuals could not exist, even in their own minds, without social categorizations and relations. Much like language not only commits the individual to a set of rules and vocabulary, but it is also through that language that an individual gets defined and defines themself. This is what Karl Polanyi (2001 [1968]) was alluding to in noting that "social reality" led to the fundamentally social nature of human agency. This is a perspective in which individual action is deeply shaped by social ties and shared ideas, rather than the reverse (Block and Somers 2014).

In social life, we come to understand ourselves instinctively through shared meanings and solidarities. We depend on "recognition" by our social environment. People experience the salience of recognition most readily in the negative, namely in the experience of humiliation and disrespect. "Subjectivity" is dependent on "intersubjectivity." The social bond is, as the philosopher Alex Honneth put it, "woven from the fabric of mutual recognition." Any prescriptive approach must—for any realistic possibility of even partial success—consider such organic, social engagement. The law, for example, is not (or, better put, should not be) a system of constraints to be (in the liberal tradition) minimized to create the space for liberty. People flourish when the law (and the associated institutions) allows us to mutually realize who we are—in Hegel's terms, of "being with oneself in another." The law thus embodies (or should embody) the civic community.[9] Citizenship is, at its core, about recognition: recognition by others, and our recognition of them, in a shared sociality. Stripped of the primordial, recognition mutually arrived at is the only means to be—as an individual and as a (civic) collectivity.

Making the ego paramount, and frequently associating the ego with essentialized, primordial characteristics (e.g., ethnicity, race, class, or nation) is inherently problematic. It will then follow that those relations are necessarily structured to be transactional. "Egos" get instrumentalized. The intrinsically competitive models that emerge seed the ground (even unintentionally) for discrimination and violence. This is also true in the context of unfettered capitalism, notably in the commodification of individuals. Similarly, collectivist ideologies of both the far Left and far Right have extinguished individual "sociality" by imposing ideological blueprints and attributes of, for example, class or ethnic nationalism (Scott 1998).

16 CITIZENSHIP

It is not sufficient to have solely abstract, formal, legal, and ideological approaches—so characteristic of much of contemporary scholarship and policy approaches—to citizenship. For such abstract approaches, social solidarity is assumed to emerge spontaneously or is grounded in instrumentalist and contractual notions of community. The *promise* of citizenship turns the *practice* of citizenship on its head—or, rather, back on its feet—by bringing civic practice back to its relational, organic basis.

Interestingly, the understanding of the need for social embedment can be shared by thinkers on both the Left (such as social democrats like Polanyi, Block, and Somers) and on the Right (such as Glen Loury, a conservative and an economist). Margaret Somers (1994, 628) observes that "social action can only be intelligible if we recognize that people are guided to act by the structural and cultural relationships in which they are embedded and by the stories through which they constitute their identities—and less because of the interests that we impute to them." Loury (2021) notes that "People are not machines. Their 'productivities'—that is to say, the behavioral and cognitive capacities bearing on their social and economic functioning—are not merely the result of a mechanical infusion of material resources. Rather, these capacities are the byproducts of social processes mediated by networks of human affiliation and connectivity." (Relatedly, Loury originated the concept of "social capital.")

Across these arguments, social relations are *a priori* to economic transactions. If the prior role of social ties is ignored, as it frequently has been, there are severe psychological, communal, and political consequences. This may be in terms of individual distress to the extent of suicide, and in communal polarization to the point of extremist, even fascist, politics (Durkheim 2005; Scott 1998). Socially embeddedness does not suggest that where "the social" is prioritized we will have a democratic society. In a hierarchical society, a ranked social order based on birth (e.g., in feudal systems) legitimates hierarchical political rule. For a democratic society, the propitious social context is civic for social and political transactions to be socially embedded in a genuinely democratic manner.

Social disembedment

A key thread in the emergence of the modern state has been the erosion or undermining—sometimes as an unintended consequence, frequently by design—of social connectivity; that is, of the web of social ties. Under capitalism, this process was not "natural" but forced through the increasing

INTRODUCTION   17

"commodification" of people and through the rapid spread of the contract as the basis of almost all social relations. James Scott (1998) graphically represented how centralizing states—from democracies to, in extreme forms, totalitarian dictatorships—sought legibility, quantification, standardization of their respective societies, and the centralization of decision-making. The emergence of national states, such as republican France, saw the milling down of most local and regional identities to effect more national loyalties (Weber 1976).

In the case of the Maoist cultural revolution, any hint of local community, familial loyalties, or even friendship (as opposed to comradeship) was brutally crushed (Vogel 1965, 1969). Friendship suggested a private "particularistic" world which was, in Maoist ideology, deemed a threat to the universal ethic of comradeship. The communist and fascist "experiments" of the twentieth century proffered their blueprints of, in their terms, utopian societies, to be smashed through existing social institutions. Scott (1998, 203) observes in the case of Stalin's farm collectivization that it was a "means whereby the state could determine cropping patterns, fix real rural wages, appropriate a large share of whatever grain was produced, and politically emasculate the countryside." Tens of millions of forced deaths and untold misery followed.

State intervention is not negative or positive, as such. The question is, does such intervention support or undermine social embeddedness?

The Concept of Seams Better Describes Present Trends, and Provides Better Prescriptive Purchase, than Borders and Boundaries

In a world of extraordinary global flows, transnational identities, and dual citizenship (together with, of course, counter trends of renewed nationalism and re-bordering), we can rethink the assumed monopoly of hard borders and boundaries. Such boundedness was never completely hegemonic, even at its twentieth-century highpoint, and it is even less so today. Similarly, the demographic categories of race, gender, class, and nation are, in fact, too precise, too bounded and, ultimately, contrived. Indeed, the "preciseness" applied by social scientists and policymakers in terms of such demographic descriptions is generating a self-fulling reality—but even then, it is a chimera, a distortion of underlying social and political dynamics.

18 CITIZENSHIP

Unlike boundaries, the concept of seams recognizes, in civic contexts, the mutual dependence and opposition of connected parties. Civic life, in its authentic sense, is "seamed"—it is not about *a priori*, essentialist attributions. Seams, in the sartorial metaphor, are both a line of delineation and of a suturing. Unlike boundaries, the concept of seams captures the dialectical relationship of connected parties. Such parties are mutually constitutive, dependent yet in opposition. Seams at the dyadic level—wife and husband, boss and employee, or governor and citizen—are at the nexus of demarcation and of conjoining. Seams also capture the mutual enmeshment of interpersonal relationships and institutions—notions of privacy, for example, thread together the personal and the institutional. The seamed lens can show how formal and legalistic categories can, in fact, compromise the civic process. In contexts where seams are facilitated, *we begin to move beyond "insiders and outsiders,"* and toward more scalar understandings of relational ties. We even get beyond the foregrounding of categories like ethnicity, class, and caste in favor of mutual civic projects.

Geographic borders and social boundaries generate a constant interrogation about who belongs, who is in the ingroup, and who should be exiled or refused entry. Thus, the question of who counts as a woman in the context of transgender politics or who shall be literally counted (and how) in census canvassing itself becomes a political struggle. There is power in groupness, and thus a group's definitional control is considered critical. Elites benefit, in manipulating and in patrolling group boundaries—the group becomes a source of power of the associated elite. This similarly plays out in racial (and other) caste societies, like Apartheid South Africa. When it comes to the nation, the issue of who belongs is a core public concern and the basis for often abrasive quarrels over immigration and refugees. The demand for "preciseness" in defining groups is an artifact of group politics because political power inheres in such groups. Boundary and inclusion issues have quite evidently become among the most vexatious in our democracies.

Citizenship, however, creates in principle a basis for a new form of social connectivity, and for bringing to the surface civic relations that are not legally (or analytically) recognized. Citizenship is legally binary, but here is where the present law diverges from the underlying grammar of citizenship, which is relational and scalar. In the last three decades, membership has been changing and, indeed, becoming more scalar. We are now well beyond the simple citizen–alien distinction. Noncitizen residents' rights have expanded, dual citizenship has rapidly grown as a legal status, nonresident citizens are getting more attention, and transnational ties have been strengthened through internet communications. Myriad ways are available for political engagement or disengagement, regardless of citizen status. Noncitizens can be political activists and contribute money for campaigns in countries like the United States (Spiro 2017). We have "scaled" memberships—in effect, creating gradations of citizenship. For this reason (among others), we must complement notions of hard borders and boundaries. In this context—but also for prescriptive reasons—we introduce the concept of the seam.

The seam, however, is not just descriptive of a static relationship. The seam is animative, a catalyst, and thus also expressive of a dynamic process. The seam is the "engine" for engagement—it generates political, economic, and affective relationships. On the dyadic level, think of desires and tensions across gendered seams. Or, economically, the seams between adjacent poor and rich countries. The seam activates and drives relationships and their transformation (Jacobson and Goodwin-White 2018).

The underlying logic of citizenship is about seams rather than borders or boundaries. In thinking prescriptively, and in shaping institutions to rejuvenate citizenship and democracy, the "seamed" approach must be core—domestically and internationally. Borders, as such, will not end and the state's role is critical in several respects. But borders and social boundaries will need to be understood in a more nuanced way. One can observe in certain areas that relationships across borders can be highly seamed—diasporic communities, news media, low and high culture, medical research, and (in a less positive light) crime networks. In other areas, of course, borders remain definitive—cyber warfare, national security, conflict with Russia and China, seeking national advantage over COVID-19 vaccines. But much as we speak of "international borders," increasingly one can observe emerging "global seams."

The Twenty-First Century Guild as a Response to What Ails Contemporary Citizenship

We put forward a guild model, adapted for the twenty-first century, as a modular nucleus for a more developed civic polity. The guild, wrote the German historian Otto von Gierke, is a "miniature commonwealth" (quoted in Black 2003, 12). John Maynard Keynes (2010 [1926]) argued that although capitalism was efficient, we need a social organization that would lead to a more "satisfactory way of life." Keynes proposed, in passing, a turn to a medieval conception of separate autonomies, essentially guilds, from craft cooperatives to universities.

The corporate environment is, we argue, increasingly propitious for a guild model. What can be termed a "second wave" in human rights is increasingly evident in the corporate sector, as well as in public organizations, and comes under the rubric of environmental, social, and corporate governance (ESG). The developments include a gradual shift to stakeholder (as opposed to the stockholder) principles and to corporate social responsibility. Employee activism is clearly more evident. The digitization of the economy has made for much more transparency. ESG has different components— from the use of ESG criteria to guide socially conscious investors (e.g., through ESG targeted index funds) to corporate, local, national, regional, and global compacts to advance human rights, the environment, and employee governance—and brings different stakeholders to the fore. The ESG "movement" does not promote a guild model, as such, but it provides the conditions for which guilds could be structured. We can learn from the medieval guilds in Europe (and to some extent in China) how corporations, public bodies, and workplaces more broadly can become the nexus linking citizenship to governance.

An analysis of over thirty-six hundred United States-based firms from 1991 to 2016 indicates that we have hit an inflection point when it comes to ESG. Enough corporations are embracing components of ESG to suggest a movement toward a progressively expansive normative practice under ESG (Jacobson et al., 2022).

Building on ESG developments and adjusted for the twenty-first century, a prescriptive guild form can address several concerns. The corporation, especially now, is so extraordinarily important in shaping people's lives and the world itself, from the environment to human rights to wellbeing. Yet the ability of the state to regulate corporations has been declining significantly. On the other hand, corporations, as Satyajit Bose and his colleagues (2019) note, have "scale and power [that] dwarfs the resources available to the governments of most countries to regulate the societal impact of corporate activity." The twenty-first century guild can help democratize corporations and provide a new pathway to revive citizenship while harnessing the corporate sector for civic goals.

Furthermore, the twenty-first century guild can provide an alternative pathway to political engagement beyond the corporation itself, confronting the democratic distrust and deficit and shoring up the legitimacy of the state. The civic demands on corporations have also been growing through pressure from primary and secondary stakeholders and the public on issues from climate to punishing Russia for the invasion of Ukraine. By developing mechanisms of employee governance (e.g., through innovative board structures and stakeholder engagement), the democratically unaccountable structure of corporations can be addressed.

In the digital society in which we now live, high-tech companies and AI pose significant threats to citizenship and democracy from the top-down technocratic approach, algorithms that shape behavior, and the ways social media drives populism. Guilds can ensure "the people's gaze" as a form of discipline and accountability.[10] On the positive side, digital platforms show promise for innovative forms of guilds (e.g., to address the severe marginalization of independent gig workers, such as rideshare drivers).

The guild can be a nexus of citizenship. In the medieval model, citizenship in communes and cities was dependent on guild membership and vice versa. In a moderated version, we propose how this may be applied in our contemporary context. The guild model is a palpable measure of stakeholder engagement at both the primary and secondary levels, including in the broader community. Equally, guild engagement reveals the "genuineness" of stakeholder connection, and it can do so in a scalar manner.[11] Through the intersection with the place of work, the new guild can help shape the practice of citizenship. Rights are not simply "enjoyed" in such a context. Rights are *enacted*. This includes choosing members, including those who are not yet citizens nor engaging politically. In this regard, the guild is republican in a lived way. As the workplace includes a mix of citizens and noncitizens, the guild effects a seamed republicanism without the sharp binaries of insider and outsider. This has implications for secondary stakeholders, including across borders.

The guild, structured correctly, can overcome the rupture between the politics of rights with the politics of consent, which has been so damaging for democracies (e.g., in the delegitimization of court decisions). By combining juridically required civic goals with democratic participation, the guild functions as a civic project and thus engenders civic social and political embeddedness. It is a kind of "juridical democracy." The civic goals stimulate a relational and seamed form of engagement, rather than interest-driven transactional politics (which have impaired attempts at employee engagement at companies like Google).

22   CITIZENSHIP

Until recently, ESG was associated with mostly climate initiatives. But ESG has expanded well beyond that. Gillian Tett (2022) of the *Financial Times* observes:

> [E]vents such as COVID-19 or the Black Lives Matter campaign have made it hard for corporate boards to ignore social welfare at a time when social media tools and increased digital transparency has made it easier than ever for activist groups to monitor what companies are doing and launch campaigns against them if they breach social norms. Or to put to another way, the concept of ESG has moved from being a narrow area of activism—driven by people who want to change the world—to a sphere of risk management for corporate boards—where it is shaped by the knowledge that companies which ignore ESG issues can face reputational damage and the loss of customers, investors, and employees . . .
>
> Meanwhile, the amount of money earmarked for ESG funds has exploded . . . while there are numerous different ways of measuring the size of this field, analysts estimate that around a third of all investments are managed with some ESG lens . . .
>
> Today . . . there is not just a new era of digital transparency, but a collapse of popular faith in the power of governments to fix problems. As a result, companies are being forced into the frame of policy issues, whether their leaders like it or not. And while the issues that corporate leaders are being asked to address seem like an ever-shifting kaleidoscope of problems—ranging from Russia to gender rights to carbon emission to biodiversity—the key point is this: returning to a world where the public thinks companies should "just" chase shareholder returns is unlikely any time soon.

Key elements of a seamed, global world, such as the impact of the internet and global media; the role of transnational ties and communities; the experience of a singular global space impacting ideas, politics, and culture; the global production of knowledge and research; and, above all, the crisis of legitimacy of institutions, from state agencies, to courts, to media, to academia, are not likely to go away—at least not in the democratic world. The discord and alienation of different publics is reaching an extraordinary pitch. In thoughtful ways, we need to re-think the architecture of citizenship. Ironically, that may mean going back to citizenship's fundamental roots.

Notes

1. The literature on these regions in this light is extensive. See, for example, Nicolet (1980), Hall (2002), Levinson (2002), Raaflaub (2004), Knoppers and Levinson (2007), Lewis (2007), Liverani (2007), Vishnia (2012), Çıpa and Fetvacı (2013), and Casale (2015a, 2015b).
2. We see more complex social structures emerging at the beginning of the Holocene period, about eleven thousand years ago. As the archaeologist Charles Stanish (2023) notes, the late Pleistocene consisted of small bands of hunter-gatherers, rarely exceeding several dozen people. At the start of the Holocene, group sizes increased considerably. Societies with over two thousand to three thousand individuals required a "structural adjustment to maintain cooperation and to pursue collective pursuits." New social structures, backed by norms necessary for sustained cooperation, emerged. See also Graeber and Wengrow (2021) and Harari (2014), and *infra* note 4.
3. The discussion on the role of these civilizations is also vast. See, for example, Grosby (2002), Raaflaub (2004), and Yavari and Azhar (2017).
4. It is important not to equate early cooperative structures with democracy, as Stasavage (2020) does, suggesting that democracy is "natural." As John Keene (2021, 236–237) notes, "Democracy is much more than people and leaders needing each other and engaging in mutually agreed compromises." Democracy "casts doubt on all claims to 'natural' privilege based on such criteria as brain or blood, skin colour, caste or class . . . Democracy spreads doubts about talk of the 'essence' of things, fixed habits, and supposedly immutable 'natural' arrangements. It encourages people to see that their worlds can be changed."
5. On the linkages between democracy and racism, see Fitzgerald (2014).
6. Marshall's (1950) classic text threads rights into the narrative of citizenship's development. Other scholars add other dimensions. For example, Linda Bosniak (2006) notes the roles of status, equality, and identity in addition to rights—but rights are still embedded in definitions of citizenship in essentially unqualified ways.
7. An extensive conversation has emerged, especially of late, on the relationship of *ethnos* and *demos*, or cultural and republican models of citizenship (among other descriptors). See Beiner (1999), Yack (1999), Reeskens and Hooghe (2010), Lucka (2019), and Pogonyi (2022).
8. Jennings (1963) is quoted in Bauböck (2007, 2412).
9. See Honneth (2020). The discussion in this paragraph benefits from an essay by Peter Gordon (2022), from which the quotations by Honneth and Hegel are drawn.
10. See Foucade and Green (2020) and Brubaker (2023), discussed further in Chapter 8.
11. On "genuine" ties see Shachar (2009) and Bauböck (2019a), and also the discussions in Chapters 7 and 8.

2

The First Revolution

The Ancient and Classical Periods

Citizenship, in theory and abstracted, strips the individual of their "natural" clothing. Birth no longer conjures up one's status in society. It no longer determines, intrinsically, whom you shall marry or what your occupation shall be. Citizenship *denaturalizes*.[1] Citizenship also universalizes by legally "de-recognizing" particularistic characteristics—leading to a civil rule of law that condemns parsing individuals by race, gender, religion, descent, sexuality, and class. Such denaturalization from the dictates of statuses and identities determined by birth gives the citizen their "freedom," their "liberty," and their autonomy. The human is stripped bare, now vulnerable but also, in principle, able to take on the clothing of their choosing.[2]

Citizenship as the organizing principle of society breaks from kinship. Citizenship cannot rely on blood descent as the predetermined basis of human affiliation and rule. It must be grounded in long-term civic understandings and aspirations. Citizenship is such that human association itself becomes a project that is dynamic, evolving, and instilled with a sense of historical and political agency. When realized, citizenship as a project nurtures a membership with much more import than simple affiliation; it is about the engagement with the project of citizenship itself. As opposed to this underlying "grammar" of citizenship, the *practice* of (formal) citizenship has devolved today for many into a thin membership with a bundle of rights, interests, and identities largely disconnected from a civic project.

With human agency unshackled by the ahistorical imperatives of kinship, questions of membership and rule are thrust to the forefront. Such agency, however, came very late in human history. All societies in which kinship plays a central role, from hunter-gatherer bands to tribes, from Ancient Egypt to the Incas, from the Confucian Middle Kingdom to feudal Europe, demanded service and subjectship. Slavery is an extreme (but historically common) expression of the body at the service and subjectship of

Citizenship. David Jacobson and Manlio Cinalli, Oxford University Press. © Oxford University Press 2023.
DOI: 10.1093/oso/9780197669150.003.0002

others. The individual's place in this hierarchy was a function of birth, with extremely limited opportunities for mobility. Family, status, and rule were largely expressions of a primordial process. It is in this regard the figuration of "blood," as in bloodline, becomes so important.

For this reason, kinship societies were (and are) overwhelmingly patriarchal and gender roles were the cornerstone of such societies. Determining bloodline was a *condicio sine qua non* of social life. Patriarchy followed almost universally, as the frequently extreme control of women—for example, enforcing virginity before marriage—was a function of protecting the bloodline. The individual's life in kinship-based societies is at the behest of the larger social order, notably as a woman and as a man, and in terms of rank. The concept of honor reflects this. Honor is served by fulfilling socially *fixed* roles as a woman, man, peasant, or aristocrat. You are subject to the chieftain or lord—but you are also subject to your father, husband, caste, religion, and beyond.

Roots of Citizenship

However tempting it may be to arrive at a teleological story based on a narrative of inexorable progression from kinship to citizenship, the lesson from history is that citizenship has regularly evolved, appearing and disappearing throughout social and political life, in often ad hoc and fragmented ways. Forms of citizenship—as they emerged in ancient civilizations from the Ancient Near East to the Indian subcontinent—mostly vanished with the collapse of those civilizations themselves. While reaching a significant foothold in Rome, and in the Greek polis before then, citizenship came almost to an end with the emergence of the Holy Roman Empire.

In Europe, civic principles were revived under Pope Gregory VII, in the mid-eleventh century, in his recognition of civic "corporations." Also in the Middle Ages, from the eleventh century, robust civic political practices took root in the Italian city-states and in guilds and communes in wide parts of Western Europe. History continued to be marked continuously by these shifts up until the constitution of post-World War II democracies, with an unprecedented emphasis on civil, political, and social rights (Marshall 1950). But post-war developments in citizenship followed the dramatic assertion of fascist ideologies based on proclaimed kinship of "blood and soil," and of racial and *voelkisch* nationalisms.

26 CITIZENSHIP

However, if we look back "genealogically," with no assumption of a predetermined historical path, we can begin to elicit progressively the different intellectual and institutional fragments of citizenship coming into view. These "fragments" were articulated and combined in different ways, and so the concept of citizenship is historically formed and developed (Somers 2008). The development of citizenship has always involved actively looking back at historical antecedents: the Romans learning from the Greeks; the Italian city-states of Venice and Florence citing Rome and Ancient Greece; the seventeenth-century Dutch Republic inspired by the arguments on citizenship of Venice, Florence, Rome, Greece, and Ancient Israel.

In our "genealogical research," we elicit different rearrangements of citizenship, with its array of developments, at different points of time. We do not claim that there is an ineluctable, grand narrative. But historical sequencing of certain ideas and institutional practices is evident, if not inevitable. Citizenship, like other institutions, is at the nexus of the past and the present. History is not absent as to where we are now. Humans do not live only in the present—individually or as a society. All kinds of actions and social patterns perforce draw on the past. Thus, we use the term genealogy more broadly than the poststructuralists, who deny any form of historical "narrative," with its own internal coherence. Even if history is often disjointed, we have much to learn from it.

In sum, a genealogy of citizenship does two things for us. First, it reveals the intellectual bases of citizenship, which remain in near continuous dialogue from the classical period to the present day. From such, in part, we can elicit the grammar of citizenship. Second, the genealogy can reveal the practices of citizenship, the ways kinship practices intersected with citizenship across different historical contexts, and the effects of such "practice-bound norms" (Pollock 2006). Such learning also affords us a better foundation to critically analyze our present and to consider how we may move forward on civic matters.

From Kinship to Citizenship: The Ancient Near East, Greece, and Rome

The story of citizenship and public law in the Western imagination begins with Athens and Rome (Barchet 2015; Davies 1993).[3] Ancient Israel's model, through the prism of the Hebrew Bible, came into focus regarding citizenship following the Protestant Reformation. Although Rome chronologically follows Athens, for the cities, republics, and states that followed them a thousand years later, Athens and Rome provided alternative approaches to citizenship and, notwithstanding their respective developments across different historical periods, could be looked upon as if side-by-side in history. It was Herodotus, the ancient Greek historian, who in his book, *The Histories* (2003), compared the East, represented by the Persian Empire as—wrongly—the epitome of tyranny. He proclaimed that Greece, by contrast, embodied freedom. In doing so Herodotus likely shaped the West's sense of the Ancient Near East in the following centuries, and the crediting of Ancient Greece as the birthplace of civic political principles.

Yet it is in the Ancient Near East, as far as we can tell, we first observe the lineaments of citizenship across the articulations of both society and state (Charpin 2012; Clifford and Richardson 2017; Liverani 1991). These incipient civic developments are not uniform in a region that was politically deeply varied, both geographically and over time (Khurt 1995; Snell 2020; Van de Mieroop 2016). Consider just the area of Mesopotamia: significant political differences were evident from the Kingdom of Hammurabi, the Kassite Kingdom of Karduniash, to the Second Babylonian Empire (Joannès 2001; Pollock 1999; Postgate 2017). Relatedly, it is in the Ancient Near East in which agriculture was first systematically practiced, which in turn supported cities and territorial states with centralized governments, developed religious institutions, and organized armies.[4] Similarly, bordered territory becomes a way of identifying a community of people beyond strict blood ties.

The scholar of the Ancient Near East, Eva von Dassow (2018), notes the following markers for eliciting emerging citizenship in the Ancient Near East:

> The subject's liberty was freedom in the legal sense of having autonomy of action and rights over one's own person . . . further, it had the political dimension of a (theoretical) right and duty to participate in the governance of one's community. In other words, the subject is related to the state as a citizen, not as a servant. As such, the subject was obliged to support—to serve—the state of which he was a citizen. Women as well as men possessed free status, albeit women's freedom was normally limited by their legal dependence on men [and only] exceptionally could women participate in governance.

What then, von Dassow asks, was the state?

28 CITIZENSHIP

If the idea of citizenship has meaning, it entails conceptualizing the state as, fundamentally, the governmental embodiment of a community, not as a superstructure extrinsic to the population it rules. The validity of this proposition too can be demonstrated from the evidence of ancient Near Eastern sources.

This point is illustrated with the following example from a Babylonian advice manual: "Don't hang around the assembly or they will have you decide a dispute, you will be made into their witness, they will bring you to settle what's not your affair." This passage shows, although ironically, that membership in such a political community accorded with Aristotle's definition of the citizen as a stakeholder who may participate in judgment and office (Dassow 2023; Aristotle 2009 for citizen's definition in §1275a22-24 and §1275b17-22). "Citizenship" also included rights to legal protection by the state. Rules were written down and formalized as fully fledged laws to regulate social life and to avoid arbitrary abuse of authority; here one can mention the Code of Ur-Nammu around 2100–2050 BCE, the codex of Lipit-Ishtar around 1930 BCE, and the Akkadian Laws of Eshnunna around 1770 BCE (Roth 1995; Westbrook 2003).

At different times and places, rights could include access to magistrates, up to the king himself, for the resolution of disputes and protection from the state interference over the citizen's person, family, or property. Duties included availability for the defense of the polity. Citizenship also included the right, and even the obligation, to participate in the governance of the community—including checking the power of the king. Citizens participated through assemblies, representatives or liaisons, and local leadership. These bodies, von Dassow (2011, 2018) notes, were at different scales—such as a senate, court, city, or tribal assembly—drawn from heads of free households in the relevant community.[5] In cases in early second-millennium Assur, for example, such representative bodies could conclude treaties with other states. The enslaved were, by definition, excluded from all acts of citizenship. Most people in the civilizations of the Ancient Near East were free, not enslaved. Women, however, rarely partook in such assemblies, and free women's status was dependent on their ties with free men.[6]

The idea of the citizen, however, was not abstracted from the person. The civilizations of the Ancient Near East, dating from about 3000 BCE to 500 BCE, did not develop political abstractions such as "state" or "citizenship."

THE FIRST REVOLUTION   29

Although a word that could be translated as citizen appears absent, Raymond Westbrook (2003, 36) notes that the free native-born had "a notion of belonging to a political unit, which, if not having the clear-cut contours of citizenship in the modern sense, was associated with privileges and duties, and attended by legal consequences." The exception, regarding the abstraction of citizenship may be in, as we shall discuss in a moment, Ancient Israel. More developed political theory and abstraction started with the Greeks, outside of the Ancient Near East.

While Ancient Greece was hardly a homogeneous notion given the differences across time and city-states, one finds that in general to be a free person was largely a function of birth, of kinship (Lewis 2018; Morgan 2003; Raaflaub 2004). Yet, even free persons still had to be "claimed by the community they claim."[7] Terms of kinship evolved to capture broader civic affiliations. For example, the notion of the "son of" of a particular father—the patrilineal line was generally privileged—which has been rooted in establishing kinship lineage for millennia in the Middle East (and elsewhere) to this day, took on an additional form. That kin affiliation was expanded by describing an individual as the "son of" a territorial unit, from "son of the village" to "son of the land," such as in Babylonia. Displaying the intersection with kinship principles and yet transcending them at the same time, new practices had to build on existing vocabulary and experience. Literal kinship was complemented with what the sociologist Steven Grosby (2018, 2020) calls "territorial kinship." In the Hammurabi period, for example, to be a citizen one had to be both a native *and* a free person (von Dassow 2023). Notably, citizenship was expressed both on the levels of participation in social life and of rulership—what we call respectively the social and political dimensions of citizenship. Critical to both is a notion of "freedom" for all citizens.

Extensive evidence shows that ideas of rights and liberty were part of Ancient Near East society and state well before such theories emerged in Greece (Charpin 2012; Clifford and Richardson 2017; Liverani 1991). What is striking about practices and legal propositions in the Ancient Near East, in places such as Babylonia and Assyria, is that they engaged in both social life (membership) and in rulership. At the foundation of both dimensions of citizenship was the idea of individual freedom (Snell 2001). Freedom—the autonomy over one's own body—was essential for the citizen to be engaged in the polity, as well as to participate in the civic community. The idea and practice of such individual freedom, albeit predicated on the lottery of birth,

30 CITIZENSHIP

is evident in extant documentation from the Ancient Near East (von Dassow 2011, 2018).

Territoriality—bounded and fixed in time—became a foundational mechanism of citizenship for determining civic community. The Ancient Near East serves in this regard as perhaps *the* precedent. The pivotal shift to territory as a marker of identity gave the basis of a thicker and more inclusive notion of membership. The territory or "the land" is not simply real estate, nor is it presented as static in time. It is sacralized soil that gives birth to the nation in both space and time (Grosby 2018). The territory is frequently presented as part of a historical narrative, with a genesis (such as the Puritan "plantation" in America) and a more-or-less linear path to collective and individual freedom (marked by momentous events, such as the Declaration of Independence and Lincoln's Gettysburg Address).

Moreover, the land is bounded so that processes of exclusion between "insiders" within the land and "outsiders" beyond it can take shape across borders. However, within a given land, social life could thrive. Territorial membership transcends individuals and melds them into a shared, holistic, and transcendent community. In the telling, mythic in its import, division is overcome, and marginalized groups can socially bring themselves into fold. This story nurtures the experience of an "as if" primordial community, and the ultimate, sovereign expression of its members. The social melding of individual and collective has been compelling (in both senses of the word— intellectually compelling to the individual member, and compelled through the state apparatus, through civic education to the law). Citizens have felt compelled (again, in both senses) to go so far as to sacrifice themselves to protect their own land, as millions have done in wartime.

We observe such examples of more expansive social and political communities in the Ancient Near East, and of territorially defined membership when distinctions were drawn as early as the early dynastic period (2900–2350 BCE) between the Sumerian city-states (Grosby 2023; Westenholz 2002). The respective states could do so when their control extended over a relatively large territory with defined borders and with a reasonably stable legal system.

As Steven Grosby (2023) writes, we have the contours of nationhood and nationality in the Ancient Near East:

> The nation is a "we"—a social relation where its members recognize that
> there is a property that each of them have in common in contrast to those

who do not . . . [a] property recognized in [one] another to be significant such that it becomes a part of a distinguishing self-classification [that] may vary, for example, [by] language or religion . . . Distinctive of the category of nationality, distinguishing it from other categories of social relations such as family, friendship, business firm, religious sect, and so forth, is the ascendancy of the significance attributed to being related *by virtue of birth or residence within a territory.* (emphasis added)

It is revealing that as far back as five thousand years ago, we see political forms which, in part, resonate with the modern nation-state. The "virtue of birth or residence within a territory" as the basis for collective identity directly parallels modern national developments. This suggests that underlying social structural forces shape collective identity, as new forms emerge as social complexity grows, without fully dispensing with kinship-like criteria. These historical developments anticipate the dialectic of what would later be called *demos* and *ethnos*.

In the Hebrew Bible, the Hebrew term *ʾezrāḥ haʾareṣ* is generally translated as "native of the land"; *ʾezrāḥ*, or "native," is associated with free Hebrew individuals in a civil relationship (Milgrom 2000, cited in Grosby 2020). Free Israelites are legally distinct from both the resident non-Israelites (what one ironically could term "resident aliens") and the foreigner, *nokrî*, who lives outside the nation's borders. In modern Hebrew, a citizen is referred to as an *ʾezrāḥ*. Whether the Biblical *ʾezrāḥ* should be translated as "citizen" is a matter of debate. But as Grosby (2020) notes, *ʾezrāḥ haʾareṣ* indicates birth and residence (a "native") in a bordered land, and so the legal community is a territorially designated membership or nation. Accordingly, in the historical experience of Ancient Israel, the bounded territory became the means to nurturing a "covenant" by which nationality and citizenship are closely related to each other—a pattern, or key relationship, we observe in later, modern times (Elazar 2018; Liverani 2007).

Thus, the embryonic structures of nationhood, resting in citizenship, are not a modern phenomenon, nor are they first rooted in Europe. The generally accepted view that the Treaty of Westphalia of 1648 or the American and French Revolutions mark the beginning of nationalism and national states is misplaced. The evidence shows that emerging conceptions of "nationhood" and the associated ideas of a clearly bordered territoriality are found in the Ancient Near East. Indeed, the Ancient Near East civilizations indirectly, and directly in the case of Ancient Israel, influenced the early modern and

32 CITIZENSHIP

modern concepts of nationhood (Smith 2006). This sense of "territorial kinship" makes for a subtle interplay between kinship practices and citizenship
practices. One can trace, conceptually, a thread from such notions of territorial kinship to citizenship of the modern state and the distinction for basing
citizenship on *ius sanguinis*, or blood descent, and on *ius soli*, or birth on the
land. The intersection of kinship and civic concepts remains into the modern
period and in our contemporary readings of citizenship.

After the Protestant Reformation—in, for example, the Dutch Republic,
the Puritan settlement in America, and even (if less accentuated) Anglican
England and Lutheran Scandinavia—one can identify the influence of
Ancient Israel as represented in the Hebrew Bible. This is expressed in the
aspiration to a shared body politic, a felt "inextricable" relationship with a
"sacred" land, and a soteriological role in history. Following the example of
the "New Israel," the "New Jerusalem," and other invocations of the biblical
Holy Land, many nations in post-Reformation Europe talked in the same
light of a "providential chosenness." That sense of chosenness could sometimes be of a liberal character, spreading the rights of self-government to
the world, as in the American Declaration of Independence and, later, in
Lincoln's struggle against slavery; and sometimes of a chauvinist character,
such as South Africa's Dutch Reformed Church's historical justification of
Apartheid.[8]

In the ancient world, it is not just in the Ancient Near East that we observe
territorial states, with incipient forms of "freedoms" or protections vis-à-vis
the king. This development is evident in, for example, the late Vedic period
in the Indian subcontinent (1100–500 BCE).[9] As in the Ancient Near East,
so in the late Vedic period were *concepts* of kinship used to convey the emergence of a political order that transcended, as well as incorporated, *actual* kin
social and political structures. The historians of India, Hermann Kulke and
Dietmar Rothermund (1990), note on the Vedic case:

> [There] is a good deal of evidence in the texts for the dissolution of tribal or-
> ganization and the emergence of a new political order [in the late Vedic pe-
> riod] . . . [This] can be traced by looking at the changing meaning of words.
> *Jana*, which used to refer to a tribe, refers to people in general in later texts,
> and the term *viś*, which indicated a lineage or clan in earlier times, now
> referred to the subjects of a king. At the same time a new term appeared—
> *janata*—which meant "a people." The area in which such a people was
> settled was called *janapada*. *Pada* originally meant "step," so *janapada* was

the "foothold of a tribe," but it was now used to designate the territory of a people. The new kings called their realm *mahajanapada* (great territory of the people).

That the linguistic transition is so similar across these regions, with no evidence of cross-regional transmission of such ideas, is again suggestive of an endogenous social-structural change. Social change, even radical, is rarely, if ever, de novo, and per force existing cognitive categories are adapted for new circumstances. Unlike the Ancient Near East, however, Indian political development in that period had no apparent influence on the subsequent development of citizenship in Western Europe or in the world at large.[10] Nonetheless, this example further illustrates that the social forces underlying what we now call citizenship are cross-cultural and were not rooted in Europe as such.

History shows that experiences of "unbounded" territoriality revealed distinctive social and political forms in contrast to that of territorial nations. Take the Ottoman sultanate. The Caliph al-Mansur built his new capital in Baghdad in the middle of the eighth century. He designed a round city. Why? A circular city meant that the sections of the city would be equidistant from him, in the center. The caliph was at the center of the city, Baghdad was the center of Iraq, and Iraq was the center of the world. To emphasize al-Mansur's caliphate's centrality, his chroniclers describe it with the metaphor, "the navel of the world." Authority for the Ottomans was precisely about the territorial distance from power, center, and periphery. Membership of a territorially bounded community was secondary to a particular form of patrimonial rule (Lewis 1988, 22).[11]

Confucian China in the Qing dynastic period between 1644 and 1912 displayed yet another form of unbounded territoriality. The Kingdom of Heaven had a "center"—the Forbidden City in Beijing—but China, as such, was not a fixed territory. Rather, Confucian China experienced the world as a series of concentric zones moving outward into increasingly culturally barbarian lands (Lewis 2012, 2007; Weller 2019). Civilization lay in the center, bestowed with the Mandate of Heaven, and the closer to the center you were the more civilized the cultural context. The Forbidden City was the *axis-mundi*. In fact, many "a-territorial" societies had sacred centers where the felt presence of the gods intersected with their human followers where in, Mircea Eliade's terms, Heaven touched Earth—and anchored that society (Eliade, 1957).

34 CITIZENSHIP

Greeks and Romans

We have thus far argued that while the historiography of citizenship still overwhelmingly starts with Greece, this overlooks the potential influence of previous civilizations, notably the Ancient Near East. One question is if the Ancient Near East societies influenced the subsequent development of citizenship?

One suggestive pathway, although not conclusive, is that of the Ancient Near East's influence on Greece itself (Burkert 1995; Noegel 2007; Westbrook 2015). Almost identical storylines exist, for example, of divine warnings of retribution against rulers who violated their peoples' rights, such as the warning of the storm god Addu to the King of Mari (in today's Syria) in the eighteenth century BCE, to a warning of Yahweh to the Israelites one thousand years later, to the storm god Zeus' warnings to Athens in the sixth century BCE. In each case, the message was delivered by a prophet, in the case of Yahweh by Amos and for Zeus it was Solon (von Dassow 2018). The influence on Greece is not conclusive in terms of transmission of such political ideas. One theory is that the transmission may have taken place orally (West 2018).

However, the second pathway of influence of the Ancient Near East on understanding of citizenship in the West is reasonably clear—the influence of Ancient Israel. This influence is most noticeable with and following the Protestant Reformation (Walzer 1982; Grosby 2002; Levinson 2002; Sutcliffe 2004). Ancient Israel itself is significantly influenced in its doctrines and mythologies by the rest of the Ancient Near East, notably following the Babylonian exile (in today's Iraq) in the sixth century BCE. The Babylonian exile followed the Babylonian conquest of the kingdom of Judah in 598/7 and 587/6 BCE. The captivity ended in 538 BCE, after Persia conquered Babylonia, although some Jews remained in Babylonia—thought to be the first diaspora (Diner 2021).

The Greeks and Romans provided distinct contributions to citizenship. The Greeks developed the theory and practice of rulemaking, in particular the relationship between rulers and ruled. The Romans in turn emphasized the social community and its legal basis. Starting with Ancient Greece, citizenship first arose as a foil to slavery through intense warfare and revolt against internal tyranny and against external domination by Persia (Lewis 2018). It was at this time that political freedom emerged as the central concept of Greek citizenship, soon becoming the basis for the rise of the Athenian Golden Age, in the fifth century BCE. It was in this period, in the time of Pericles and the Athenian Empire, that citizens regarded rulemaking as the basis of their freedom, and freedom became the justification of their rule (Raaflaub 2004). By the establishment of democracy in 430 BCE, to be a citizen meant to be a free man (women remained excluded from the benefits of citizenship). Before any type of other membership, citizenship stood out as a condition of one's own freedom in the determination of the citizen's life and that of their community of free fellows. At the same time, the use of kinship categories (women, slaves, ethnic groups, noble families, etc.) stood out as a form of identity marker of the Greek polis, combined with geographic borders (Hall 2002).

In the case of the slave, the body is at the service of others. This was only too evident as slavery was firmly grounded as a legacy of the Ancient Near East (Hall 2002; Lewis 2018). However, during the Golden Age the "free body" took on distinct connotations. In his *Republic* and *Laws*, Plato provided the basis for the famous metaphor, that of the body politic, emphasizing fitness and well-being over illness—illness of the body politic occurred when the different institutions of the state did not perform their functions.[12] In addition, the novelty of Greek citizenship went beyond the simple constitution of a unified body per se, extending in a way to spell out its own substance (what citizenship is about) rather than simply querying about who are, or are not, members. Citizenship could thus provide the basis on which any legitimate rulemaking is determined (Alwine 2018; Pocock 1993; Rhodes 2014). Normatively then, the Greek model took at its core the act of "ruling and being ruled," resting as it was in the *zoon politikon*; that is, in the political human being (Aristotle 2009). This was a crucial step as it put, at least in terms of ambition, the centrality of public offices at the core of citizenship in the Golden Age. Kinship continued to have a crucial weight, however, due to the importance of descent (Blok 2017).[13]

Rome's historical experience shows a different path to citizenship based on rights and obligations. Citizenship was less about empowering the choice of the governed vis-à-vis the decisions of governors, and more about legal protections of citizens themselves. Rome brought to the fore membership through an emphasis on the idea of civic community. For example, even if the ultimate foundation of authority was in the *populus*, the role of the Citizens and Centuriate Assemblies remained passive and, furthermore, lost powers in the passage between the Roman Republic and the Roman Empire (Forsythe 2007). What did not change, however, was the fact that in Rome a citizen was, as Pocock (1993) writes, "someone to act by law, free to ask [for]

36 CITIZENSHIP

and expect the law's protection, a citizen of such and such a legal community, of such and such legal standing in the community."

Describing Rome's "model" based on "suing and being sued" may be reductive but the term captures a certain essential quality of citizenship as a judicial concept. "By claiming to be a Roman citizen, [the individual asserts the protections of] the various patterns of legally defined rights and immunities available to the subjects of a complex empire made up of many communities" (Pocock 1993). In this context, the Roman citizen could "sue and be sued" in contrast to the Athenian citizen's political role to "rule and be ruled." Not surprisingly then, even the leading voices of Roman Republicanism expressed a broader patrician fear that an "excess" of political representation could have dangerous outcomes for Rome (Cicero 2009).

The broader the population included as citizens, the more likely that territorial bordering could play a role in determining membership, both functionally and ideologically. Accordingly, citizenship in Rome fundamentally altered the meaning of Greek citizenship, suggesting a form that, as a legal fiction, was universal and multiform (Pocock 1993). Multiple statuses could, and were, defined, ranging from citizens to the alien foreigner. Multiple forms of law could and were "told," including natural law, municipal law, civil law, and onward. Freeborn women had a second-class citizenship as they could not vote or hold public office, even if of patrician background. Various others were excluded from citizenship. But a geographically expansive citizenship, as a legal status even in its multiplicity, allowed for building civic loyalty to Rome over the centuries and throughout an ever-increasing empire.

Rights and immunities radiated from legally grounded citizenship. As such, courts and jurisprudence loomed large. In this way Rome stood out as the point of departure in the Western tradition of legally grounded citizenship. Rome is not, however, simply important in the sense of setting legal precedent. This intertwining of judicial institutions in the composition of membership becomes, we argue, a socio-legal pattern from Rome to the present day—a pattern that has grown in importance in our last half-century during the "rights revolution" in the West and globally regarding human rights. In contrast to the legislative emphasis of Greece, Rome's legally situated basis of civic membership foregrounds the judicial dimension of governance.

Indeed, the political community in Rome was not just about a bordered membership. Romans of all classes perceived that they were part of the same community—they shared the same religious and political calendars, the same deprivation, and the same apparent readiness for death in the name of Rome. Membership was rather open-ended, with an eye to adapting Roman membership in the light of shifting political goals rather than focusing on membership for its own sake. Critically, citizenship became associated with a political project, whether it was about a Roman political community ruling over Italy, or an *Italia* built with Rome at its core, or later in the life of Roman history, a broader multicultural empire committed to citizenship for all free men. That idea of citizenship as a project is a thread that extends to our present day.

In contrast to the Athenian citizen *leaving* the "world of things," to be tended by women and slaves in the *oikos*, Roman citizenship entailed *embracing* the world of things (Pocock 1993). The individual had possessions, and their possessions tied them to the community across the Roman Empire. Those possessions demanded relationships, such as those of the market and trade: the individuals were, in this conception, the sum of those possessive relationships, reinforcing their connection to the broader community of fellow citizens as well as their personal involvement in the direction of the *res publica* (Millar 1998; Mouritsen 2001; Erdkamp, Verboven, and Zuiderhoek 2015).

Rome's embrace of property was also the first step to thinking of citizens in terms of their "intrinsic properties," notably in respect of their rights. Rights emanated from the "real" property of the land, later reflected in early modern European history where citizenship status demanded landed property. An individual with interests (worth defending) would be, so it was reasoned, more civically trustworthy and committed than an individual without interests (and nothing to lose). This was not only a convenient stratagem for the ruling class; it was felt that citizens anchored through their interests and properties in the community would benefit the community itself. Those rights, those properties, would over time become detached from actual land to the "properties" of the human being and their inherent rights.

Thus, Rome also planted the seed of that nexus between individual "interest" and collective interest—a crucial moment. The individual's property (and interest) could be the basis for collective interest. The Enlightenment, and the development of Natural Law under its auspices, would put self-interest at the core of the individual and, by extension, at the center of the market and of politics. "Interest" thus became foundational to conceptions of citizenship, as it came to be practiced. From there, interest became embedded in the foundation of modern democracies.

38   CITIZENSHIP

Rome helped shape key traits of citizenship for the modern democratic era. While democratic participation furthered citizenship as an embodiment of a people's collective association, there was more to membership than solely political community. In Rome, membership was about what citizens "are owed" (such as rights) rather than simply about which community they were a part of. Another important point: Roman law was the basis on which a multitude of people shared thoughts, sentiments, and feelings about a common political, social, and civic space—even though they did not know each other personally. Tangible property, including private land, was legally inscribed as an early basis of rights. And so this would later extend, notably in the modern nation-state, to the territory—the country—of "the people" as a whole. That land, legally demarcated, is a felt projection of a people, their place in history, and their collective rights.

Membership in Rome was more expansive and inclusive than in the Greek polis. In the latter, citizens lived in a contained space, knew a reasonable proportion of their fellow citizens, and physically experienced the same environment with no strong ambition to extend their domain. In its abstraction and universality, Rome's public sphere was incomparably larger than the narrow agora in a Greek polis (Calhoun 1997). Rome was thus projected to serve an ever-widening community. Even in the passage from the Republic to the establishment of Roman imperial law, the sovereign ruled (in principle) on behalf of a society of individuals who were the ultimate bearers of rights (Weintraub 1997).

Citizenship in Rome could be granted at birth; it could otherwise be gained or even lost, willingly or unwillingly, according to changing rules throughout centuries of Roman history. Even if kinship never lost its grip, as ethnic Romans retained a better political access also in the passage to a multicultural empire, what mattered most was the content of citizenship itself (Calhoun 1997). To be Roman was about being equal before the law within a broad political community. This also contributed to linking citizens further among themselves, such as in their quality as taxpayers, in their availability to leave their private life to hold a public office, to fight for Rome when needed, or to share in nationwide festivities.

The legacies of Rome—and of Ancient Near East civilizations and Greece—would serve as a long-lasting precedent. It was a precedent that would influence medieval thought, Italian city-states, and subsequently modern nation-states, centuries after the fall of the Roman Empire.[14]

Notes

1. When a noncitizen becomes a citizen, they "naturalize"—and denaturalization is formally an individual's renouncing of their citizenship. The irony of this term, and why it is used, is a matter we will address further in the book.
2. We use the notion of the human "stripped bare" in a distinct sense from that of Agamben (1998).
3. Other Greek states, like Sparta, could also be included in this discussion on citizenship but Athens has been the lodestar for the construction of citizenship in the West, especially because of philosophical elaboration by Plato in his *Republic*.
4. Other civilizations, or societies, around the world, may have done the same in this period. But we do not presently have evidence of these cases affecting, say, Greek or Roman thinking or the subsequent trajectory of citizenship in world history. We are all bound by the historical record that has been revealed to us.
5. For a contrasting view of state development and the status of subjects in Babylonia, see Clifford and Richardson (2017). For the general understanding of society in the period Richardson focuses on, see Charpin (2012).
6. See Stol (2016) and von Dassow (2023, 2011); for a perspective on women's autonomy and their contributions to public life, see Chavalas (2014).
7. Quote from Sarah Viren (2021), used in a different context; quoted in von Dassow (2023). See also Blok (2017) and Hall (2002).
8. See, for example, discussions in Moses (2010) on Protestant churches and German unification, Shalev (2010) on "biblicism" in the early American Republic, Guibbury (2014) on the Jews' readmission to England and the idea of an Elect Nation, Jones and Shain (2017) on Jews and Westphalia, and Ilany (2018) on Germany.
9. On the "protections" and the Indian case, see Brekke (2012).
10. Emergence of language and practices that resonate with Western political developments date to the third century BCE through *The Arthashastra*, dealing with principles and practices of state government (Ramaswamy 1994; Boesche 2003); for later developments under Asoka the Great, see Nikam and McKeon (1978) and Ahir (1995).
11. A broad literature is available on civilizations and bordering. On specifically Ottoman and Islamic Empires, see Kafadar (1996), Lowry (2003), Karpat and Zens (2004), Finkel (2007), Peacock (2009), Casale (2015a, 2015b), and McDonald and Moore (2015).
12. The metaphor was expounded upon by Jean-Jacques Rousseau in his *Discourse on Political Economy*: "The body politic, taken individually may be considered as an organized, living body, resembling that of a man. The sovereign power represents the head; the laws and customs are the brain; commerce, industry and agriculture are the mouth and stomach; the public income is the blood; the citizens are the body and the members, which make the machine live, move and work" (Rousseau 1994).
13. The gendered distinctions of public and private spheres, inherently discriminatory, is a source of rich critique among feminist scholars (see discussion in Gavison 1992).

Citizenship was an "emancipation from the world of things," and this necessitated the support of the (male) civic activities in the public sphere from the *oikos*, the household based on the exploitation of women and slaves (Pocock 1993; Blundell 1995; Katz 1992, 1999).

14. See, across these periods and regions, Jones (1997), Hirschi (2012), Waley and Dean (2013), and Molho, Raaflaub, and Emlen (2018).

3

The Second Revolution

The Medieval Roots of Modern Citizenship

In conventional understanding, the roots of modern civic and corporate associations began with the Enlightenment in the eighteenth century. More recent work has shown that we need to go much further back in history, starting in the eleventh century. Furthermore, geographically we must go beyond Europe, notably in the case of guilds in China in the Qing period. In Europe, these roots are not secular and modern, but rather medieval. They rest in Christian, mostly urban corporations. These corporations did not remain focused on voluntary religious or social matters; they soon turned to issues of participation in political rule (Lewis 2007; Van Dijck, De Munck, and Terpstra 2017).

Corporations developed rapidly in Europe from the eleventh century, under the sanction of the Church. The corporate form is based on voluntary associations of one kind or another, rather than resting largely in kinship ties, which are critical inflection points for the development of citizenship. These corporations are at the heart of the development of guilds and Italian city republics, and indeed to the emergence of business corporations and nation-states. This is, in part, why the second revolution should be dated from the eleventh, not the seventeenth century, via the Treaty of Westphalia, or from the eighteenth century and the Enlightenment.

Corporations, notably guilds, nurtured values of judicial equality, individual liberties, and mutual aid for their members (Black 2003; Van Dijck, De Munck, and Terpstra 2017). However, their civic impact was circumscribed by the ongoing stickiness of primordialist attributes. From a sociological perspective, one can parse how it worked for eligible Christian males and extrapolate the ways this became a nucleus upon which the corporate civic forms of association developed over time. This is analogous to the related story of democracy: an initial, highly exclusive basis of propertied males becoming much more inclusive over an extended period. Conversely, understanding how and why guilds in this period were discriminatory also can be

Citizenship. David Jacobson and Manlio Cinalli, Oxford University Press. © Oxford University Press 2023.
DOI: 10.1093/oso/9780197669150.003.0003

42 CITIZENSHIP

enlightening for understanding citizenship and the conditions under which citizenship was forcibly circumscribed.

As a second example, we draw on the Chinese case in the Qing period, the final dynasty of Confucian China (1644–1912). This period is when Chinese guilds were most comparable to those in Europe. The Chinese guilds illustrate that the emerging civic corporate principles were not uniquely endogenous to the European social and cultural milieu. The Chinese guilds also show that there were no specific religious or culturally delimited bases for the emergence of civic forms of association (Fewsmith 1983; Lucassen, De Moor, and Van Zanden 2008; Moll-Murata 2018, 2008). The "civic grammar" emerged, albeit partially, in socially propitious yet disparate historical contexts.

Corporations are a basis of association in which its members are bound by rules, understandings, and values that, in principle, supersede kinship ties. Corporations have been religious, civic, economic, and political. The corporation can scale from a local voluntary organization to a national or global movement. A guild is a form of corporation that, historically, is based on a particular occupation; that controls access to that occupation; and that promotes the economic, social, welfare, and political well-being of its members. Guilds have varied dramatically across geography, practices, professions, and history. The primary distinction for historians has been between merchant guilds and craft guilds. The merchant guilds were mostly concerned with trade. Craft guilds were organized around specific crafts and provided specific goods and services. But guilds have taken various forms, sometimes fusing different categories of guilds, and guilds were the primary basis for training skilled workers, notably through apprenticeship programs (Ogilvie 2019, 2020; Prak 2018).

Guilds are a corporate form that is of particular importance in the development of citizenship. As documented in Antony Black's (2003) seminal work, guilds across Europe were built around particular crafts and trades and brought together economic concerns with communal commitment, mutual aid, individual rights (if circumscribed), and political influence. They facilitated face-to-face engagement to simultaneously nurture civic community and political access. The corporations and guilds in this period were the "first statement," in Black's words, of participatory democracy. Their legacy is as the nucleus for the nation-state, business corporations, and civic organizations; the guild became, in effect, an analogue or prototype for the civic polity. Yet these guilds have been underappreciated in terms of their long-term impact and their role in informing present-day approaches to democracy.

But the guilds, particularly in the European case, have also been idealized in terms of their democratic character, with their exclusionary qualities elided or contextualized as a matter of the medieval early-modern environment. The knitting together of primordialist criteria with (circumscribed) civic participation was, however, a fundamental characteristic of the guilds. Sheilagh Ogilvie (2011, 2019, 2020) has made a deeply researched, empirically supported corrective to the frequently idealized picture of the guilds. She assesses guilds' inclusiveness across three dimensions: the extent to which the guilds facilitated participation by everyone in society ("societal inclusiveness"); the degree to which members of the guild participated in their own governance ("community inclusiveness"); and the level to which the guild had representation vis-à-vis political authority in, notably, both communes and city-states ("corporate inclusiveness").

Drawing on her detailed dataset, Ogilvie finds that, in terms of societal inclusiveness, the guild was left wanting indeed. Guilds excluded almost all women and Jews. Other minorities could be excluded as well, including linguistic and ethnic minorities. The guild did not, in many cases, replace clan or family ties, as Antony Black (2003) claimed, but instead tended to favor them. Some guilds favored the kin of existing guild members when deciding whom to admit to membership. A significant share of members were relatives of existing members. In a sample of 499 guilds in eleven European societies dating from 1375 to 1860, thirty-seven percent were sons of existing guild members (Ogilvie 2019, 111–114). Guilds did not replace the role of family but co-existed with it. Of the ten percent of the European population who lived in towns, one-third of households had a guild member.

Consider the case of discrimination against women, evident in both European and Chinese guilds. Ogilvie (2019, 303–306) closely examines the question of discriminatory practices against women and Jews in European guilds. One argument she quotes is that the "exclusion of women and minorities was a generalized social, religious and cultural phenomenon," and that, in effect, guilds were operating in an environment of invariant cultural norms. Guilds did not simply mirror patriarchal and antisemitic values—they actively enforced them. Indeed, there was an inverse relationship between the ability of guilds to regulate economic activity and the extent of female participation in the labor force. Women moved into different economic activities as soon as guild regulations opened up or in cases where guild rules were more relaxed, such as in retailing. Women's role in guilds was hindered, Ogilvie (2019) shows, in three ways: (1) girls' admission to

44 CITIZENSHIP

apprenticeship was restricted by most guilds; (2) women's access to the labor force through the guilds was limited in the industrial and service sectors the guilds controlled; and (3) the guilds restricted women as independent entrepreneurs.

Involvement in guild governance was, Ogilvie (2020) states, high in cases but modest on average. However, here the picture is more nuanced. As Dutch historian Maarten Prak (2018, 69) points out, the guilds had a reasonable degree of member participation in internal governance. Guild representatives had to be elected. Guild members often preferred, Prak concedes, elite and well-connected representatives; however, the guild members could still hold them to account. Furthermore, although ample evidence suggests that well-to-do members joined guilds to access municipal levers of power, ordinary guild members did manage to do the same in many places.

The picture of guilds' overall influence in terms of commune and city authorities is more encouraging. From the tenth to twelfth centuries emerging merchant guilds broke up the monopoly of royal, noble, and church groups. From the thirteenth to fifteenth centuries guilds undermined the domination of old elites. But Ogilvie (2020) notes how, having wrested political influence, guilds also used this newly found power to reduce the inclusion of broad groups of people—women, peasants, Jews, laborers—in a range of occupations, in political influence, or even in the cultural life promoted by the guilds. Different forms of inclusiveness are not necessarily positive sum in their effects and, indeed, can be zero sum, as seen in the overall impact of the guilds—some people get excluded at the expense (literally, in economic activity) of others.

We need to be cognizant of historical guilds' limitations, not only in terms of our historical understanding but also to draw lessons about what guilds can teach us prescriptively, and how the less welcome attributes can be overcome. The guilds' combination of fertile civic shoots, yet frequently accompanied by primordialist criteria, is another example of the way citizenship has always been circumscribed in some way. The modern nation-state itself has elaborated rules about who acquires citizenship, even if in recent decades those restrictions have partially opened such that, for example, explicit racial and ethnic legal criteria have been diluted or removed.

However, in a scholarly fashion, and even prescriptively, we can learn from both the successes and the failures of historical guilds as a civic institution. This is akin to contemporary engagement with the practices of democracy— we still appreciate the comparative successes of modern democracies despite the uneven distribution of benefits ranging from socio-economic to legal justice. In a more positive vein, we can ask what can be learned from civic practices in guilds for those who were included as full members. Under what circumstances can discriminatory and exclusionary practices be diluted?[1]

Civic Developments after the First Millennium

In 1000 CE, civic organizations, from incorporated towns to guilds, hardly existed. By 1300, an extensive system of corporate bodies—notably guilds and town communes—were active across significant parts of Western Europe. Although characterized by regional variations, it is possible, as Prak (2018) notes, to observe a particular model of late medieval citizenship. Even though guilds are often viewed as a form of trade or craft association, they were much more than that, with cultural, mutual aid, and political goals. They were also critical intermediaries of citizenship in communes and the city republics. Why there was, in this period, the emergence and upsurge of such corporate bodies is a matter of debate, but a key development tends to be overlooked.

During canon law reform, under the impetus of Pope Gregory VII (reigning from 1073 to 1085), the Church created and sanctioned the *corporation*. Groups of people could create their own civic association or "body" (or *corpus*, the Latin root of corporation), allowing them to be legally sanctioned as juridical persons in the emerging forms of communes, guilds, and voluntary associations. The corporation did not have to be religious in character. Merchants and artisans had already started forming their own organizations with their own elected officials. In the tenth century, bishops took a key role in establishing local town government by juridically separating the town from the countryside (Berman 1983; Prak 2018). But the sanctioning of corporations by the Church was to have a dramatic effect.

The historian of canon law, Peter Landau (2022, 579), notes the critical role of the Church in the Gregorian period for the sanctioning of corporations:

> Canon law was decisive for the history of incorporation . . . In spite of many efforts to find the beginning of corporation concepts in certain legal rules of Germanic origin, there can be no doubt about the role of the canonists for the main features of corporation theory. Many elements of modern corporation law are found for the first time in canon law. This includes the

46   CITIZENSHIP

principle of freedom of association, the use of the idea of fiction for juristic personality, and the elaboration of the concept of foundations. The corporate unit first became a subject of rights and duties in the realm of canon law.

This moment in history—the invention and legal sanctioning of the corporation—is scarcely remembered in the public imagination (in contrast to the Enlightenment, the French Revolution, and the American Revolution), let alone commemorated. What is better remembered of the canon law reform is also significant, however, for the long-term development of citizenship, albeit indirectly. Gregory VII established, in 1078, that the investiture of bishops and abbots was in the hands of the Church, not lay authorities—wresting control away from secular rulers and, ultimately, strengthening the papacy in the long-term conflict of "popes over princes" (Sisson 2016). The Church was understood as a community of faith predicated on the belief in Christ as Lord. The Church was constructed and maintained through (canon) law. Law, as we argue more broadly, is key to civic establishment and transformation—not through natural reproduction and kinship (Berman 1983; Tamanaha 2004; Ullmann 2013; Cushing 2021). In principle, law replaces, wholly or in part, presupposed kin ties as the basis of church organization. The "invented" character of the faith community is exemplified in the idea of the Church as the embodiment of Christ. In the words of Sir Thomas More (in 1514), "[Christ] doth incorporate all christen folke and hys owne bodye together in one corporacyon mistical."[2] The early understanding of the corporation was as a "body" of people—hence the term corporation—brought together by collective qualities than transcended blood ties (religious belief being one among a variety of possibilities).

Faith communities in cult-like groups, often associated with a charismatic leader, existed in Christian Europe and in the Mediterranean world in the first millennium CE and, for that matter, cults were active before then in Rome and among Jews in Ancient Israel. Cultic activities also took place in other parts of the ancient world. Early Christians were drawn to the idea of retreating into the desert to live a pure, spiritual life, as seen in figures such as St. Jerome (born in the year 347 and died 420), who also generated (literal) followers. But the difference is that when the formal Church later institutionalized corporations (and the cults transmogrified into more structured religious orders), the implications for society were vastly greater and longer lasting. The greater institutionalization of the Church overall began at the prompting of the Roman Emperor Constantine who, as a convert, had done so much to anchor Christianity. He initiated the First Council of Nicaea in 325 CE, which gave the Church a much more defined and robust organizational structure, notably regarding episcopacy, or Church governance. This process of institutionalization continued through the centuries; for example, the Rule of Benedict, written in 516 CE, stipulated rules for orderly monasteries under the leadership of an abbot.[3]

Eleventh-century canon law reforms also included the introduction of clerical celibacy. It has been compellingly argued that celibacy ensured the Church's control of property—no children of priests would remain with competing claims on the estates of the clergy (O'Loughlin 1995). Celibacy also had, we argue, the effect of helping supersede kinship as the basis of community and rule within the Church. In contrast, medieval lay authority, from the emperor to the landed gentry, was precisely grounded in family, inheritance, and kinship. Ironically, the practice of celibacy, which many today view as conservative or even reactionary, was in fact revolutionary at the time. Gregory VII was, after all, seeking in celibacy to overcome the role of family in social, political, and cultural reproduction.

Gregory VII also required, under canon law, *elected* bishops for the respective dioceses and elected abbots in the monasteries; collegial bodies would vote to place candidates in ecclesiastical offices, extending to the canonical election of a pope by the cardinals. The pontiff was supreme in his hold of all executive, legislative, and judicial power—the church was still strenuously hierarchical. But as a "community of faith," legal and religious criteria were (in principle) the basis of holding ecclesiastical office, judged and voted on by the appropriate collegial body—not kinship (see Morris 1989; Cowdrey 1998). This requirement of such elections also anticipates, albeit in a highly constricted form, the notion that if authority was no longer a function of birth, then it demanded the assent of the governed. We are not, of course, talking of a democratic organization in the Church. But given that the canon reforms pushed a religious body to transcend kinship as the organizational principle of their association, it is telling that traces of "consent" can be observed.

What an extraordinary watershed moment this was in Church history—and yet, astonishingly, its portent for Europe (and the world) since is marginally recognized (with notable exceptions—see Berman 1983; Black 2003; Prak 2018). Pope Gregory VII had no ambitious plan for a civic-minded blueprint for European communities in establishing the legal basis for the corporation. Yet he had, unwittingly, planted the seed—in the

48   CITIZENSHIP

establishment and juridical sanctioning of the corporation—for a revolution in human affairs that affects us to this day.[4] Furthermore, in going beyond "natural" communities, the inherent and foundational role of law was established—corporations, being invented and institutionalized as "fictitious personalities," had to be perforce legally defined and sanctioned. Such invented entities, which risked fragility absent the family ties so central to feudal life, demanded the involvement of its members through some level of the consent (albeit bounded and limited relative to what came later). For the corporation, the "body" of a human association, these developments were crucial for its flowering in Western Europe.

From this seed, the corporation became the nucleus, metaphorically like a modular building block for building a broad range of social, economic, and political forms of human association. The legacy of the corporation has been multifold and extraordinary, from medieval communes, town councils, and guilds to Renaissance city-states; dissenting religious sects which would grow into full force in the Protestant Reformation; the flowering of the economic corporation starting with those such as the Dutch East India Company, established in 1602; whole countries structured on the corporate model, including the United States, from the Mayflower Compact of the Puritans in 1620, to the legal basis of towns and states, to modern voluntary organizations; to the abstracted and "imagined" peoples launched through revolutions from the eighteenth century, in which the state becomes the locus of citizenship; to nineteenth century (and beyond) political movements based on socialist principles; to contemporary notion of modern corporation extending to non-shareholding stakeholders.[5]

Critically, the Church sanctioning of the corporation in the feudal context is the keyhole, the doorway, to civic possibilities in an otherwise kinship-based society in which birth determined social life, economic status, and political rule.

The European Guilds

Antony Black (2003) argues that civic corporate bodies, and especially the guild, eased the transition from the close, personal bonds of the clan. "As a small face-to-face group, the guild perpetuated some of the characteristics of . . . tribal human association," writes Black, and as such, guilds in effect cleared the pathway to the "dispersed and impersonal relationships of modern society and the state." Ogilvie's research suggests that Black's description is an idealized depiction. However, the guild provided a civically embedded form of community, and a novel model of such, although significantly limited by exclusionary practices.

A typical town in the late Middle Ages had dozens of craft and merchant guilds, and just as many, if not more, confraternities, charities, and religious organizations that also worked as social welfare associations. The towns and communes also had citizen militias, which on occasion became another means of citizen demands and empowerment. Citizenship was extensive, if predominantly male. Commonly, one- to two-thirds of households in each town or city were headed by a citizen. Although working-class households were less likely to be headed by a citizen relative to the middle and upper classes, citizenship cut through the social hierarchy (Prak 2018). Citizenship in the period up to the French Revolution in 1789 is local. Communities are direct and "felt," not the "imagined" communities of nation-states; as such, citizenship in the nation-state itself became more abstracted (Anderson 1991).

Membership in guilds implied membership in the wider town or city. In England, the guilds were the pathway to citizenship. In continental Europe, to become a member of a guild one frequently had to first become a citizen of the commune. Guilds provided a wide range of services to the community at large, such as the upkeep of public spaces, defense, tax collection, and fire control (Prak 2018). Guilds training in crafts and other skills served a larger public good. Their long-term impact, and potential future role, is illuminated in the guilds' role in the establishment of universities. The universities of Bologna (1088), Oxford (1096), and Paris (1150) originated as guilds of students or masters (Hastings 1895; Staley 1906).

Guilds could be welcoming to foreigners joining the guild; however, not all guilds were welcoming of "foreyns." In London, for example, guilds could see non-members as threats to their livelihoods. Petitions and statutes sought to limit access to markets and labor to members only. But evidence also suggests that noncitizen work was essential to the guilds. Economic conditions ameliorated enforcement of statutes. Guilds restricted membership, and thus citizenship itself, through their apprenticeship system. But this was rarely static. For example, in the forty years after the Black Death of 1348–1349 guilds rarely restricted the number of apprentices masters could take on (Davies 2018; see also Ogilvie 2019). Foreigners could also be violently targeted, such as in a notorious case in which guilds were involved in

50   CITIZENSHIP

an anti-Jewish pogrom which also targeted foreigners in Frankfurt-am-Main in the 1614 "Fettmilch Uprising" (Friedrichs 1990).

Overall, in Europe there was extensive acquisition of citizenship status—Italian archives of the thirteenth and fourteenth centuries abound with documents of citizenship acquisition. That status impacted, most significantly, access to the guilds and access to high office. Citizenship provided more than a legal affiliation; it was a path to an "expansive" membership, from the guilds to communal government to participation in the militias. Citizenship made each member a part of a civic project. How citizenship was structured varied between cities. Siena, for example, had distinctions between generational citizens, new citizens, and citizens from the periphery of the town, "out-burghers." There was no singular model of citizenship in Europe. Local authorities brokered relationships between their own citizens and state authorities (Prak 2018).

Membership in these communities involved various statuses, but two categories were most widespread: full citizenship and resident status. Noncitizen residents had few formal rights. Formal citizenship in this period had its greatest impact in two respects: access to guilds and access to high office. But, as today, formal citizenship lagged actual practice, which involved a kind of "informal citizenship." Noncitizen residents could be secure in their property, get a fair trial, and even access public welfare. Generally, noncitizen residents could not participate in elections nor serve in high office. They could have jobs, although in most towns they were excluded from the guilds, which in turn disadvantaged them economically (Prak 2018; Ogilvie 2019).

The nexus of guilds for citizenship is of interest in thinking about the shaping of citizenship today, a topic we will return to in Chapter 8.

Republics and Guilds: Florence and Venice

The age of small, independent Italian communes started as early as the ninth century with Venice, Gaeta, and Amalfi, and was followed by just about every other significant town in the Centre and North of the country. By the end of the fifteenth century, almost all Italian city-states were absorbed and consolidated by greater powers. A few republican city-states, however, remained. Florence and Venice, the famed historian Jacob Burckhardt claimed (2019), were the beginning of the modern world. The passive medieval subject was left behind in these republics to be replaced by, Burckhardt

THE SECOND REVOLUTION   51

wrote, the ambitious, forward-looking individual who would transform the arts, politics, and science in the modern world (see also Gilbert 1968; Comino, Galasso, and Graziano 2017).

Many would contest Burckhardt's sweeping claims of Florence and Venice as *the* source of the modern world, but these two city-states have undoubtedly played a crucial role. In the Middle Ages, outside the urban centers, social, political, and economic inequalities were celebrated, be it that of the nobility and the peasantry, the monarchy and its vassals, or of the papacy's hierarchical distribution of grace. But it was not simply inequality that was celebrated. So was the ascetic life epitomized by monasticism. Sexual restraint was not, in principle, just the province of the cloistered monk and nun: the Church father St. Jerome taught that "the wise man should love his wife with cool discretion, not with hot desire," also suggesting that "[n]othing is filthier than to have sex with your wife as you might do with your mistress" (quoted in Withol 2010). This world was viewed as incorrigibly corrupt, to be redeemed only by withdrawal from the pleasures of the wayward and the sinful joys of lust and lucre. True salvation lay only in soteriological escape—in death (see Brown 1990).

The humanist language of Venice and Florence confronted the assumptions of hierarchy and inequality. The social and political order, writes the Renaissance scholar Hanan Yoran (2007, 335), came to be "perceived as a contingent and changeable product of human actions [and] notions of political equality and liberty become plausible . . . Liberty and equality are therefore inscribed, if only as potentials, in modern political discourse in a way that they were not in premodern thought and imagination." Accordingly, the civic humanists of Italy turned the Middle Ages on its head. As Yoran (2007, 327) notes:

> While medieval high culture considered the renunciation of sexual activity, private property, and power as its ideal . . . the civic humanists affirmed family life as natural and as conducive to the fulfilment of our purpose as social animals. By the same token, [they] regarded economic activity and material wealth in a positive light, natural for the individual and necessary for the community . . . The civic humanists rejected the medieval preference—based on Christian, as well classical, premises for the *vita contemplativa*, the life of philosophical contemplation, internal meditation, and prayer. They affirmed, instead, the *vita activa*, active life of man as *pater familias*, as economic actor, and, above all, as an engager in the public sphere.

52   CITIZENSHIP

The idea of *vita activa* similarly presupposed the citizen as active and engaged, not simply a passive recipient of rights. *Vita activa* also presupposes citizenship as an act of creation, a project, rather than a "given" world determined by tradition from "time immemorial."

The Florentines and Venetians drew on, and compared, their civic republics to Ancient Greece and Rome. They invoked Aristotle, Plato, and Cicero. Petrarch described Venice as "a city rich in gold but richer in repute; strong in power but stronger in virtue; built on solid marble but more stably and solidly established on the more secure foundations of its citizens' concord, fortified and made safe by the intelligence and wisdom of its sons rather than by the sea which surrounds the city" (quoted in Gilbert 1968, 46). Venetian nobles were drawn to humanist treatises which described Venice in terms of the admired Greeks and Romans.

Rome and Greece's Influence on Italian Cities

The Italian cities put a strong emphasis on active membership, with citizens in a state of direct, rather than indirect, solidarity and mutual responsibility. They did so through a panoply of signorias, republics, and city-states that emerged from the ninth century. For Italian theorists of civic government, Roman citizenship was something of a foil. Rome's conception of civic community was, in this perspective, too thin, providing a mere affiliation. At the same time, the limited geographical scope of Italian cities invited comparison with the Greek polis. In their determination to thicken their notion of membership, the Italian cities engaged in shaping organizational and legal structures that could link membership to decision-making. In doing so, the Italian city governments could be, in principle, better informed of the preferences of the governed—progressively so, beyond the experience of Athenian democracy.[6]

Venice's model of mixed government also provided a lasting impact, not only intellectually in the writings of the humanists, but in shaping subsequent republican constitutions in Europe and beyond. This, too, was influenced by the Roman legacy: "the Doge [chief magistrate] represented the monarchical element; the Senate the aristocratic element; and the *Consiglio Maggiore* [chief political assembly] the democratic element" (Gilbert 1968). The Venetian concept of mixed government was emulated throughout Europe and beyond, including in the United States (Gordon 2009; McDougall 2018).

Citizenship did require residency. In Florence, further, only those who were members of a guild could become citizens. The judicial element—the role of adjudicators, mediators, and judges—was most prominently exercised *within* the guilds (Najemy 2006, 1979; Putnam, Leonardi, and Nanetti 1994). This leads us to another key characteristic of civic life in the Italian cities, the role of associations that were voluntary and not derived primarily from kinship ties—notably, in qualified ways, regarding the guilds. In kinship-based societies it is hard to unwind the different threads—kin ties, economic ties, social ties, and political ties—in contrast to the way we think of, for example, economic corporations today being driven largely by concerns of, ultimately, profit and loss. The role of the family as the basis of different associations was as true in Italy as it was elsewhere in the Middle Ages—that is, until the mid-1200s. Italy, however, also has a history of building associations which, over time, became voluntary in character and were not predicated purely on family and blood ties (Weber 1966; Eckstein and Terpstra 2010; Jurdjevic 2010).

In voluntary associations, in principle, office was determined functionally, and collaboration was built on mutual exchanges among members. Accordingly, cities knitted together the populace based on neighborhood associations and civic ties. Neighborhoods formed groups responsible for mutual defense, business relationships, and assistance. Guilds were formed for social, political, and occupational purposes by craftsmen and tradesmen (see, for example, Farrell 2020; Richter 1890). The oldest guild-statute, from Verona and dating from 1303, stipulated those members shall provide, *inter alia*, "Fraternal assistance in necessity of whatever kind . . . hospitality towards strangers, when passing through the town . . . and the mutual obligation of offering comfort in the case of debility" (quoted in Putnam, Leonardi, and Nanetti 1994, 125). The violation of the statute was, it stated, to be met by ostracism and boycotts of the guilty party.

It is remarkable how the guilds became the strike force of political reform and a key instrument of citizenship (Najemy 2006). They contested family-based forms of authority, notably that of the patricians and the landed aristocracy. The guilds were the foundation for the political organization of local communities and neighborhoods. They were thus a crucial civic dimension that further extended membership, including to outsiders and foreigners, in qualified ways. At their best, these guilds were not merely a matter of affiliation with rights and duties but they demanded a commitment to mutual responsibility and solidarity among citizens themselves (Assente 1998). Some

54   CITIZENSHIP

guilds took the form of *popolo* ("the people") pressure groups that were organized by guild or by district, to protect the interests of commoners (usually merchants and tradesmen) from the nobility (Cohn 2022, 2008).

The guilds also addressed the main concern for transformation of preferences from below, softening top-down decision-making. The guilds, and the *popolo*, developed organizational and legal structures. Elected officials of guilds participated directly in decisions of the commune. The decisions of the guilds could sometimes supersede that of the commune, while guilds and other associations provided the *capitano popoli* of their own militia, a particularly cogent form of political expression. In fourteenth-century Pisa, the *Podesta* (chief magistrate) was forced under oath to assure that he and his judges would not interfere in disputes of the populace. *Capitano popoli* occasionally had separate authority to summon citizens. City officials were elected through *popolo grasso*—the high-ranking guilds, such as judges, bankers, doctors, and the like. Finally, after several revolutions, some of the lower ranking *popolo minuto* obtained a degree of access to the levers of power (Weber 1966; Poloni 2022).

At the core of the Italian city, the guilds stood out as a collective project, driven by a mix of economic, legal, social, welfare, and political concerns. The guild, in essence, became the locus of citizenship for its members, whether they were formally citizens or not, roughly in as much as today members of a corporate body—say a university or a business—have legal protections regardless of citizenship status. But guilds and the multitude of other associational bodies in Italy's republican city-states—for example, the *vicinanze* (neighborhood associations), the confraternities (religious societies for mutual assistance), the *populus* (parish organizations), and the *consorterie* ("tower societies")—provided the most meaningful locus for political community, as well as the nexus between the governors and the governed and in so providing the structural foundation of the city itself (Putnam, Leonardi, and Nanetti 1994; see, in general, Guenzi, Massa, and Caselli 1998).

It is no surprise that the marking of sharp geographic borders in this context became less of a concern. Borders as such in these city republics had a limited role in defining citizenship, and indeed the actual geographic borders were ambiguous, in line with broader patterns in Europe. The surrounding rural areas had a symbiotic relationship with the cities, and cities had much control of, and keen economic interest in, those areas; however, the rural surroundings were not "of" the city-state as its inhabitants pictured it (see Chittolini 1989; and, in general, Vitale 2016; Abulafia and Berend 2017).

THE SECOND REVOLUTION   55

The *experience* of geographic borders, in such circumstances, was uncertain and was more of a "zone" than the sharp borderlines drawn on political maps. Even today, it would be hard for the typical city dweller to say what exactly are the boundaries of their city and answers to such a question would most certainly be varied. Reinforcing such fuzziness—or seamed—character of such boundaries, Italian city-state governments, which relied heavily on lawyers and functional experts in areas from planning to accountancy, drew on such expertise from other parts of Italy. Lawyers tended to come from Bologna, while their commerce and trade relied in part on diasporic populations of Venetians and Florentines, who lived in other cities (Chittolini 1989; Martines 2015; Tanzini 2018).

Sharply delineated borders, on any scale, nurture endogenous identities—such as in the case of the nation-state. The Italian republics did not rely on bounded territoriality in the same way, and thus they provided a distinct civic model. Absent a strict territorial vision, associations and organizations were the key nexus for social and political ties and in shaping the character of the civic community, including the acceptance of outsiders and foreigners. Such associations and organizations were, institutionally, legal "fictions" or creations, which, in their voluntary and civic character could at least partially supersede kinship and make the potential for more expansive membership. Law also gives substance to civic engagement. Only through the law could the "invented" categories of guild, city, and, later, nation have social, economic, and political cogency. The citizen, in principle, was enmeshed in civic association (from the guild to political authority) through engaging, in different ways, "the law." The boundaries of civic communities and city-states in Italy were more supple than territorial states. The story of the guilds, their role in terms of citizenship (both for rule and for belonging), and the seamed character of boundaries in the Italian city republics have much to teach us for our present moment.[7]

The Guild and the Civic Habit

"Most historians [have] considered the supposedly more secular culture of the Enlightenment," Van Dijck and his colleagues (2017, 2) note, "as an essential precondition for the rise of European civil society in the modern era." Scholarly literature on the concept of civil society has grown dramatically since the 1970s, but the Enlightenment baseline interpretation has remained

56   CITIZENSHIP

the consensus about the roots of civic society. Scholarship has continued to highlight the independence of civic and voluntary associations from religion and the state as a key marker of civil society (Gellner 1994). "The crux of the matter," as one scholar stated, echoing the consensus, "was liberation from feudal and religious 'shackles' " (Baker 2001, quoted in Van Dijck, De Munck, and Terpstra 2017, 2). For Jürgen Habermas (1989), civil society was intrinsically tied to individualization, secularization, and capitalism—all associated with the Enlightenment.

While it has been assumed that "liberal individualism" was associated with the emergence of the modern central state, Black (2003) shows how corporate groups like guilds and their values were integral to state formation and legitimation. Furthermore, guilds are a key source of the theory and "habit" of democratic rule—the basis, in other words, of the self-governing citizen—albeit circumscribed by gendered and religiously discriminatory practices. Further, the guilds' economic motives, individual freedoms, and communal commitments reinforced one another. The guild, as such, contradicts the conventional historical telling of a transition from a medieval tight-knit community to a modern market or "contract" society—what Ferdinand Tönnies (2001 [1887]) famously referred to as the movement from *Gemeinschaft* to *Gesellschaft*.

The nation-state would, however, be pivotal to the mass expansion of citizenship, including to larger and larger populations and to excluded groups, such as women, Jews, and racial minorities. State expansion was in a dialectical relationship with the growth of citizenship rights; the state's legal and government bureaucracy grew in tandem with expanded responsibilities to the citizenry (also legitimating taxation and the mobilization of citizens for war) (Tilly 2007a). However, while the modern state was built on the corporate example of the guilds and other medieval corporations, the state, market, and civil society became increasingly institutionally differentiated.

The Chinese Guilds

The European guild as a corporate form is emulated (consciously or otherwise) in a variety of contexts, from business corporations to voluntary organizations. The European forms of corporation became dominant models globally initially due to European colonization, particularly from the nineteenth century—not least in the idea of the nation-state itself. But guilds were not "of" Europe. They were a social form that arose in specific circumstances, where kinship-based organizations were no longer solely capable of responding to social, political, and economic change. This was the case due to growing social complexity and scale, and because of the emergence of central authorities that transcend kinship-based societies, such as feudal or clan-based societies. Thus, we can observe guild-like organizations elsewhere, from Confucian China to the Ottoman Empire. The role of kinship does not, however, disappear and, as in the history of citizenship and civic association, incipient civic forms are often in complementary association with kin associations. The Chinese guilds are illustrative.

The Chinese merchant and craft associations that most shared similarities with European guilds originated in the sixteenth century but became much more extensive from the mid-eighteenth century. This is in the period of China's last dynasty, the Qing Dynasty (1644–1912). The number of guilds soars from the mid-nineteenth century following the first Opium War (1839–1841) and the Taiping Rebellion (1850–1864). However, Chinese guilds were not precisely the same as European guilds. They had similar functions, such as fulfilling, to varying degrees, the economic, social, and cultural needs of their members. But the political setting was very different, notably in the character of the relationship with the Chinese state—the Confucian bureaucracy—or local authorities (Moll-Murata 2008).

Three sets of questions arise. First, to what extent did Chinese guilds provide examples of going beyond clan and kinship bases of association? How inclusive were they to, for example, non-kin and outsiders? Second, what was their influence in terms of political authorities, either at the local or national level? And third, to what extent do we see democratic inclusion in internal guild governance? The first question addresses the social dimension of citizenship (even if not articulated as such in the Chinese case), and the latter two questions address the political dimension of participation.

The available data on Chinese guilds is more limited than that of European guilds, particularly following Ogilvie's (2019) extensive collection of data on European guilds. Here instead we focus on the extent to which Chinese guilds demonstrate the emergence of civic practices as "corporations" that went beyond solely kinship forms of association and, in addition, provided a form of civic governance. Chinese guilds display a wide geographic and historical diversity. But quantifiable generalizations of the kind that Ogilvie's empirical research provides for the European case are lacking. General patterns notwithstanding, the flowering of civic practices—whatever the

58   CITIZENSHIP

extent—is key to our understanding of the guild as a new corporate form. That, in turn, illustrates that the emergence of civic forms is independent of any cultural, religious, or geographic determinism (European or otherwise). This observation applies to citizenship more broadly, and its origins or future possibilities.

Outsiders and the Chinese Guild

In a theme that became familiar, Max Weber (1966) argued that capitalism did not develop in China because of the privileging of clan attachments. Urban dwellers favored their ties to their ancestral villages and, as such, never nurtured autonomous urban affiliations. In contrast, for Weber, European guilds provided a form of association in guilds that was an alternative to clans (Greif and Tabellini 2017; De la Croix and Doepke 2018). But subsequent scholarship has shown a more complex picture in China, as well as in Europe.

W. T. Rowe (1989), in his classic study on Hankow, noted that while common kin origins had been an important basis for membership in guilds, the nineteenth century saw a growing emphasis on common trades as basis of membership and diminution of common origins. Large syncretic businesses also developed in this period. The city of Hankou, Rowe argues, had achieved the highest level of what in today's terms would be called urban civic identity in China before China's absorption of European practices. Hankow came to be distinguished by the "multiplication rather than the substitution of social identities," such that its residents could view themselves as Hankow denizens while still maintaining their affiliation with their respective ancestral villages (Rowe 1989, 17). The civic functions of the guilds expanded greatly, and by the late nineteenth century they were providing services often through cross-guild alliances. Services included schools, street maintenance, and fire brigades, and they were available to all denizens, not only guild members. The autonomous activities were not legally recognized by the imperial government, but Rowe argues that de facto autonomy had emerged.[8]

Christine Moll-Murata (2008, 217, 223) writes that "as a rule" Chinese guilds did not so much keep outsiders out but instead sought to force those in a particular trade to join the relevant guild. Guilds established in the sixteenth century were founded by traveling merchants with wide geographic mobility. Such guilds stood in contrast to earlier forms of business that were installed at the order of the government since the eighth century. The itinerant character of such merchants and voluntary quality of such guilds would, relatively speaking, "open up" these associations. However, critically, women are rarely mentioned in guild documents—mirroring the story of European guilds.

We do not have the comparative Chinese data available to state whether the Chinese or European guilds were more inclusive (Ogilvie 2020, 188). Sidney Gamble and J. S. Burgess (1921, 168, cited in Ogilvie 2020) found that not a single Peking craft or trade guild had restrictions on entry based on kinship or place of origin. South Chinese crafts were exclusive, Gamble and Burgess stated, only if they demanded a "particular skill, [had] special trade secrets, or whose work is especially remunerative." Just one of the forty-two Peking guilds of porters that J. S. Burgess analyzed restricted admission to sons and brothers of guild members (1930, cited in Ogilvie 2020). Conversely, Moll-Murata (2013: 234) found that the Jingdezhen potters guild included, according to a twentieth-century stele, initially just four surnames and then twenty-four surnames. These surnames formed sub-groups or networks which organized the affairs of the guild on a rotational basis. This meant that access to this guild was restricted by family.

Influence of Chinese Guilds on Political Authorities

Where the Chinese guilds were distinctly different from the European guilds involves the vertical relations with political authorities. Joseph Fewsmith (1983, 619–620) writes how:

> [the] Confucian monopoly on moral knowledge and legitimate political action was institutionalized in a bureaucracy which . . . attempted to insulate itself from society. In a constant effort to maintain the centralization of authority, the government relied on a relatively small bureaucracy which regularly rotated its officials. To expand the bureaucracy to further "penetrate" the society or to choose officials from the local areas, as some writers in the "feudal" (fengjian) tradition desired, risked the "capture" of the bureaucracy by society . . . The bureaucracy monopolized communication to the throne and hence dominated without penetrating.

Guilds were not formally recognized, and they had no place in the law. But the limited penetration of the state bureaucracy made for a significant

60 CITIZENSHIP

political space at the local level that was filled by the guilds, together with clans and secret societies. Such extra-bureaucratic "private" associations could fill important roles, yet with uncertain legitimacy. This ambiguity created an inconsistent environment. Overall, Chinese guilds were not as politically influential as European guilds, as they did not formally participate in the governance of the city or town. Their reach politically could be forcibly restricted. On the other hand, the rules were frequently not put in writing, which allowed for some flexibility. Consequently, in at least some Chinese cities, such as Peking, Suzhou, Shanghai, and Hankou, guilds could informally participate in municipal governance (Fewsmith 1983; Moll-Murata 2013; Miaotai and Jingdezhen 1991, cited in Moll-Murata 2013).

Guild Internal Governance

Guilds mostly focused on the control of their own occupations, rather than concerning themselves with municipal politics. The guilds required individuals in a particular trade to join the appropriate guild. "Guest merchants" had to sell their goods through the guild system. In the enforcement of such practices the guilds had considerable juridical authority. Disputes were resolved within a guild, or a plurality of guilds. Sometimes they even had policing authority. The grain guilds, for example, ensured that arriving merchants did not overcharge through tipping the weight of their merchandise by dousing it with water (Fewsmith 1983, 621).

In terms of their internal governance, guilds were run through management boards, and the directors were drawn from the members. In some cases, the guild office was hereditary, but a practice of rotating the leadership also had a significant presence. One nineteenth-century British observer described the rotational system as "almost pure democracy." Peng Nansheng (2003) describes the Chinese guilds as a mix of "democracy, authoritarianism, and customary law." Democratically, some guilds rotated leadership annually while others held elections. Some guilds demanded a quorum for important decisions and secret ballots could be used for controversial decisions (Moll-Murata 2008, 224; Peng Nansheng 2003, cited in Moll-Murata 2008; Morse 1909).

A critical difference from the European case is that the guilds did not serve as a nexus between guild members and citizenship. Formal citizenship did not exist in Confucian China. Moll-Murata (2020), using Engin Isin's

(2012) definition that citizenship is the "right to claim rights," points to the protections of *min liangmin*, which she translates as "people," or "respectable subjects/citizens," who were entitled to the protection of their persons and their belongings. But "rights" are only a partial, subsidiary aspect of citizenship. The larger citizenship question—and to avoid a tautological definition of citizenship—is to ask how the Chinese guilds facilitated questions of rule and of membership. The Chinese guilds represented some progress, yet they were more limited than European guilds when it came to citizenship and political representation.

But, as Fewsmith (1983, 622–623) notes, "while guild jurisdiction was largely autonomous, it did not, as in Europe, constitute a separate structure of authority." Furthermore, guilds "could appeal to local custom or the magnanimity of officials . . . but they could not point to customary law and plead their cases in court." Thus, even though guilds played an essential role in the Chinese economy, and nurtured corporate forms of association, they did not have the legal standing to become an alternative form of authority. That absence of recognition of the guild as a "separate structure of authority" was fundamental—the guild in such circumstances was limited as to the extent it could become, endogenously, the nucleus of a broader flowering of the "corporate" model. The guild could not, or at least was severely restricted, in becoming the *pouvoirs intermediares*, the intermediary nexus, linking state and society (Fewsmith 1983, 617). As such, the Chinese guild was circumscribed as a means for nurturing citizenship within the Confucian framework.

It is telling, however, that as Confucian governance and institutions began to collapse following the Opium Wars, the guilds became essential in the functioning of towns and cities. That flickering civic promise would be extinguished by civil war and dictatorship in post-Qing China.

The Promise, and the Cautionary Tale, of Medieval and Early Modern Guilds

The key contribution of the Middle Ages in Europe, under the impetus of the eleventh-century Gregorian reforms, was the corporate form epitomized by the guild. For those who could be members, the corporation, especially the guild, provided key elements of citizenship: civic engagement, both socially and politically; citizenship as a civic project, which engendered a social solidarity well beyond its economic functions; socially embedding the

62 CITIZENSHIP

individual into a shared identity; conviviality; mutual aid; and, internally, a relatively democratic form of governance. Citizenship was simultaneously a social and political *act*, woven into the fabric of everyday life, including work. Citizenship was not a passive entitlement, individually enjoyed. Citizenship was immediate and palpable, a virtuous nexus between social and political commitment, with the profit-driven imperative leavened by, and in symbiosis with, noncontractual commitments.

Yet, the guild as then practiced had severe and profound deficits, notably in its exclusion of women and Jews and, depending on the guild, other exclusionary practices from certain linguistic groups to peasants. The inner civic life of the guild was encrusted by the hard shell of primordialist exclusion.

Guilds declined rapidly after the French Revolution and, with the rise of the nation-state, the autonomy of the guilds essentially disappeared. The nation-state was built on the corporatist form, but at its most abstract level. The corporate body politic became a national community, an "imagined community." We must recognize the nation-state's civic successes. Over time it provided examples, especially by the twentieth century, of embracing the excluded: women, racial groups, religions, and sexual minorities. It was the locus of an expanding panoply of rights. And we must also recognize the nation-state's horrific failures, from imposing or abiding slavery and racism to promoting colonialism. Today, liberal democracies are facing down antediluvian demons.

The nation-state did not manage to fully liberate itself from what has weighed on the civic project from the beginning, even in its most promising liberal republican shoots. The dialectic of *demos* and *ethnos*, and the "naturalization" of human characteristics (the individual, race, sex) and institutions (notably the market) was, ironically, sedimented in Enlightenment doctrine.

Notes

1. We will leave aside the issue of the guilds' contribution to, or hindrance of, economic growth, a matter which occupies economic historians.
2. Thomas More, *Treatise on the Passion* in *Works*, 1348/2 (published in the year 1514). See More 1976 [1514]. More was the Lord High Chancellor of England (1529–1532) and was beheaded by King Henry VIII for objecting to several steps taken by the king that marked an irrevocable break from Rome. More authored the book *Utopia* about, tellingly, an imaginary island society. One could argue that the book is a marker of a

THE SECOND REVOLUTION   63

growing human capability (given a changing sociological environment) to radically reimagine societies based on ideas, or what would later be called ideology.

3. See Chadwick (1967) and Brown (1995). We are grateful to the patristics scholar Celia Rabinowitz for her communications on church history (August 12, 2019).

4. Medieval canon law had far-reaching influence beyond the Catholic Church, and not only in engendering corporate mechanisms and governance. For example, the origins of international law are grounded in the writings of the canonists, and the canonist writing on the relationship of Church and State had a fundamental impact on constitutions and institutions. See Berman (1983).

5. On the modern corporation that extends to non-shareholding stakeholders, see Mansell and Sison (2020).

6. The character of Italian city-states was not, of course, completely static and we emphasize the periods when civic communalism was most at the fore. Karataşlı (2016) distinguishes periods of "communal patriotism," "civic nationalism," and "city-state chauvinism" in the communes and city-states from the eleventh century to the sixteenth century.

7. See Black (2003, 2017) and Burckhardt (2019). But also see Stanley (2011) for an argument tying civic humanism to the preservation of oligarchic authority.

8. Wakeman (1993) critiques Rowe's argument, questioning the extent of the autonomy of at least some guilds in Hankow, from the state or from bodies elsewhere—for example, pointing to a tea guild as apparently under the supervision of Shanghai compradors. Furthermore, Wakeman argues, guilds in Hankow were characterized by a "combative factionalism" rather than a shared urban identity, and that the urban landscape was riven by interethnic gang fights. Rowe (1984, 1989, 1993) responds in turn to Wakeman to argue that autonomy is not an "all or nothing thing" and guilds could operate in areas the state deemed inconsequential or seek state sanction if operating in areas of greater consequence. On conflict, Rowe argued that interethnic violence (which he pointed to in his original study) did not contradict an overall atmosphere of tolerance across ethnic and cultural divides.

4

Practices of Citizenship

From the Enlightenment to the Nation-State

The eighteenth century, the century of the Enlightenment and arguably the first revolutions in human history, is customarily seen as marking the beginning of the modern world. Much of our discussions on citizenship stem from the understanding that citizenship today, together with the nation-state and capitalism, is rooted in the Enlightenment. The Enlightenment is seen as providing the intellectual foundations of what was not just a politically groundbreaking period but a marker of an epistemological transformation. Principles—that monarchs ruled by divine right, that the pursuit of gain was a cardinal sin, and that one's place in society should be based on birth—were put into question, and ultimately repudiated. If hitherto philosophers aspired for the City of Man to emulate the City of God, now the City of Man could flourish on its own terms. Citizens could now come together, bound by social contract and untethered from ecclesiastical fiat. From nature to society, the human experience of "being in the world" was fundamentally altered. Or so scholars have generally viewed the Enlightenment.

The understanding that political ties were a series of interlocking feudal duties and obligations, from serried ranks of prince to vassal to peasant, had already been overcome in the examples of the Italian city republics and in guilds and consociations. But the nation-states that emerged from the eighteenth century, most notably in the American and French Revolutions, vastly expanded the demographic, geographic, and political scope of such earlier civic endeavors. The idea of a nation was a monumental abstraction drawing on purportedly shared ties and commitment across society and politics to form a modern political community. In Benedict Anderson's (1991) phrase, it was an "imagined community," imagined here conjuring up the thought that it could be a spectral supposition with little substance. Even the idea of the social contract, on such a vast scale, sounded like a conceit. What, in both

Citizenship. David Jacobson and Manlio Cinalli, Oxford University Press. © Oxford University Press 2023.
DOI: 10.1093/oso/9780197669150.003.0004

PRACTICES OF CITIZENSHIP   65

substance and the felt experience of the citizenry, *mediated* these emerging national communities?[1]

In practice, kinship and primordialism were not so much transcended in the Enlightenment as sublimated. Essentially, two claimed models of nationhood materialized: "territorial kinship" and national "fictive" kinship—what would be respectively associated with republicanism and ethnonationalism. In the first case, the land itself was associated with the people and its narrative. Its borders defined not just a territory but played a core role in defining national identity itself, both along the social dimension of mutual acknowledgement among inhabitants of the same land, and in their political allegiance to governors ruling on the same territory. In the case of ethnonationalism, the people are, in the German word, a *Volksgemeinschaft*, putatively associated through blood descent, a tribe writ large but now also claiming its own bounded country, a nation of, in its most assertive formulations, "blood and soil." Violence is iconographic across both the republican and nationalist imaginaries, through narratives of war and independence (Armstrong 1982; Smith 1987; Hutchinson 1987). The imagery of violence accentuates the sense of communal boundedness, and thus unity.

The emergence of individual rights, albeit partial and gradual, was not in opposition to central states but in dialectical support. As citizens increasingly depended on states for their rights and, in time, material support, so the state was strengthened. Local authorities, notably feudal, were weakened in the process. However, liberal individualism, commonly thought to be rooted in the Enlightenment, had prospered previously, albeit not universally, from guilds to Italian city republics. But with the emergence of nation-states, such liberal values played out on a much larger, more abstract stage. The pathways forward, from defining the civic community and the basis of belonging to the principles of governance and rule, would be diverse and generate myriad fragilities.

For all its radicalness, the question remains as to why the Enlightenment, even on an intellectual level, failed to fully discard the fetters of kinship or kinship-like based groups and primordialism at national and subnational levels—all limiting or undermining the realization of more fulsome civic polities?

66 CITIZENSHIP

The Enlightenment's Conservative Revolution: "The Laws of Nature and of Nature's God"

Under the revolutionary impulse of Enlightenment thinkers lies a profound conservatism, itself rooted in an abiding concern with social order. On what basis could social order be assured once God and monarch, and the legitimacy of divine rule, were taken out of the picture? The fear of disorder was fundamental, as for many of these thinkers the motivation of individuals was selfish and, if untethered, would wreck chaos. This was reflected most memorably, and with profound impact, in Hobbes' conjuring of *bellum omnium contra omnes*, "a war of every man against every man," of a humanity unleashed.[2] Tracts of the day suggested various ways to restrain humanity's base impulses, but a common ideological foundation is the turn to the "laws of nature." It was a turn at once reactionary, in that it drew on ideas of nature from traditional medieval Church doctrine, and revolutionary, in using claims of "natural rights" for a transformative dogma. But the longer-term reactionary effects are frequently overlooked.

In turning to Nature and natural law, the Enlightenment thinkers were following a rich tradition in the Catholic Church, particularly as espoused by St. Thomas Aquinas in the thirteenth century (Goyette, Latkovic, and Myers 2004; Zuckert 2007; Elders 2019). Natural law, for Aquinas (1948 [1265–1273]), is the Eternal God's reason applied to Creation. Through natural law the "rational" person participates in nature, a nature created by God. The rational person could thus discover knowledge and use reason to govern one's actions. These are the laws of nature. Aquinas had gone beyond prior Church doctrine by stating that revealed divine law was distinct from natural law, and in that regard natural law opened the possibility for human discovery and agency. For Aquinas, positive, human-made law had to be judged based on its reflection of natural law. That demand—that human law reflect natural law—provided a political basis to challenge unjust rulers. Aquinas, however, had no account of natural *rights*, rights that are inherent in human beings by their very being.

"Nature" for Aquinas and in Church doctrine had a particular meaning. Nature denoted the essential qualities—the innate properties or attributes—of life, such as expressed in the phrase "the nature of man." The laws of nature refer to the underlying patterns or rules governing this quality. The association of nature with landscape and flora was absent for the medieval thinkers on nature and its laws.

The Enlightenment thinking that followed, and which informs us to this day, absorbed, expanded, and transcended the Thomist exegesis on natural law. The association of nature with the qualities of humankind was extended and encapsulated in landscape, flora, and animals in ways in which we today take as self-evident. It was not simply an expansion of nature to include the ambit of the material and organic worlds, but it included an intense preoccupation with finding the laws—the qualities—of those worlds. This preoccupation merged with the ethos of reason, science, and empirical observation that so characterized the Enlightenment. Universities and the emerging genre of scientific journals were animated by a particular fascination with natural history, which extended to fields like biology, zoology, geology, and botany. Isaac Newton's distilling of the cosmos into a handful of mathematical equations gave faith that science and reason could reveal the keys to the natural order and, by extension, to the social order as well. Science could be, in the felt epiphany of the students of the Enlightenment, the foundation for politics, economics, and society (see, in general, Israel 2002).

Aquinas had, ironically, created a new pathway for Enlightenment thinkers to engage learning, politics, identity, and self-interest. By separating divine law from the law of nature, and imbuing nature with reason and rationality, a new world was opened. The Enlightenment thinkers could reject the claims of divine rule of monarchs and seek a science of the natural and human order. The relationship of God and nature also meant they could continue, in the main, to call themselves Christians or deists. Man himself (gendered as their thinking was) was *of* nature imbued with the rights of the "laws of nature and of nature's God."[3] In nature "man is born free and everywhere he is in chains," in one of the most remembered phrases of the Enlightenment, in this case of Rousseau (2004). Theories of the social contract, in the varying versions of Rousseau, Locke, and Hobbes, evoked images of a pastoral nature in depicting the Original Man.

The law of nature and natural rights thus became, in the words of C. S. Lewis (1961, 61), "an absolute moral standard against which the laws of all nations must be judged and to which they ought to conform." In this respect, albeit with a twist, the Enlightenment thinkers were following Aquinas' dictum that positive, human-made law had to be judged based on its reflection of natural law. In this we see the basis of rights from the American Declaration of Independence to the French Declaration of the Rights of Man and of the Citizen, to the Universal Declaration of Human Rights, and indeed to constitutions which followed worldwide. When today we speak of certain

68   CITIZENSHIP

rights—for example, the right not to be tortured—as having "universal juris-diction" in which any court worldwide can (in principle) adjudicate, we can thank the early proponents of "natural rights."

The thread from natural law to the "natural sciences" to the "social sciences" was, conceptually, relatively unproblematic. Equally important, what would become known as the social and behavioral sciences had the apparent promise of revealing the foundations of social and political order now that divine rule was to be cast to the dustbin of history. The empirical and reasoned methodologies of the natural sciences, which had proved so successful, would now be used in the social sciences—a spirit which informs the social sciences to our present moment.

Take the notion of "self-interest," a concept that would become a cornerstone of modern economics and politics. Albert Hirschman (1977) has described how Enlightenment thinkers had to contend with medieval sentiments that saw human conduct as being driven by "passions," often dangerous. They confronted beliefs that the pursuit of gain was the sin of avarice, a "passion" that as such was irrational, unpredictable, and menacing. A science of society and economics demanded (for the day) a Newtonian-like predictability, transparency, and orderliness. This underlies the transition from medieval "passion" to modern "interest." Interests, in contrast to passions, were predictable, transparent, and rational. Even if the interest was ego-driven, it could be harnessed to benefit social life. The philosopher Helvetius declared that as "the physical world is ruled by the laws of movement, so is the moral universe ruled by the laws of interest." Adam Smith co-opted the idea of the passion and transfigured it into interest; "non-economic drives," he argued, "powerful as they are, are all made to feed into economic ones and do nothing but reinforce them, being thus deprived of their erstwhile independent existence" (quotations in Hirschman 1977).

By instituting the "first principle" of the rational, predictable, and transparent actor, scholars could also build purportedly scientific laws of politics. What Adam Smith established for the market and the social good, Montesquieu would do for the legitimacy of political institutions (Montesquieu 1989 [1748]; Smith 2010b [1776]). Upon self-interest, he promoted the idea of balancing factions and branches of government—so influential on the framers of the United States Constitution (and many other legal systems). That same principle was extended to international politics, captured in the premise of "balance of power." The third Earl of Shaftesbury, a figure of the Enlightenment, declared that interest "governs the world," and

PRACTICES OF CITIZENSHIP 69

that indeed became a self-fulfilling reality (Cooper, the third Earl of Cooper the 3rd Earl of Shaftesbury 2001 [1737], 52). Since then, interest has become the cornerstone of society and politics, so much so that it is difficult today for us to think of any actors—be they individual, corporate, or state—as anything other than in terms of models and systems built upon concepts of self-interest.

In sum, mechanisms such as self-interest could, imputably, serve as the foundation of an orderly society and an orderly politics—a well-balanced political community could be reached absent the heavy hand of divinely-ordained kings and queens.

Regardless of the merits of the approaches of Enlightenment philosophers, in what way were they conservative in this most revolutionary age?

Enlightenment figures turned to the law of nature to advance the rights of the individual and the citizen and to delegitimize divine rule, but ironically that same natural law approach helped seed primordialist and kinship-like principles into the politics of post-Enlightenment Europe—and into concepts of interest and identity. This influence included even territorial, ostensibly civic republican models of statehood.

Nātūra, in terms of its Latin origins and its medieval development, connoted nature, birth, character (or essential attributes), genitalia, and "the creative power governing the world." *Nātūra* shares a common root with *nasci* (to be born), and with *natio* (nation or race). Tellingly, in the Middle Ages these "natural" qualities were understood as bestowed by God and arose out of divine creation. Subsequent references to such ostensibly natural attributes are seen as innate or shaped by experience, absent any reference to divine origin.[4]

Thomist principles of the medieval Church claimed nature, as shaped by God, represented "essential attributes" in, *inter alia*, human character but did so such that nature represented universal qualities (as God himself was universal).

The Enlightenment thinkers, by making humans "of nature" from whence humans derived their rights—while still also absorbing the Thomist understanding of nature as representing "essential attributes"—created the paradox of implanting primordial understandings at the very foundations of modern politics, the market, and society. These Enlightenment thinkers *naturalized* categories ("essential attributes") of what became the constituent elements of modern democracies: the individual, the nation, ethnic groups, race, and even the idea of the political state. The Latin etymological associations of

70 CITIZENSHIP

nature—with their kinship references from birth, genitalia to *natio*—were raised to the level of organizing principles.

Primordial understandings became intertwined with democracy, particularly in cases where primordialism took on a particularly dark turn, notably in *Voelkisch* forms of nationalism. But republican experiments were far from free of this provocation. This is a matter beyond the struggle around slavery, racial discrimination, and gender discrimination, in which the most republican minded always saw such primordial understandings as exogenous to democracy and thus to be confronted. The primordialism in republicanism was, rather, embedded in qualities with "fixed attributes" referring to the individual, ethnicity, race, and a variety of "interests." Accordingly, the idea of interest—self-interest, interest group, and national interest—arose from and reinforced such primordialist assumptions.

Enlightenment appeals to nature, now including the sense of nature as also landscape, lent themselves to the sacralization of the soil of the country that came to characterize civic-republican nation-states as much as ethnonationalist nation-states. The "natural history" of the Enlightenment and post-Enlightenment science was not so much in opposition to but in mutual support of the romanticization of the landscape. While the natural history of botany, zoology, and biology developed in the eighteenth century, so, too, did romantic poetry. Nature was beginning to now be identified with the color green. In the words of a poet popular in the eighteenth century, James Thomson:

> to wander o'er the verdant earth,
> In various hues; but chiefly thee, gay green!
> Thou smiling Nature's universal robe!

The Romanticism movement, not just in poetry but in art and literature, is seen as arising in opposition to "the modern," to rationalism and industrialization, but its roots are intertwined with changes set off in the Enlightenment period. The sacralization of a supposedly inextricable relationship between the land and a people is anticipated as early as the seventeenth century among, for example, the Dutch Calvinists and the Puritans in New England, in their sense of being a providential people in a chosen land.[5] A growing sense of "territorial kinship" continued to strengthen throughout the eighteenth century and beyond. An equally powerful moral connection to the land—also drawing on Romanticism—was felt among ethnonationalist movements, most evident from the nineteenth century. Yet, such a felt connection of a land and a purported people was anticipated thousands of years previously in the Ancient Near East.

The prevailing perception, among scholars and more broadly in the "educated public," is that the Enlightenment is the source of modern citizenship and republicanism. While the Enlightenment set the ground for dramatically broadening citizenship it also, in the longer term, helped bring forth a primordialist bacillus that came to chronically ail both society and politics.[6]

"Constitutional Patriotism" or Nationalism?

A key discussion in social and political theory with roots in the Enlightenment concerns the problem of social integration (a correlate of the Enlightenment concern with social order [see, e.g., Gordon 1994]). A case in point: on what basis can political communities cohere across domestic divisions such as class, ethnicity, and religion? Immigration has intersected with these concerns, and questions of integration have framed policy, popular, and scholarly engagements on migration issues. The question that emerges is, in essence, can citizenship be the foundation of integration solely based on common standards for the good social life and for political legitimacy? Or does integration depend on the prior existence of a historical, common nationality identity that can (in its more liberal versions) serve as a foundation for absorption of marginalized groups and immigrants? By implication, at least, a common historical national identity contains some level of kinship-like descent (such as ethnicity), as in the White Anglo-Saxon Protestant historical core of the United States.

The debate goes to the nexus of the relationship between citizenship and national attributes. Habermas famously argued that for a truly civic society to emerge the Gordian knot with nationalism had to be cut, even in its more liberal versions. A "majority culture," Habermas (1998b) argued, even if expansive and culturally absorbent, such as arguably in the case for the United States, will distort civic principles. This "fusion," argues Habermas, "must be dissolved if it is to be possible for different cultural, ethnic, and religious forms of life to coexist and interact on equal terms within the same political community." Instead, Habermas called for a polity based on "constitutional patriotism," which should replace ethnonationalism as the focus of a common identity. Liberal nationalists responded that a sense of nationalist

72 CITIZENSHIP

affiliation generates the sense of trust and commitment that can make citizenship effectively function socially and politically. This is especially the case in the context of large entities, like states, that are at such a vast scale that precludes, for example, pervasive direct ties to nurture such trust (Miller 2000; see overview in Leydet 2017).

The "civic constitutionalists" do not dispute as a historical matter the importance of nationalism in the rise of citizenship, but they reject that the relationship is anything more than contingent. A civic polity, in other words, can be nurtured to grow out of its nationalist roots. This is critical as, in the spirit of Habermas, only through such a development can a legacy of exclusion of minority cultures be overcome. For liberal nationalists, by contrast, the national foundations of the majority are essential to citizenship; this does not mean that such societies cannot be inclusive, but they build on the progressive widening scope and embrace of the majority culture. Here again the American example is illustrative, up to a point, as the White Anglo-Saxon Protestant culture over (albeit lengthy) time embraced Catholics and Jews. However, present-day America presents a much more fractionalized picture (Herberg 1983; Miller 2000; Leydet 2017).

What is clear from the liberal national critique nonetheless is that civic and postnational approaches to politics do need to respond to a number of challenges. The populist backlash we have seen in recent years suggests a vulnerability in the claim to building a reasonably integrated political community based on civic principles. This is further illustrated by the sensitivity to migration issues. A political community in which the majority has trust in its institutions is indeed more welcoming of migrants—in other words, in circumstances where the majority feels on firm footing.[7] Furthermore, per the arguments of liberal nationalists like David Miller (2000), the scope, complexity, and cultural diversity of modern democracies are a far cry from the face-to-face democracies imagined by Jefferson of New England townships, anchored by farmers, or of the citizens of the Athenian polis. We do not, at present, have the institutional structure that sufficiently develops social trust and political legitimacy organically. For the civic foundations to act as a fixture of modern societies, these concerns must be addressed.[8]

This tension between a civic basis and a kinship or primordialist approach to politics and social cohesion is thus not transcended by the influence of the Enlightenment, and these interlocking threads appear as if inextricable, constraining citizenship from its earliest Ancient Near East beginnings. Still the Enlightenment did provide the foundations in place for an extraordinary expansion, over time, of citizenship beyond a small aristocratic, male, landowning class. But the Enlightenment did not cut off the thread of primordialism—a true Gordian knot—which, in the long term, also proved problematic for a civic society. Part of the challenge lay in the highlighting of issues of membership, of "belonging." Determining membership of the state became a cardinal vector for state-building from the seventeenth century.

Privileging Membership

The Treaty of Westphalia of 1648 was foundational on matters of state membership.[9] The treaty, also called the Peace of Westphalia, ended the Thirty Years War that had pitted Catholics against Protestants, side-by-side with other quarrels that involved German princes, the Holy Roman Empire, France, and the Hapsburgs, and involved countries from Sweden to the Netherlands. The peace treaty—actually two treaties signed in Osnabrück and Münster—brought not just the war to an end, but it created organizing principles for relations between states. The consequences of those principles impacted first Europe and subsequently, centuries later, the world at large. Most importantly, at Westphalia the principle of *cuius regio, eius religio* was institutionalized (building on the Peace of Augsburg of 1555)—namely that each prince would have the prerogative of determining the religion of their own state. In principle, this came down to choosing between Catholicism or Protestantism (Onnekink 2016).

The Peace of Westphalia is widely regarded by scholars as the foundation for the modern nation-state system. Except for certain outposts, it ended the war between Catholicism and Protestantism. Protestantism was recognized as a permanent feature of Europe, thus ending the Holy Roman Empire. Indeed, a furious Pope Innocent X named the treaty "null, void, invalid, iniquitous, unjust, damnable, reprobate, inane, empty of meaning and effect for all time."[10] Most importantly, the Peace of Westphalia established the architecture of contemporary international law and relations: each state would have sovereignty over its territory and people. Three hundred years later, the principle of sovereignty was still a centerpiece of encoded international law, written into the United Nations Charter, which states that "nothing . . . shall authorize the United Nations to intervene in matters which are essentially within the domestic jurisdiction of any state." A correlate of state sovereignty in international law was the inviolable nature of recognized borders and the

74 CITIZENSHIP

principle of non-interference in another state's sovereignty and domestic jurisdiction. Only late in the twentieth century does international humanitarian and human rights law begin to add caveats to such restrictions on the inviolability of state sovereignty (Falk 2008; Benvenisti and Harel 2017).

This history of the Peace of Westphalia is well known among scholars. However, what is missed is another profound effect for citizenship. The diplomats were largely indifferent, in reaching the settlement at Westphalia, as to the *form* of government. Most states were headed by monarchs but, significantly, the Peace of Westphalia recognized the, arguably, first early modern republic, that of the Dutch Republic. The Dutch Republic was de facto an independent state since 1609, following the Twelve Years Truce, in which the Hapsburgs of Spain gave up in their attempts to defeat the Dutch Calvinists—a critical moment in the Reformation Wars. But at Westphalia the Dutch Republic was recognized as a sovereign state and a formal member of the concert of states (Esser 2007).

Thus, what was at stake was not the basis of rule but rather the question of membership in these states. The Peace of Westphalia created a state structure that was designed to determine membership and "belonging," rather than generate social and political transformation. The privileging of the question of membership and identity was marked through sharply bordered territories. Because borders were fraught with intertwined political, economic, security, and, initially, religious concerns, they now sharply delineated domestic and foreign, inside and outside—a clear break with medieval society, or even with the Italian city republics. Although it appears that the diplomats at Westphalia were, in the main, seeking primarily a means to end a long, costly war, the long-term impact of the treaty was extraordinary in advancing a narrow notion of citizenship—and, in effect, nationalism (Verhoeven 1998; Blaney and Inayatullah 2000; Smith 2002).

In a dialectic that winds itself through so much of the human endeavor, Westphalia was at once a radical endeavor—a watershed in European and in, ultimately, world history—and at the same time highly conservative. Nations and their borders would come to be soon experienced as "natural," as primordial, as if rooted from time immemorial. It was a belonging of a people and a land that was mythologized as a sacred relationship, in cases blessed by "Providence." The Enlightenment, subsequently, also had its radical and conservative threads. Politically, the Enlightenment introduced a much more promising civic vision, one which in principle was more dynamic and which de-naturalized the primordial view of humanity. The Enlightenment helped erode the notion that humanity should be ordered hierarchically, by caste and rank, determined by blood descent. But the conservative dimensions of Westphalia—putting an onus on membership and belonging—created politics which over time nurtured the conservative dimensions of the Enlightenment and its long-term legacies.

The primordial was indeed increasingly emphasized—in the most evocative sense of the primordial, in birth. Birth, on the soil of the nation (*ius soli*) and in the bloodline of the nation (*ius sanguinis*), came to be pivotal in determining membership and citizenship. The thinking that came out of the Enlightenment played an inextricable role in this development. It is ironic, but also revealing, that Rousseau would prove inspirational for both French Republicans and German ethnonationalists (Smith 1983; Garrard 1994; Simon 1995).

The seemingly Gordian knot of citizenship, in which the civic thread was intertwined with a primordial thread, is evident in different ways in both republican experiments, such as France, and in ethnonationalist accounts, such as Germany. Indeed, the tendency of social scientists to talk of "models"— such as the French model or the German model—can distort more than it reveals. The idea of models has at times implied that national "qualities" are essentially invariant (see Favell 1998; Ireland 1994; Brubaker 1992; Kohn 2017 [1944], 1955, 1962). Nevertheless, the civic thread can be traced back in Germany from the pre-unification period, just as the primordial thread is evident in France, certainly from the Second Republic (Lebovics 2018; Kocka 2010; Weil 2008).

One can elicit historical "threads" that can be illustrative of periods in which ethnonationalist and republican threads can be respectively dominant—but also the way they can weave together or fade. Therefore, far from being a question of essentialized models, the thread that comes to the fore is historically contingent in a highly dynamic process.

Consider the French, German, and American cases.

France's Republicanism

The French Revolution introduced an expansionist and outward-looking republicanism. Civic integration progressively grew in France as a key objective. The break from primordial, kinship-based models of society was made clear, figuratively as well as literally, in the guillotining of the King and the

76   CITIZENSHIP

Queen and numerous members of the nobility. But French Republicanism only briefly took on as its prime concern the issues of limiting monarchical rule. Quite quickly, the revolutionary spirit turned to questions of public virtue, and about the "sociability" that would anchor French society. In other words, by 1792, the horizontal matters of social life gained purchase over the vertical matters of political legitimacy and rulemaking. The revolutionaries were concerned with inventing "the social." Royalists in France, and elsewhere, did not recognize a self-governing social realm—everything involving social exchanges was at the behest and intervention of the sovereign authority. Everything was, in that sense, political. "The invention of the social field," writes Daniel Gordon (1994, 5), "required a demonstration that meaningful activities can be self-instituting, that in some situations humans can hang together, that, in short, humans are sociable creatures." In that regard, the nurturing of civic, horizontal ties took root early in French social thought.

France's Declaration of the Rights of Man and of the Citizen, proclaimed in 1789, is historically pivotal, and not only for establishing the French Republic. The document established foundations for republican citizenship and, in addition, for universal human rights—which the framers self-consciously aspired to in the very title of the "Rights of Man *and* of the Citizen" (emphasis added). Rights are declared as "natural, unalienable and sacred," co-opting "nature" from kinship systems through natural law. The citizen is bestowed with protection of their interests, namely in terms of "liberty, property, security and resistance to oppression." Privileges by birth limiting individual equality were, in essence, banned and feudalism was declared over: "All the citizens, being equal in the eyes of the law, are equally admissible to all public dignities, places, and employments, according to their capacity and without distinction other than that of their virtues and of their talents." The Declaration established popular sovereignty, in contrast to the divine right of kings that characterized the French monarchy, and social acknowledgement of shared equality among citizens. In turn, the Church was identified as a reactionary force and an integral part of the *ancien régime*. The Republic was declared to be secular.

While rights were extended to a wide population, there were hierarchical components. By a decree passed following the Declaration of the Rights of Man and of the Citizen, so called "active citizenship" was limited to essentially male property owners in a clear acknowledgement that rights serve interests (through the link that property constitutes citizens). "Passive citizens" concerned those without property (so without material interests) as well as those who had been excluded from political rights in the Declaration— women, foreigners, slaves, and children. The distinction between active and passive citizens caused much upheaval among groups excluded from "active" citizenship during and after the revolution. However, the Declaration of the Rights of Man and of the Citizen had set a precedent for the idea and practice of rights, both inside and outside of France.

France initiated the rights-based orientation to citizenship in modern Europe. French Republicanism was highly individualistic, rejecting family and birth as the basis for building social trust and political legitimacy. But it was also highly assimilationist. The regional and communal differences across France were flattened through revolutionary ardor or fiat. This radical civic challenge to other primordialist-based forms of affiliation became even stronger under the Napoleonic Wars. Accordingly, the universalizing expansion of republican efforts shifted from inside France to the outside, challenging the very order that had been established in Westphalia. But, in turn, France's Napoleonic failure brought back a primordial revival with the return of the *ancien régime* at the Congress of Vienna of 1815. France itself was drawn to state nationalism: across Europe, the revolutions of 1848 propelled nationalism and its highly bordered frontiers in tandem with a broader liberal spirit.

Race and the "soil" of France historically plays a quite distinct role from either the German or the American cases. If the French Revolution created two nations, the monarchical and the republican, also Catholic and secular, by the nineteenth century, observes the historian of France, Herman Lebovics (2018), the Right accepted that France was "one nation." However, the Right sought to define the "French nation" in its own terms. The New Right emerged with the Dreyfus affair and culminated in *Action française* and in Vichy France.[11] Neo-monarchists had found a haven in the French army command, and they were the source of the antisemitically motivated charges against Dreyfus, a Jewish officer, accusing him of spying for Germany.

The New Right contrasted rural France, the country, and the peasants as the true and eternal France, the *pays reél* itself. This was in a period when the French countryside was undergoing a state of permanent cultural change, in Eugene Weber's (1976) depiction, when peasants became French. The New Right attacked republican politicians, businessmen, speculators, lawyers, and Jews as not being the "True France." Vichy traditionalists later "envisioned beliefs, customs, practices as somehow growing from *nature*" (Lebovics

78 CITIZENSHIP

2018, 171). It is in antisemitism that the role of race enters the French national debate, later to be extended to other colonial subjects and minorities in France. But because "race" is conflated with (French) "culture," the notion of race tends to be rather porous compared to the racism of Nazism or of the American South, where race is depicted as genetic and biological. For example, Vichy France at first (in 1940) targeted foreign Jews, rather than Jews of French nationality, in roundups and internment. But by 1942, Vichy France collaborated under German orders to round up all Jews, French included, to be sent to the camps.

"Race" and the French soil came together in the New Right depiction of the Jews as the foil to True France, identified with the urban businessmen, speculators, and lawyers. The Jews were the "rootless cosmopolitans" that threaded together the New Right ideology, as it did for antisemites outside of France.[12]

A Germanic Response

Germany is frequently pointed to as the example, historically, of an ethnic, kinship-like, nationalist "model." The argument, which can go so far as to imply that *Volksgemeinschaft* has been even an essential quality in German nationality itself, is overstated. Others have argued that scholars suggesting a German ethnonationalist model have too readily extrapolated back into history from the Nazi period (Brubaker 1992; Kohn 2017 [1944], 1955, 1962). The cultural historian George Mosse (2021) argued, however, that the antecedents of Nazism did indeed extend to the Wilhelmine period.

The civic thread is also evident, originating in German town burghers and guild organizations that go back centuries. But history also shows that Germany became, from the late nineteenth century, after unification in 1871, the most prominent European exponent of a *Völkisch* nationalism. The roots for such nationalism go deeper, to the backlash to French Republicanism, following the Napoleonic invasion of Prussia in 1806. Ideologically, the nationalist reaction is famously articulated by the German philosopher Johann Gottlieb Fichte in his seminal address, "To the German Nation," in 1808. Here Fichte (2013, 158) proclaimed:

[T]he first, original, and genuine natural frontiers of states are without any doubt their internal frontiers. Those who speak the same language are immediately and naturally linked by very many invisible bonds to each other . . . ; they belong together and are naturally one, an indivisible whole. A people like this cannot desire to absorb and integrate another of a different heritage and language without at least initially confusing themselves and without profoundly disturbing the regular development of their culture. The outer demarcation of residence only follows as the consequence of this inner frontier, which is drawn by the intellectual nature of man himself. And in the natural view of things, it is not at all because men live among particular mountains and rivers that they are a people; rather they live together—and, if they are fortunate, are protected by mountains and rivers—because they were already a people beforehand by a far higher law of nature.

Further, Fichte (2013, 178) wrote in his addresses:

If you proceed onward in torpor . . . then all the evils of servitude will soon await you . . . If on the other hand you rouse yourselves and take notice you will survive, finding above all a bearable and honorable existence, surrounded by the blossoming of a race that promises both you and the Germans the most worthy remembrance. In your mind's eye you will see this race exalt the German name to be that of the most glorious of all peoples; you will see this nation as the means for the rebirth and restoration of the world.

The intermingling of nature, nation, and race—and the supposed risks of mixing with those of a different "heritage"—is already clear in Fichte. The nation tied to its "soil" precedes the state: "the love of fatherland must itself rule the state as the supreme, ultimate, and independent authority, above all constraining the choices . . . Freedom . . . is the soil within which a superior cultivation germinates" (Fichte 2013, 100). The purportedly inextricable association of the *Volk* and "its" soil would be even more accentuated after German unification in 1871.

In the period Fichte is writing there was still a reasonably vibrant, if proportionately small, civically minded class. The historian Jürgen Kocka (2010) notes that, in German, *Bürger* stands for "citizen" and "bourgeois" alike and indeed the history of the bourgeoisie merged with the history of civil society in what became Germany. (This amalgamation of citizen and bourgeoisie virtues is, to one degree or another, true in other Western countries,

80   CITIZENSHIP

even if the linguistic conjoining is absent.) The *Bürgertum*—the bourgeoisie or middle class—was a culturally recognizable group within towns and cities, including such social types as artisans, merchants, and shopkeepers. The *Bürgertum* accounted for five to eight percent, Kocka calculates, of the population in the nineteenth century. Though in principle not closed to outsiders, the *Bürgertum* were exclusive, and were sharply demarcated from the working class. Bourgeois status was, in practice, identified with the cultural attributes of a citizen. Jews were unable to attain full citizenship status in the first two-thirds of the nineteenth century; tellingly, Jews and others saw Jewish assimilation into the bourgeoisie as essential for their attainment of citizenship.

However, the cultural and political influence of the German middle-class remained limited. "The line of distinction," Kocka writes (2010, 23–24), "between the *Bürgertum* and nobility continued to be neatly drawn, more sharply than in France or in England. Aristocratic background remained important for being recruited into top positions at the court and in the army, in government, and in the rural power structure, particularly in the East." The German middle class became less liberal toward the end of the nineteenth century. Kocka continues:

> For the most part, the German bourgeoisie had made its peace with a political system that, after national unification under Prussian hegemony, maintained strong authoritarian traits (besides some liberal concessions and democratic elements). It became common to give support to a kind of nationalism that increasingly moved to the right, with imperialist aggression and chauvinistic radicalization. Racism and antisemitism gained ground within the bourgeoisie and, particularly, the lower middle classes. Faced by an ever-growing oppositional, social democratic labor movement on the left, large parts of the bourgeoisie became more defensive. In important ways, bourgeois support for the universalistic elements of civil society weakened.

Mosse (2021) takes this observation even further. He argues that many of the bourgeois were disappointed by German reunification in 1871, and that it had not risen to the level of "spiritual unity" they anticipated. This drew them to *Völkisch* ideology, its mystical attraction to nature, and the supposed bond of "blood and soil." It created a kind of religious-like hold, anti-modern and deeply antisemitic. The Nazis, Mosse argued, grew out of this *Völkisch* movement.

German nationalism is said to grow out of Romanticism, with its emphasis on nature, beauty, intuition, authenticity, and, in turn, its opposition to scientific modernism and rationality. This, in large part, is true and it is evident in Fichte's writings. But the man most responsible for Germany's unification, Otto von Bismarck, spoke the language of *macht* and realpolitik. In his "blood and iron" speech of September 30, 1862, when he was Minister President of Prussia, he proclaimed:

> The position of Prussia in Germany will not be determined by its liberalism but by its power . . . Prussia must concentrate its strength and hold together for the favorable moment, which has already been missed several times. Prussia's borders under the treaties of Vienna are not propitious for a healthy body politic. The great questions of our time are not decided by speeches and majority decisions—that was the great mistake of 1848 and 1849—but by iron and blood (*Eisen und Blut*).[13]

Romanticism and realpolitik complemented each other, however; the common leitmotif was the realization of the German nation in terms of a shared acknowledgement of common identity. Territoriality was imbued as a sacred projection of the nation, connected by *Blut und Boden*. The term was a nineteenth-century invention, and it conveyed the sentiment of a pure nation united with its land, which was imbued with mystical qualities. *Blut und Boden* lent itself to a racialized notion of nationhood and a bedrock of German antisemitism already in the nineteenth century. The Jews were the foil as a "rootless" people compared to the "rooted" and grounded *Volk*. Rootedness—the metaphor itself—conjured up the purportedly sacred ties between a nation and the land, a people *of* that soil. The metaphor has, however, also been used in non-racialized contexts of civic society (Clark 2016; Santa Ana, Waitkuweit, and Hernandez 2017; Smith 2006).

Blut und Boden also, in its imagery, *naturalized* the civic model. Such nationhood could be *felt* as self-evident, and a difference of degree rather than of kind vis-à-vis the kinship model. *Blut und Boden* reached its malign apogee in Nazi ideology, although present in other genocidal ideologies

82 CITIZENSHIP

(Kiernan 2008; Kott and Patel 2018). The *Volk* is imagined to be akin to an extended family, one with deep mutual commitment and shared outlook. The supposed "natural" relationship of the German *Volk* with lands historically occupied by Germans became a driving force for "re-claiming" such lands outside of post-Versailles Germany. This was a cornerstone of Nazi ideology and expansionism, put into violent effect at the dawn of World War II in, *inter alia*, the Sudetenland in Czechoslovakia. Germany in this period expressed an especially virulent form of the "nation to state" model.

Such ethnonationalism reached emphatic forms among, *inter alia*, Afrikaners in Apartheid South Africa, and, in its most extreme form, in Nazi Germany. When "blood" gets so accentuated, inevitably "outgroups" suffer, to put it mildly, such as Jews in Nazi Germany and Black Africans in Apartheid South Africa. Ameliorated, liberal forms have emerged as well, for example, in postwar Germany (especially from the 1990s) or Norway—countries more open to immigrants becoming citizens, relative to the past. We like to think the age of the *Volk* is in the past but, clearly, this is not the case. Across Europe, hard right groups from Sweden to the Balkans evoke an antediluvian *Volksgemeinschaft* (Sommer 2008; Kelly 2019).

In contrast, the main response in Germany from the late nineteenth century to the question of basing political legitimacy between the rulers and the ruled on liberal precepts was marginalization to outright hostility. This was clear in Bismarck's sentence, in his iron and blood speech, that the "position of Prussia . . . will not be determined by its liberalism but by its power." By the German citizenship law of 1913, the die of German ethnonationalism was cast, not to be broken until the second half of the twentieth century, with its most cataclysmic expression—for Germany, and for the world at large—from 1933 to 1945.

However, as noted, softer and even liberal forms of ethnic nationhood are evident, not least in postwar Germany and Japan. The unification of Germany after the collapse of the Soviet Union implicitly, at least, relied on a historical memory of *Volksgemeinschaft*, roughly translated as "the people's community." The translation does not, however, fully convey the sense of a people organically tied together in a "natural" kinship-like relationship. The term itself is now associated with the Nazis, who exploited it for their own propaganda purposes. But the term was rooted in the sociologist Ferdinand Tönnies' (2001) distinction of *Gesellschaft* and *Gemeinschaft*. Tönnies strenuously objected to the Nazi use of the term, and in fact it had been used by some in World War I and the interwar years in more unitary ways, including, for example, by some German Jews (Fritzsche 2009).

The German approach was, for a lengthy period, starkly different from France. Civic models can lean in one direction or another, as is clear in principles of *ius soli* (highlighting territory) and *ius sanguinis* (emphasizing "blood" and blood descent). At the same time, the idea of political development from "state to nation" (a state forming a national people) converged, in significant degrees, to the "nation to state" (a preexisting "nation" or people becoming a sovereign political entity). Although France has been frequently presented as a model of republicanism and Germany as a model of ethnonationalism, in fact we can observe the combination of civic and primordial threads across both their histories. While the national differences are discernable over lengthy periods—France and Germany (and the United States) are not completely convergent—in the *longue durée* the "models" are fragile and contingent. Thus, even in the more promising republican experiments, such as in France and United States, the civic practice was severely limited by, for example, antisemitic, anti-republican movements such as *Action française* (culminating in Vichy France) and institutions like slavery in the South of the United States.

The Winding Road of American Republicanism

The duality of nationhood and the land, and of sacrifice and soil, is evident in the "state-to-nation" model of republicanism as well. The articulation of national identity leans into universalistic rather than particularistic forms of expression. In that vein, the land is used to build an inclusive, rather than exclusive, nation. Abraham Lincoln is especially notable in this regard. His presidency was active in roughly the same period as German romanticism reached the threshold of its objective, that of a united Germany in 1871. Toward the end of the Civil War, Lincoln consciously took steps not simply to bind the wounds of the nation, but to use the territory, the land, the soil of the United States to define a new citizenship. Lincoln explicitly evoked the American landscape as the verdant soil of an egalitarian and united Republic. Furthermore, he compared slavery to the ascriptive, kinship principles of monarchies. In other words, the United States (the country was referred to

84 CITIZENSHIP

in the plural before the Civil War, as in *these* United States) had both a civil tradition and an explicitly caste, kinship model of society based on slavery in the South.

Lincoln evokes the land in terms of speech but also in a set of institutional measures that tied a bounded territory, the people, and a new citizenship. It is Lincoln who initiates cemeteries dedicated to the military (before they even emerge in Europe in World War I), using them as symbols of national unity and associating the civic sacrifice of soldiers with the soil (Mosse 1990). Lincoln establishes national parks with Yosemite. Lincoln also is behind the Homestead Act, again linking the land, independence, and civic virtue.

In the most notable of these acts, on November 19, 1863, he made the dedicatory remarks that became known as the Gettysburg Address, consecrating the first military cemetery. The Address invokes the soil and the bodies of lost Union soldiers intermingled, symbolizing civic duty and sacrifice and the roots of a reborn people. The blood of the martyrs fed the soil of the nation: the land, the people, and republicanism again became one. The Union was now an unbroken landscape. In the metaphor of John Cotton, the Puritan minister, in his sermon before the Great Migration of 1630, the people were "planted" in the land, in America.

In contrast to the *Blut und Boden*, "nation to state" mythology, the land overcomes kinship divisions above all slavery and racism. Furthermore, in Lincoln's Second Message to Congress, December 1, 1862, he suggested that the land was indeed the most durable part of the Republic:

> A nation may be said to consist of its territory, its people, and its laws. The territory is the only part which is of certain durability. "One generation passeth away and another generation cometh, but the earth abideth forever." It is of the first importance to duly consider and estimate this ever-enduring part. That portion of the earth's surface which is owned and inhabited by the people of the United States is well adapted to be the home of one national family, and it is not well adapted for two or more.

That territory, that soil, summoned for Lincoln a certain moral geography, that of republicanism. Before the outbreak of war, in the presidential debates with his opponent Stephen Douglas, Lincoln declared, "slavery is an unqualified evil to the Negro, to the White man, *to the soil*, and to the State" (emphasis added).

Universalistic and inclusive as Lincolnian republicanism may be, it's a citizenship that forces individuals and communities to adapt to its own organizing principles. A painful irony of American history is this: the very way the land was inscribed with a distinct, republican moral geography would lead to the destruction of pre-colonial American Indian culture. Genocide of tribes was one way destruction took place. But even nineteenth-century progressives deemed that Native Americans must be converted from nomadic lives to farming, to be sedentary and live in bounded plots of land and reservations. One government official wrote how, "We want to make citizens of them, and [in order to do so] they must first be anchored to the soil." The moral geography, and the soil, that was celebrated in confronting slavery would later be bemoaned for its treatment of native peoples. But that moral geography had its own internal logic, for better and for worse.[14]

The desire to "naturalize" citizenship models, of the *ius sanguinis* and the *ius soli* variety, is striking. The ethnic models could evoke the language of kinship, now writ national. This is explicit in the German model whereby ethnic descent was the basis of citizenship (and still is, although now dimensions of *ius soli* have been introduced for non-ethnic Germans born in Germany). But it is evident in the *ius soli* models themselves as well. Thus, Lincoln pointed to the Declaration of Independence assertion that it is "self-evident" that "all men are created equal." Such rights, he then deduced, were a birthright and, as such, a product of nature, like the nation itself is (purportedly) a product of nature, of the land itself. Rights are natural, a function of birth. From this follows the process of "naturalization," meaning the once alien or foreigner is now made of this country, of this land. That now new member of the body politic is "naturally" a citizen, an American.

Migration becomes such a major issue no matter what the specific "national model" because it goes to the issue of defining borders and boundaries. Geographic, social, and political boundaries are seamlessly superimposed one upon another in the nation-state in a way that was rare in prior history. This highlights the key role of bounded territoriality and bloodline for defining civic-republican and ethnonational political communities, respectively. The very act of saying, through legislation, who may or may not enter, who does or does not belong, and who may or may not become a fully-fledged citizen defines the character of the border, the regulation of which, in turn, defines the national community itself. The relationship represented by the metaphors of soil and blood is an intricate relationship. In the nation-state, the primordial looms large.

Notes

1. Benedict Anderson (1991) pointed to the media, specifically newspapers, as the literal "mediator" of nationhood. But here we ask about the substance, not the means, of a shared and felt experience of nationhood.
2. See Hobbes (2020a, chapters 13–14). The Latin phrase is in Hobbes' *De Cive* (2020b).
3. The phrase comes from the US Declaration of Independence.
4. See discussion on the etymology of the word "nature" in Lewis (1961) and the entry on "Nature" in the unabridged *Oxford English Dictionary*.
5. See Groenhuis (1981) for the Dutch case, and Jacobson (2002) regarding the Puritans in New England. Regarding biblical Israel, Protestantism, and conceptions of nationhood, see also Appelbaum (2013).
6. Not all Enlightenment figures were democrats in their disposition. Notably, Voltaire believed in enlightened absolutist monarchs as the most effective means for reform, and Johann Struensee effected reforms in Denmark through his roles as physician and minister to King Christian VII (O'Brien 1997).
7. On different spheres of politics and trust see Hetherington (1998), Levi and Stoker (2000), Eder, Mochmann, and Quandt (2014), and Treib (2014).
8. See further discussion on postnational citizenship in Chapter 5 and on the "twenty-first century guild" in Chapter 8.
9. See Croxton (1999) and Teschke (2003); see also critiques of a "Westphalian myth" in Osiander (2001) and Havercroft (2012).
10. Quoted in Wedgwood (2005, 506). Pope Innocent X called the treaty thus in the Papal Bull, *Zelo Domus Dei*.
11. *Action française* was a monarchist, extreme Right, Catholic movement founded at the end of the nineteenth century, in response to the support of Dreyfus by society figures and intellectuals.
12. The ambiguity that complicates the French republican narrative is also revealed in the way principles of *ius sanguinis* as well as *ius soli* informed French immigration rules. See Weil (2008).
13. See German History in Documents and Images (GHDI) at https://germanhistorydocs.ghi-dc.org/sub_document.cfm?document_id=250&language=english. Translated by Jeremiah Riemer. Accessed October 23, 2022.
14. This discussion draws from, and the quotation is in, Jacobson (2002).

5

The Turn to Human Rights and Its Vulnerabilities

What job are rights expected to perform? The answers we come up with are critical for the formation of citizenship and for the kind of citizenship that emerges. Definitions of citizenship typically point to "rights," such as the "right to claim rights," but such definitions overlook a key point (Marshall 1950; Isin 2012). From the approach of citizenship, rights are a tool and not an end, as such. The objective of citizenship is, in principle, a fully civic society and polity. We must ask how rights, or the way rights are conceived, advance, or indeed inhibit, both now and historically, civic goals? What job do rights perform and have they done so in a way that addresses the key concerns of citizenship regarding membership and rule?

The answer is nuanced. In democracies we see over time advances in, for example, the inclusion of more racial and gendered groups with more expansive rights, and liberalizing criteria on immigration and access to citizenship. On the other hand, the way rights have been constructed and applied has served the "naturalization" of race, ethnicity, and primordial interests, on both the Right and the Left, to an extent that is threatening our democracies.

In principle, by transcending primordialist attributions human rights provide an opportunity for overcoming the kinship-like circumscribing of citizenship. However, in practice, a number of critical errors in the rights revolution from the 1970s has limited the potential gains for the civic project. This is not to say that enormous gains were not made under the aegis of human rights—in the expanding of rights, and the awareness of rights, to populations formerly with few protections. But the potential of human rights has only partially been fulfilled, particularly in shaping citizenship as a force for a civic society and not one governed by the centrifuge of identity politics.

What has limited the "job performance" of rights? Going back at least to the Enlightenment, rights were rooted in property, beginning in its literal sense. Property gave its owner an independence and a basis to participate in civil society. This was, of course, historically a highly privileged group, although

Citizenship. David Jacobson and Manlio Cinalli, Oxford University Press. © Oxford University Press 2023.
DOI: 10.1093/oso/9780197669150.003.0005

88   CITIZENSHIP

the notion was partially democratized in, for example, in the United States' Northwest Ordinance of 1787 (Taylor 1987; Williams 2012; Onuf 2019). This history is well known, but the problem is that property became, metaphorically, the basis of rights even when real estate no longer governed the idea of rights. Rights became construed as natural "properties" of individuals, albeit of preferred demographics. (Obscenely, the different notions of property could be juxtaposed when humans *were* property—as enslaved persons yet owned by another individual with their purportedly inherent "natural rights." Thomas Jefferson was a notable example of such hypocrisy.) That evolution of the meaning of property had a direct source in the Enlightenment.

The Enlightenment thinkers, as we observed earlier, by making humans "of nature," from whence humans derived their rights, implanted primordial understandings at the center of modern politics, economics, and society. They naturalized categories (the "essential" properties or attributes) of what became the constituent elements of modern democracies: the individual, the nation, ethnic groups, race, and sex. Through the inscription of law, the citizen and (initially) his rights became natural and essential "properties." Such fixed properties were also imputed to abstracted actors in politics and in the marketplace. The abstraction of actors, such as *homo economicus*, derived from the notion of essential attributes. This in turn led to rather mechanical understandings of the functioning of the economy, politics, and society— understandings that are, *mutatis mutandis*, still with us.

Property, in its literal and metaphoric senses, has had an extraordinary impact on our understanding of rights. As Charles Reich (1964, 771) wrote:

> Property draws a circle around the activities of each private individual or organization. Within that circle, the owner has a greater degree of freedom than without. Outside, he must justify or explain his actions, and show his authority. Within, he is the master, and the state must explain and justify any interference. It is as if property shifted the burden of proof; outside, the individual has the burden; inside, the burden is on the government to demonstrate that something the owner wishes to do should not be done.

Note the highly bounded notion here of "property"—the derived rights are per se. The derivation of the term property itself reinforces the territorial-like quality of rights. As Reich puts it, "property performs the function of maintaining independence, dignity and pluralism in society by creating zones within which the majority has to yield to the owner" (1964, 771). More than ever, Reich notes further, "the individual needs to possess, in whatever form, a small but *sovereign island* of his own" (1964, 774; emphasis added). So, rights are a property, understood as an essential attribute and frequently as a "natural" phenomenon. This has at least two major implications.

First, bounded, enclosed, self-interested actors, institutions, and states—sovereign islands—could only be contained and harnessed through a static, ahistorical, Newtonian-like mechanical model. So emerged the concept of balancing factions and branches of government, or of states, through essentially the same premise of "balance of power." This thinking, so influential in the structuring of institutions of democracies, as well as between states, emanated in the thinking from Montesquieu to, in the twentieth century, the political scientist Hans Morgenthau. Democracy, institutionally, in such a context, generally becomes a means to balancing adversarial interests.

Second, as legal rights (as "properties") have expanded dramatically in democracies in recent decades—in numbers of codified rights, of those claiming rights, and in the cascading of rights into the operations of corporate and public organizations—a striking cognitive shift has developed. The individual lays claim to their "territory." As rights expand in scope, a sense of rights as entitlements (which, indeed, legal rights are entitlements) impacts the citizen's approach to politics. The individual experience of citizenship (and even by resident noncitizens) over time becomes increasingly one of implicit and explicit rights claims. Governments must justify penetrating the individual's sovereign island for a larger public interest, but so do fellow citizens. As rights expand, the circle around the individual owner of rights becomes even more accentuated. Rights become less a matter of enabling civic engagement and political compromise but rather "properties" to be protected and expanded.

The effect is to reinforce adversarial politics as rights are experienced as absolute, as an essential property. These claims are not just mediated by courts but are a matter of everyday discourse. The expectation of "total justice," in Friedman's (1985) phrase, comes to the fore. There is now no longer an area of life not potentially a space of rights claims. It is important to note the accentuation of (metaphorically) personal property, of space, is not just legal as such; it spills into the intricacies of quotidian social life, into what Erving Goffman (1959) referred to as the territories of the self. Such rights are made "corporate" when the purportedly essential qualities of the individual, such as ethnicity, are raised to a collective level, leading to a fusion of identity and interest.

90 CITIZENSHIP

Rights, *when framed as properties*, demand an administratively and judicially minded state to mediate, rather than embody (or represent), the "sovereign islands," whether defined in individual or corporate (such as racial, gender, or business groups) terms. The judges, experts, administrative officials, and fellow employees sitting on quasi-judicial committees judging matters like discrimination or sexual harassment have been progressively critical for governance, and increasingly over recent decades have been responsible for public policy decisions that were once in the orbit of elected officials.

In lieu of popular governance, the concept of what serves the "public interest" is frequently determined through these bodies—individual and organizational. The proponents of administrative and judicial instruments have sought to promote democracy. But the problem is what is understood by the public interest when it is not determined by the public as such? Charles Reich noted (1964, 774) that although public interest framing has been laudable, the great difficulty is that they are simplistic; the "[c]oncentration on a single policy or value obscures other values that may be at stake."[1]

In sum, the problem comes down to a profound challenge in judicially driven human rights, namely that the nexus between the governed and the governors is significantly weakened. The judicial and administrative approach demands the trust—frequently blind trust—of the citizenry in experts and judicial figures. Where that trust in government and its agencies erodes, as we can clearly see in increasingly dire survey data in many democracies across the last two decades, we are confronted by what we see today. Democracies have, in this regard, a serious challenge. The suspicion of government and elites in general (including of media and academia, increasingly identified with the governing class) not only leads to declining legitimacy. It creates the room for conspiracy theories; increasingly illiberal attitudes, including racism and antisemitism; and dark visions of a "deep state."

Political legitimacy correlates with social trust, and as political trust declines so trends social trust; equally, there is a clear correlation between trust in others and in public institutions (OECD 2015).[2] Societies become, and democracies have become, more fractionalized. Rights, when framed as properties, already lend themselves to identity politics (of both the Right and Left), where kinship-like identities are fused with perceived interest. This gives further ballast to fractionalization, which in turn reinforces primordialist identities. Where social trust is low, tolerance of immigrants and foreigners is less (see Messing and Ságvári 2021; Jeannet et al. 2020). Where the response to such illiberalism is to use the administrative and judicial tools to counter illiberal groups and to advance liberal goals on issues, such as immigration, so the vicious cycle is reinforced (see Kyeyune 2022).

In sum, the way rights, and specifically human rights, have been used has had a two-edged effect. On the one hand, extraordinary progress has been made in expanding the scope of rights and of the populations that are now protected by such rights. Great success has been made in chipping away at practices that discriminate based on kinship-like attributions of race, national origins, sex, and sexual orientation. Asylum law, for example, has steadily progressed from, in practice, protecting a narrowly defined group of politically persecuted individuals from particular countries to extending its embrace more globally and to groups such as gays and victims, or potential victims, of female genital mutilation. Sometimes states have gone well beyond the letter of the law, such as in German Chancellor Angela Merkel's *en banc* acceptance of refugees from Syria's civil war. Activists express understandable unhappiness with measures such as the offshoring of asylum procedures and the remaining forms of discrimination. But we lose sight of the considerable progress.[3]

On the other hand, the way rights have been framed and used risks undermining the human rights project. It significantly contributes to the crisis for democracies both on the levels of political legitimacy and social trust, respectively the vertical and horizontal dimensions of citizenship. The framing has reinforced the centrifugal forces of "propertied" rights.

Ultimately, the question is how the civic project can be best advanced, and how rights can be most effectively used to that end. Human rights, by in principle transcending primordialist attributions like race, began to have a profound influence on the shaping of citizenship from the 1970s. This turn came to be called in the scholarly literature "postnational citizenship" from the 1990s (coined first by Soysal 1994). Human rights introduced some remarkable normative changes.

It is important to note two common misnomers about postnational citizenship, which come up commonly in critical treatments.

First, the human rights revolution came to be increasingly, but wrongly, identified—not just by the public but also by significant numbers of scholars of multiculturalism. Critics often blurred the relationship between postnationalism and multiculturalism (e.g., Joppke 1999; Koopmans and Statham 1999; Bloemraad 2006). The relationship between human rights

92 CITIZENSHIP

and multiculturalism has been much more nuanced. By the early twenty-first century, however, and certainly by the police murder of George Floyd in 2020, the discourse of rights became more transnational but also much more hooked into explicit identity politics—to the extent that other rights, such as freedom of speech and academic freedom, were seen as at risk.

The second misconception is that postnational citizenship is arguing for or describing a world of disappearing borders. The legal scholar Ayelet Shachar (2020), for example, refers to the postnational argument as part of "[an] alternate globalist vision of a world in which extant borders are, or soon will be, traversed with the greatest of ease, to the extent that they become all but meaningless. In combination with the sheer number of people on the move, this has led some scholars to argue that the grip of borders, or even the fundamental principle of territoriality itself, is waning" (13). In parallel fashion, scholars such as the political scientist Randall Hansen (2009) have suggested that the postnational argument is "anti-statist."

But these readings of postnational citizenship are mistaken. The fact of the matter is that international human rights law, and the legal regime around human rights, is almost entirely dependent on states for the implementation of human rights law. The state is *intrinsic* to the human rights architecture, and as such to the postnational argument. It is through the judicial mechanisms of democratic states that human rights legal instruments made up significant ground from the 1970s. Nor is it correct that borders are being legally effaced, or being suggested as such, in the postnational argument. International human rights law does not make a frontal challenge on the state's right to regulate its borders (Jacobson and Ruffer 2003).

States can even take drastic measures, like offshoring (within limits) border control, from a legal standpoint. What the human rights instruments do is make the criteria follow universalist and non-discriminatory standards. It is in that context we saw rapid decline in democracies in immigration criteria that discriminated by race, ethnicity, and sex. Similarly, asylum law cannot discriminate because of, for example, national origin—a discriminatory practice that was rampant in the past. Human rights activists may seek a borderless world, but we need to distinguish the legal regime from the desires of the activists. Furthermore, the term "postnational" refers to, in part, the partial decoupling of nationality and the state, or conversely making nationality (again, under certain parameters) a human right. Progress in that regard has in turn led to neonationalist backlashes—something proponents of human rights advances (including activists) need to account for more thoughtfully. But it is important not to read "postnational" as "post-state," as Hansen (2009) does in his claim that the postnational argument is "anti-statist." That claim is turning the postnational approach on its head.

The arc from liberal nationalist proponents of citizenship, like David Miller (1995), to proponents of postnational citizenship, has turned in on itself with primordialist assumptions shifting from the national to the sub- and transnational levels. How did postnational citizenship emerge, and how did this almost dialectical arc toward identarian politics, especially around race and gender, take place? Beyond that contemporary question, how do we build on the successes of the postnational turn, and learn from its failures, to promote the civic project? In part, that will involve a better understanding of "what job" rights should perform.

Our focus here regarding the postnational turn is primarily on Europe and the United States, but it is important to note the dynamics described here take place elsewhere in the democratic world. The case of the Korean minority in Japan—a group that has suffered severe discrimination—is especially telling. In the post-war period, resident Koreans made national claims and emphasized their linkages with their "homelands"; however, internal divisions between those who supported South Korea and those who supported North Korea hampered the movement. But, as sociologists Kiyoteru Tsutsui and Hwa Ji Shin (2008) illustrate, from the 1970s activists turned to universal human rights law and norms. Especially among the younger generation, this enabled the building of a coalition across the Korean community and other minorities, leading to key policy changes. As in Europe and the United States, the judiciary was key in pushing forward the human rights agenda in Japan.

Human Rights and the Turn
toward Postnational Citizenship

In the wake of World War II and its horrors, the banner of human rights was raised, in word if not fully in deed. The Cold War provided further impetus for the West to promote human rights—albeit in its civic and political terms, less so its economic aspirations—as a means to confront communism and the Warsaw Pact. In theory at least, human rights provided a new paradigm for state, society, and international politics. Human rights challenged primordialist assumptions based, as human rights are, in individual rights

94 CITIZENSHIP

regardless of sex, race, national descent, or religion. Developing international human rights law, and its national forms, did have a dramatic effect in democratic countries from the 1970s and 1980s.

The promise of a modern international human rights normative order rests in the Universal Declaration of Human Rights (UDHR), adopted by the United Nations General Assembly in 1948; the International Covenant on Economic Social and Cultural Rights (ICESCR); and the International Covenant on Civil and Political Rights (ICCPR). Both the Covenants were adopted by the UN General Assembly in 1966. There are numerous other human rights treaties but the constitution-like foundations are those of the UDHR and the two Covenants (Sohn and Buergenthal 1973). The UDHR, and to some extent the Covenants, have also served as the legal grounding and inspiration for regional human rights treaties and constitutions from Europe to South Africa.[4]

Lineaments of a human rights legal structure appeared before—notably in the anti-slavery legislation of the nineteenth century and the minority treaties after World War I.[5] An extraordinary array of human rights treaties followed the UDHR, for the rights of refugees, children, migrants, and women, among others. Still, in *practice* the import of the human rights legal architecture was marginal in its first decades. In practice, the realpolitik of states and of the alliances built around the bipolar Cold War (or tripolar world after Mao broke from Stalin in 1956) shaped the dynamics of international politics. Except as a means for Western governments to expose the depredations of totalitarian regimes, notably of the Soviet Union and the People's Republic of China, minimal pressure was imposed upon countries to conform with international human rights standards. The exception to this picture was at the level of social movements and NGOs, notably in the mobilization against Apartheid in South Africa.

Even the authoritarian allies of Western countries—in Africa, the Middle East, Latin America, and Asia—were largely left alone. Indeed, American leaders and intellectuals justified the alliance with authoritarian governments on the grounds that their human rights record, although regrettable, was (allegedly) less severe than that of the communist bloc. In any event, so the argument went, the West needed these governments in the struggle with communism. Brutal military dictatorships were accordingly supported by the United States against left-wing guerillas in countries such as Chile.[6]

Although rooted in the birth certificates of nation-states—notably the French Declaration of the Rights of Man and the Citizen, the US Declaration of Independence, and the US Constitution—the UDHR and subsequent human rights treaties would pose a fundamental challenge for citizenship. The challenge of the international human rights law for citizenship (as then practiced) was not fully comprehended at the time. In part, this was due to states having a near veto, in effect, over the implementation of human rights law. States had to sign off and then ratify the treaties—and even then, enforcement was another matter. It took roughly twenty-five years for most states under the jurisdiction of the European Court of Human Rights in Strasbourg to accept individual petitions to Strasbourg, not just state parties. Yet the seed of individual human rights and protections had been planted, and state-centered assurances would be diluted in the decades ahead (Bates 2010).

Scholars have tended to view normative change as a function of activism through, for example, "shaming" countries on their moral failures (Sikkink 2011). Or normative change is viewed as epiphenomenal, such as when the "organized hypocrisy" of international realpolitik drives the dynamics of international (and domestic) relations (Krasner 1999). The changes in human rights practice, particularly in and by democracies, have been more subtle than either of these approaches. For some decades, starting with the Universal Declaration of Human Rights, the architecture of the human rights regime was built up. States, beyond lip service, overwhelmingly ignored these developments in any substantive sense. The organized hypocrisy prism to state and international behavior was apparent to just about any observer—scholarly or otherwise. But, in fact, the legal architecture of international human rights instruments proved critical; they provided the foundations for an *on-ramp* toward real normative change. That on-ramp was provided somewhat serendipitously by changing structural conditions which indirectly provided for bringing human rights to the fore within democracies (Jacobson 1996; Jacobson et al. 2022).[7] Migration was a key factor for Europe and the United States in that regard. In other cases, as in the noted example of Japan, resident minorities that had long faced pronounced discrimination turned to international human rights instruments to seek remedy.

Policy responses to challenges are frequently ad hoc, and often conform with the law of unintended consequences. A case in point: Western European governments saw the importation of migrant "guest workers" in the 1950s and 1960s to address economic needs as a temporary solution and they expected those workers would soon return to their home countries. The last thing on their minds was a demographic recasting of Europe

96 CITIZENSHIP

that, in fact, transpired. Similarly, few saw the quietly revolutionary potential of international human rights law. Even fewer (if indeed anyone in the early years) realized that the Universal Declaration of Human Rights and the subsequent human rights legal machinery and treaties—from new regional courts to specialized human rights codes regarding subjects from refugees to children—were helping seed the ground for a revolutionary change in the understanding of citizenship. The seeds would take decades to germinate and so it has been a revolution of a most unusual sort.

Under such conditions, human rights have had considerable effect, primarily through judicial and quasi-judicial mechanisms. Consequently, a "politics of rights" supplemented—and partly supplanted—the democratic "politics of consent." The process of "judicialization" is not just institutional but it is associated with a cognitive shift. It changed the way people broadly think about politics and engage politically. Rights, in this light, are construed as absolute—from anti-abortion proponents to activists of identity politics—that are not (or should not be) conditioned on the give-and-take of political bartering and compromise.

Much of the postnational citizenship debate overlooks, by its proponents and its critics alike, this cognitive shift when it comes to rights. Here a reference to Pierre Bourdieu's (2020) concept of the *habitus* may be useful. The law and its institutions are particularly important in this regard by, in Bourdieu's terms, insinuating in subjects (say, citizens) a particular sense of "subjectship." Judicialization has shifted (partly but significantly) the *habitus* of rights from its republican moorings. The density of rights, and the related lattice of institutional and organizational rules, helped evolve the "subjectivity" of the citizen—and a variety of other claimants as well. The now oft-used definition of citizenship as the "right to claim rights," of Isin (2012), in effect captures this sense of subjectivity.

Postnational Citizenship and Its Sources

Under international human rights law, the individual has certain rights irrespective of citizenship and nationality in the country in which they are present. Individuals, not just states, have become objects of international law. Some rights violations (e.g., torture) have "universal jurisdiction," which means that charges can be (in theory) brought to any court in the world, regardless of where the violation took place. A case in 1980 that set a precedent in the United States concerned a Paraguayan police officer who had tortured another Paraguayan in Paraguay; in this case, a US federal court punished a non-US citizen for an act of torture committed outside the United States against a non-US citizen on the basis of international human rights law.[8] But in most cases, human rights concern issues in which national or regional courts and tribunals (like the European Court of Human Rights) are the loci for addressing concerns such as asylum and immigration. States are still free to regulate entry to their countries, but the criteria must be non-discriminatory as defined in international human rights law. Activists have sometimes acted as if human rights demand open borders—and states on occasion have had very open policies, such as that of Germany's Chancellor Angela Merkel's welcome of Syrian refugees in 2015. But under these instruments state prerogative over their borders remained, and remain, central (Shain 2019).

The postnational turn was, however, significant—even if the changes were gradual, uneven, and largely limited to the democratic world. The character of "nationhood" was significantly challenged and indeed compromised. Notions of national or ethnic descent as criteria for entry to residency or citizenship eroded (although not disappeared) rather rapidly in Western democracies—while being resisted in new democracies in Eastern Europe. The extraordinary shift in democracies from the 1970s from relatively monochromatic countries to the ethnic and religious diversity of today attests to some of those dramatic effects. The European Union as a regional entity made the most progress, especially under the aegis of the European Court of Human Rights, and especially after individuals (not just states) could appeal to the ECHR from the 1960s (Keller and Sweet 2008; Føllesdal, Peters, and Ulfstein 2013).

Human rights had the effect of breaking down the sharp, binary citizen–alien distinction, not legally but in practice. By partially decoupling nationality from the state, dual citizenship was increasingly legitimated, and it increased dramatically from the late 1990s—both in its sanctioning by different states and in the numbers of those who carried dual citizenship. Noncitizen residents in democracies were increasingly secure and protected by rights, even if not at the level of citizens themselves. In many cities voting was even extended for noncitizens. By blurring the binary of insiders and outsiders, *in practice* citizenship became more scalar rather than binary, with, in effect, multiple, quasi, and semi-citizenships. In this light, Rainer Bauböck (2017a, 2017b) argued for a "transnational citizenship."

98   CITIZENSHIP

Postnational citizenship informed the architecture of citizenship in a transnational political entity, like the European Union, and impacted all dimensions of citizenship, from membership to governance. Postnational citizenship also challenged and diluted the assumed duality of "nation" and "state" as inextricably linked. The postnational citizenship architecture, in terms of legal developments and scholarly argument, provided a framework in which the basis of domestic state legitimacy could be re-oriented from the long-institutionalized notions of "sovereignty" to one that had more subtle interplays between state autonomy and responsibilities under international human rights. The changes impacting national sovereignty and the assumed connection of "a people" and a territory became, clearly, one basis for populist backlash.

The postnational citizenship argument faced scholarly criticism in a lively debate following the emergence of the argument in the 1990s (Soysal 1994; Jacobson 1996; see also Balibar 2003). In particular, criticism focused on the resilience of the state as the main actor for shaping attitudes and political behaviors of migrants and ethnic minorities (Howard 2009; Koopmans and Statham 1999; Koopmans et al. 2005).[9] But commonly recognized across the debate was the impact of large-scale migration (from guest workers to undocumented migration into Europe and the United States) on citizenship in the post-war period, especially from the 1970s. States responded to those populations, who had to be legally accounted for, with the gradual, ad hoc expansion of their rights. International human rights codes, rooted in personhood rather than citizenship per se, were a ready mechanism to account for populations who straddled the insider–outsider dichotomy, so key to the law of citizenship. The rate at which states turned to human rights varied. Germany, whose citizenship regime at the time rested on *ius sanguinis* principles, turned to international human rights norms more readily because the "foreign" residents, mostly Turks, did not fit the ethnic criteria. The United States, in contrast, defined citizenship (in principle) in more legal and political terms and found ways to include such populations through "stretching" constitutional law to account for resident noncitizens (Jacobson 1996). These differences in legal regimes declined by the late 1990s as *ius sanguinis* criteria, under the impact of human rights norms, were watered down in Germany. Consequently, there is now a skepticism about the notion of durable "models" of nationhood beyond their heuristic value (Finotelli and Michalowski 2012; Joppke 2007).

An American example of stretching the domestic law to account for migratory pressures is *Plyer v. Doe*, in which the Supreme Court ruled, in 1982, that states could not constitutionally deny students a free public education due to immigration status (including undocumented aliens). The court in this case rejected basing the decision on international human rights law and instead turned to the Constitution to buttress its decision. As the preponderance of rights in the Constitution are bestowed upon "persons" as opposed to citizens per se, courts can, so to speak, stretch the Constitution to account for noncitizens. From the legal perspective of international human rights law, however, this is perfectly acceptable. The objective is that legal practices concord with international human rights law. Much "human rights activity" will take place within domestic legal frameworks.[10]

Various individuals and non-governmental groups have quickly adapted to this process, appealing to human rights for their claims, either formally in courts or in popular discourse. Human rights also facilitated a change from the idea of the nation as a monocultural body to a more diverse image of society. This may account for why, for many scholars, multiculturalism came to be viewed, mistakenly, as synonymous with postnational citizenship (such as Joppke 1999; Koopmans and Statham 1999; Bloemraad 2006). In fact, multiculturalism is indeed sanctioned under international human rights legal norms, but only when an individual's identification with a culture is voluntary. We will return to this point later in this chapter.

The Cascade of Judicial Rights

The populist sentiment that came to the fore across much of the democratic world (and countries crossing into authoritarianism, like Hungary) is perhaps most familiarly expressed in phenomena like Donald Trump, Brexit, and the far-right groups like the National Front in France. Migration and refugee law is the first prominent area in which international human rights criteria have circumscribed traditional understandings of sovereignty and citizenship, with an extraordinary role for courts and administrative bodies (not infrequently in opposition to public opinion in Western countries). In this light, the salience of immigration in the populist agenda is not a surprise (Cinalli and Van Hauwaert 2021; Fetzer 2012; Shehaj, Shin, and Inglehart 2021).

100   CITIZENSHIP

Thus, it is key to understand the role of "judicialization" regarding formal institutions of courts, the dramatic growth of quasi-judicial entities, and the discourse of rights. The judiciary has played not only an essential role in the postnational turn—rights get mediated and, in effect, advanced primarily through judicial mechanisms—but the shift goes beyond courts and judicial bodies. In the democratic world we see the growth of rights of different kinds, more specialization of law, more kinds of courts, courts increasingly drawing on international law, and judicialization within private and public organizations, notably adjudicating on race or sexual discrimination (Jacobson 1996; Jacobson and Ruffer 2003). This phenomenon has had a substantial impact on the underlying DNA of our institutions.

The cascading of rights over the decades is exceptionally important. It is not simply that mechanisms become available to advance rights claims to any legal (and even undocumented) resident—formal citizenship is generally secondary to claims made in organizational contexts—but it has deeper sociological implications. The assumptions of human rights increasingly infused human interaction at every level, and they continue to do so today. Human rights are not just for contesting the state, nor is the state necessarily the final arbiter. Human rights claims and struggles now take place in every context: universities, corporations, government agencies, Hollywood, and personal relationships. The "propertied entitlements" of human rights play out in almost every human interaction. The cognitive shift shapes social relations, from gender concerns at the dyadic level to race relations in work organizations writ large.

The changes are quantitative and organizational. Equally significant are the qualitative shifts. The growing web of rights in all kinds of organizational contexts enable agency, in the first instance legally but now embedded deeply in social and felt ways. Growing rights generate claims. Individuals can "litigate" internally, for example, over race discrimination. We also witness the growing specialization of law in areas from intellectual property to the environment (Bently et al. 2021; Hofmann and Naurin 2021). Rights talk has become common in our everyday language, so much so that rights are invoked without forethought. The discourse of engagement within and across organizations is increasingly flecked and informed by claims and interpretations of rights. Judicial bodies may be the ultimate backstop but the impact of the "rights revolution" goes well beyond the legal domain. Indeed, this may be the most significant effect.

Lawrence Friedman (1985) noted that accidents at work in the past—say a railway worker breaking their leg in nineteenth-century America—would be considered bad luck. Today, legal mechanisms would kick into play, from sick leave to, potentially, a malpractice lawsuit. Law *enables* the individual. This changes citizens and noncitizens alike in fundamental ways, including how people engage with each other, institutions, those in authority, and politics. Politically, juridical agency is a form of engagement which both rivals and complements the traditional democratic route of voting, civic participation, and political mobilization. The "politics of rights" is not about the "politics of consent." Judicial and administrative mechanisms, as opposed to the legislature, become central in this process. This is distinct from republican concepts of participation to shape and form the commonwealth. The politics of rights is distinct from viewing citizens as *zoon politikon*. This enabling role of law, and its impact on political engagement, is reinforced in that in contrast to the past, no area of life today is beyond the potential reach of the law. Individual access, or potential access, to the dense web of judicially mediated legal rights is ubiquitous (Jacobson and Ruffer 2003).

Judicialization, the associated importance of administration, and the growing role of expertise have eroded the salience of "representation" and, thus, the linkages between rulers and the ruled. Herein lies the problem of the democratic deficit, a term usually associated with the European Union but which is a much broader concern across the democratic world (Lax and Phillips 2012; Norris 2011). Issues associated with the postnational turn in citizenship—the growing salience of the courts and administrative bodies, immigration and asylum, and globalization—have been key factors in the populist backlash we have witnessed across almost all democracies.

From *Zoon Politikon* to *Homo Legalis*

The cascade of quasi-judicial legal mechanisms into private and public organizations does not simply enable the individual's judicial agency. It changes the experience and character of citizenship. It turns the individual, in significant part, from *zoon politikon* to *homo legalis*. J. G. A. Pocock (1993) described citizenship in Athens, as we noted earlier, as a matter of "ruling and being ruled," while Rome was about "suing and being sued." We see a similar evolution here, although, of course, the change regards not only lawsuits and is of a more nuanced nature.

102   CITIZENSHIP

Yet the cascade of rights, in our present time, goes beyond the Roman case in its significance for citizenship. The political scientist Galya Ruffer (2002) has characterized the nature of organizationally based rights and protections as a "virtual citizenship" which is, in important respects, independent of legal citizenship. For example, the rights and protections that accrue to an employee on, say, gender discrimination in a corporation, public or private, are not a function of formal citizenship status (although, of course, the presumption is that the employee is at least a legal resident). Ruffer's observation is doubly important as judicial agency is not expressed primarily at the international, regional, or even the national level. Rather, the progressively dense legal webbing enables human rights claims (e.g., on gender or racial issues) at the lower-order organizational level—such as, prominently, the workplace. Formal courts become useful in addressing issues not dealt with at the level of private and public bodies. The ability to go to courts is limited in its reach because of matters of social and financial capital, which in effect creates filtered social class effects. These effects are only partly addressed by non-governmental groups, which often represent more targeted concerns, such as abortion disputes.

Nonetheless, the courts (especially higher courts) are the setting for establishing new precedents. High courts, nationally or regionally, have wide-ranging effects. For example, a ruling by the European Court of Human Rights closed-off the gender of a spouse as a criterion in determining immigration status. In this case, different rules existed for non-British wives joining their husbands in the United Kingdom than the reverse. The European Court of Human Rights ruled this as a clear case of sex discrimination. Gender ceased to be a factor, effectively, that states could consider in determining who could enter or not enter their country.[11]

More broadly, such rulings placed constraints for a broad range of organizations under the respective jurisdictions. In judgments from the European Court of Human Rights to national courts, issues such as "gender" and "race" have been legally closed off as the bases for discrimination across the democratic world. When one contemplates the extraordinary import of certain issues being taken out of the legitimate discourse of politics—for example, the almost complete delegitimation of making sexual and gender distinctions as a basis for treating women and men differently in public policy—the extent to which human rights judgments have shaped the human landscape is more readily apparent. The remarkable influence of human rights then begins to dawn on us because we have assimilated these transformative changes as, now, unremarkable (Jacobson and Ruffer 2003).

In recent decades we have seen a striking increase in the emphasis of individual rights in the sense of the growing autonomy of the individual (Koo and Ramirez 2009). This is expressed in "bodily autonomy," and it is, socially, most evident in areas of sexuality and of race and ethnicity. Taking the case of sexuality, the public assertion of gay rights, queer rights, transgender rights, and other gendered and intersectional forms of identity illustrates how the notion of individual autonomy gets increasingly refined. Within relatively short periods of time, public opinion has quickly pivoted on issues like gay marriage and even on the right of transgender people to serve in the military.

It is the partial decoupling of rights and territoriality that hooks the postnational turn to growing transnational ties, organizations, and relationships. It is not simply about economic globalization and consequent human migration patterns. It is about changing forms of human association, networks, and social capital. Citizens belong to myriad families, ethnic groups, churches, mosques, voluntary associations, places of work, colleges, and the like—and significant numbers of these are transnational, especially among immigrants. These are groups and organizations each with their own networks, collectively defined as "civil society," linking into the policy domain with other networks made of institutions, decision-makers, and political elites of different kinds (Cinalli et al. 2021; Portes 1997; Von Bülow 2010).

In the partial but significant shift from the "politics of consent" to the "politics of rights" human rights can become the alternative scaffold to build state legitimacy and political life. However, as we observe in both Europe and the United States today, the advancing of human rights through the courts and administrative bodies has exposed an Achilles' heel. When the authority of judicial and administrative bodies grew in this regard, questions of democratic accountability came to the fore. This contributed to the discussion on the democratic deficit in the European Union (see Steffek, Kissling, and Nanz 2007). Populism gained ballast from this concern, notably around immigrants and refugees—areas where human rights norms have played, and continue to play, an important role. The attention paid to these risks, among political, administrative, and judicial authorities was remarkably sparse—until the populist parties start making headway, especially from the early twenty-first century (Rooduijn, De Lange, and Brug 2014; Van Kessel 2015).

104 CITIZENSHIP

Human Rights and Identity Politics

The commentator Kenin Malik (2019) observed regarding shifting political positions:

> Conservatives saw history, tradition, and the nation as the means by which the individual became part of a greater whole. For radical critics . . . an individual realized himself or herself not through tradition but through struggles to transform society, from battles for decent working conditions to campaigns for equal rights. These struggles created organizations, such as trade unions and civil rights movements, which drew individuals into new modes of collective life and forged new forms of belonging . . . But in recent years, as trade unions have weakened and social movements crumbled, it has seemed for many that the only form of collective politics left is that rooted in conservative, Burkean notions of national or ethnic identity. At the same time, many sections of the left have also given up on traditional modes of social change, retreating instead into the vapidity of identity politics and diversity talk. In so doing, they have often abandoned not just class politics, but their attachment to traditional liberal values as well, transforming the meaning of equality and rejecting free speech.

Malik is writing of the United Kingdom, but the comment could apply, *mutatis mutandis*, across most democracies.

The turn to "identity politics" on the Left, noted by Malik, to the point that rights claims are frequently couched in terms of, *inter alia*, racial and ethnic rights contains a certain irony. One can observe a tendency to associate human rights with multiculturalism by activist groups as well as some scholars. Yet, human rights as a legal framework can sanction a variety of political systems from multicultural Britain to republican France. What is key, in terms of human rights as a legal instrument are *individual* rights and volition—with some exceptions, such as indigenous group rights in some legal systems. When human rights as an instrument of governance intersects with multiculturalism and identity claims, forms of (sanctioned) identity change in the process. Given that many cultural practices involve coercion of individuals, especially in compelling women to follow patriarchal practices (such as in the extreme but not uncommon case of female genital mutilation), cultures practices change considerably when human rights norms are imposed. Thus, as much as the state can be held accountable for human rights violations, so can a father be held accountable for violating his daughter's human rights. The numerous court cases regarding, for example, forced marriages, honor killings, and female genital mutilation in the courts of Western countries attest to the transformative impact of human rights on cultural practices (Jacobson 2009).

The "frontlines" of human rights are dynamic, and legal interpretations and public pressures extend (explicitly or implicitly) the ambit of human rights (e.g., on what constitutes racial discrimination). Of course, as with all means of legal and social control, it is partial in its effect. But the effect is considerable, although varying depending on the issue.[12]

As societies became more ethnically, racially, and religiously diverse, addressing the diversity became a deep concern by, at least, the 1990s. As trade unions and the traditional working class weakened under the impact of neoliberal policies, diversity became an alternate coalition for movements and parties on the Left. In Europe, the language of "integration," previously the domain of American social science and policy, came to be emulated in European scholarship and policy circles, and it entered public discourse. Europeans also began developing institutional mechanisms for the representation of ethnic and religious groups, which in turn impacted electoral politics (Favell 2022; Cinalli and Giugni 2013).

It is also from the 1980s and 1990s that we see the constellation of *interconnected* forces that have been harmful, even pernicious, for most democracies and civic politics. The working class, particularly the White working class, has felt increasingly disenfranchised and abandoned. This is a function of globalization and its impact on well-paying, blue-collar industries; neoliberal policies; an emerging "global elite," and professional classes more broadly, which appeared increasingly detached from the concerns of the working class; and large immigration and growing diversity, which became the basis of changing calculus and ideologies on the Left.[13] The rise of the internet was a powerful catalyst as it unleashed populist anger at the elites, directed at what Martin Gurri (2018) calls the "old hierarchical institutions," from politics to corporations to the media. Government, media, and academic experts were, in this virtual environment, increasingly derided. Figures like Donald Trump, Gurri argues, were symptoms more than causes of this populist onrush, although the populists certainly fueled the flames of anger.

It is in this light that one must understand the vulnerabilities of the advances in human rights. It has been through judicial and administrative bodies, and in Europe through directives and legal instruments from

106 CITIZENSHIP

regional bodies like the European Union and the Council of Europe, that human rights primarily advanced. Human rights have also been associated with immigrant and refugee "crises" and a sense by the "revolting public," to use Gurri's language, that their voices were not being heard.

The postnational turn was also hurt by its co-optation by a "cosmopolitan elite," including from corporations. With the partial but significant detachment of citizenship from nationality, citizenship has been increasingly instrumentalized. Immigration and naturalization criteria have increasingly focused on economic skills and investment, such that the "value" of citizenship has been progressively weighted in increasingly utilitarian terms. The notion of the "merit" of a potential immigrant fitted with a vision of cosmopolitan and professional classes who, because of merit criteria, could claim to be globally minded and fair. Such claims appeared to have an affinity with international human rights norms as, in part, these criteria were non-discriminatory. But it ignored the unequal impacts this has as to who enjoys human rights—by a class filter—and, relatedly, had the result of instituting and legitimizing inequalities among citizens (Sénac 2017).

One scholar suggested in this context that citizenship had become "citizenship light"; we now have the paradox of citizenship having less affective and emotional value, while having increased instrumental value (Joppke 2010). To have the right to a valued citizenship, and passport, is to be closely associated with the higher ends of a highly unequal global order. The most blatant example of instrumentalization are the schemes for the outright buying of citizenship (Harpaz and Mateos 2019; Joppke 2019). Neoliberal policies have, however, in the aftermath of the Great Recession, fallen further from grace (Piketty 2014; Block and Somers 2014). Prior to the Great Recession, in the post-Cold War period (from about 1989 to 2008), the main goal had been the promotion of economic growth with the premise that a rising tide lifts all boats. Equality was framed, at best, as "equality before the law," such as on equal opportunity and ending discrimination. The growing, severe inequality in many Western democracies, among other factors, further eroded the legitimacy of elites and experts.

This description does not capture the full character of the challenge. Rights, for example, have come to be, of late, increasingly fused with ascriptive characteristics, explicitly or implicitly, in neonationalist and in identity politics. There is an assumption that selective rights based on specific attributes (e.g., race, ethnicity, religion, or gender) are essential to confront a history of accumulated discrimination and institutional exclusion. Targeted efforts to rectify, for example, past discriminatory hiring practices can be necessary. However, civic and relational efforts to address past injustices will be the most enduring, rather than approaches which accentuate group attributions and transactional approaches. This is because the challenges around group differences reflect shortfalls in relational and civic ties. Ethnic differences, for example, are not "natural," even if they are assumed to be. They reflect the fact that historically people paid attention to these boundaries and reproduced them in their daily relationships—through patterns of marriage, friendship, work relations, and hiring (Loury 2020).

The only way to substantively cross those boundaries—*to turn such boundaries into seams*—is relationally and through civic engagement.[14] Such an endeavor is essential for developing the deep civic reservoir to counter prejudice and institutional exclusion in a way legal instruments *alone* have failed to achieve. That, by itself, should give pause. It is not the case that one or two laws have not done the job of eradicating, say, racism but decades of lawmaking have failed. Clearly, far-reaching progress still needs to be made in combating institutional exclusion and prejudice. But the question is, what is the most effective strategy for generating changes? And, beyond that, what kind of rights will help get us there? We must ask ourselves what job, at the end of the day, should rights perform? If it is fulfilling the goals of a full citizenship, of a vibrant civic polity, then we must rethink our present path. Or, perhaps better put, we need to have a better understanding of how rights can support an authentic citizenship—in matters of rule and membership—as forks in the path present themselves.

Notes

1. The "territorial" rights of the individual are circumscribed by the tangible territory of the state in which they reside, which in turn bestows duties as well as rights. The state itself as a putatively sovereign entity has, historically, been treated analogously like a (corporate) individual with rights such as national *self*-determination—with rights of non-interference.
2. Northern Europe and Switzerland report higher levels of trust, while southern and eastern Europe, and France, indicate lower levels of trust across all cases: trust in the political system, trust in the legal system, and trust in the police.
3. See discussion in Jacobson and Goodwin-White (2018) and Manby (2023).
4. On the text of UDHR and the Covenants see, respectively: https://www.un.org/en/about-us/universal-declaration-of-human-rights and https://2covenants.ohchr.org/. Accessed June 2, 2022.

108 CITIZENSHIP

5. The anti-slavery legislation was initiated on a national basis, starting with Britain's Slave Trade Act 1807, followed by the British government abolishing slavery throughout its colonies in 1833, freeing more than three-quarters of a million slaves. Britain pushed its anti-slavery campaign through bilateral and multilateral agreements, notably, at the Paris Peace Conference of 1814–1815. Under the 1814 Treaty of Paris, France promised to end their slave trade, the treaty noting that the slave trade was "repugnant to the principles of natural justice." In other words, slavery became a violation of an emerging "universal law," transcending sovereignty (Nadelmann 1990). Such treaties became the basis for vigorous efforts to end slavery by abolitionist movements and by some states. The anti-slavery efforts also marked a longer-term trend in that human rights, although legally and morally transcending states, would make institutional progress only *through* states—something that was understood from the start by anti-slavery activists, starting with William Wilberforce (2007).

6. The argument was perhaps best articulated by Jeane Kirkpatrick, who was US ambassador to the United Nations during the Reagan administration, in her article on "Dictatorships and Double Standards" (see Kirkpatrick 1979).

7. The "on-ramp" is discussed further in Chapter 8 of this text, in the context of the "second wave" of human rights.

8. *Filártiga v. Peña-Irala*, 630 F.2d 876 (2d Cir. 1980).

9. However, see Cinalli and Giugni (2016) for limits of this national-based approach to rights and discourse when it is applied for explaining political behavior of Muslim minorities.

10. See a brief discussion in Chapter 8 on the "Dreamers," who are, as Jamie Goodwin-White (2020) notes, "the children" of *Plyer v. Doe*.

11. The European Court of Human Rights ruling noted is *Abdulaziz, Cabales, and Balkandali v. United Kingdom* (1985).

12. A major concern, however, is that social class appears to filter, severely, the effectiveness and reach of human rights (see, through the lens of women's rights and homicide, in Santos, Jacobson, and Georgiev 2021).

13. See discussions in Lasch (1995), Goodhart (2017), Sobolewska and Ford (2020), and Klein (2021).

14. We expand on the concept of "seams" in Chapter 7.

6

Interests and Identities

Citizenship and the Problem of Collective Action

Citizenship creates a problem of collective action. It creates the problem by negating, in principle, long held kinship or kinship-like criteria as the basis for determining issues of rule and membership. Citizenship raises the question, in the absence of such criteria, on what principles can society be molded into a reasonably cohesive collectivity? So, a foundational challenge for nurturing and maintaining a civic society is figuring out the basis of the "social glue." It is difficult to overstate the centrality of that question in political theory. The idea that society had internal coherence is at the very roots of the discipline of sociology (Comte 2019; Durkheim 1984; Weber 2019). Migration studies have been perennially concerned with questions of integration and assimilation. Debates on multiculturalism and, say, French Republicanism have been abiding concerns.[1]

Considerable progress has been made in terms of promoting civic practices in recent decades, in varied ways and at different scales from voluntary associations to republican states. But, in practice, states have never, as we have observed, been fully free of primordialist practices. In terms of the cognitive and organizational framing of modern democracies, in social and political life, implicitly or explicitly primordialist attributes are made on, *inter alia*, race, religion, and the nation itself. Not only have states had difficulty in giving up on primordialist impedimenta, but social and political movements keep reverting to it. Historically, we have been used to the Right appealing to culture, race, and religion as pillars of the social order. But even on the Left, or a significant part of it, we now observe that same turn to race as a bedrock of political life.

Political theorists have grappled with this question, on what basis the coherence of society can be assured. It is a debate that goes back to the Greeks and Romans and, at least implicitly, to civilizations of the Ancient Near East.

Citizenship. David Jacobson and Manlio Cinalli, Oxford University Press. © Oxford University Press 2023.
DOI: 10.1093/oso/9780197669150.003.0006

110   CITIZENSHIP

For modern democracies, the engagement since the Enlightenment is most apposite because Enlightenment theories and arguments have so impacted the institutions of present times. The dilemmas remain in contemporary political thought. The question regarding the foundations for social cohesion is a profoundly challenging problem. It demands, among other things, interrogating questions about human motivation and its generalizability. Intricate arguments in political theory, and research in the social sciences more generally, can be built on the epistemological assumptions which, in their insistence of the determinative role of interest (or identity), remain, in essence, unproven.

The responses to this conundrum—how individuals can transform themselves into collective assemblages, both socially and politically—can be distilled via the respective organizing frames of "interest" and "identity." Interest has traditionally provided an instrumental and contractual basis for bringing individuals together into collective wholes. Identity has, alternatively, been put forward as the cognitive and emotional basis for binding individuals together into collective wholes. Interests or identities can also be the basis for concomitantly mobilizing against others. The framing of interest and identity, respectively, has had extraordinary influence in shaping the institutions of government, market, law, and society at large.

The terms of interest and identity reflect attempts to grapple with the challenges inherent in the emergence of civic politics, especially with the emergence of the modern state. Identity and interest mirror in curious yet significant ways the organizational framings of, respectively, *ethnos* and *demos*, "cultural" and "political" states, and what has been referred to as German ethnic versus French republican understandings of nationhood. The distinctions between *ethnos* and *demos* have in practice tended to be overstated, or at least to not be as stable as assumed, until recently.[2]

It may be the same for the distinction between interest and identity. Can a society be based solely on "interest"—or on identity, absent interest? The real question, as we will argue, is how the relationship between interest (and its cognate notions of contract and instrumentality) and identity are configured.

Theorists like Rawls and Habermas have, in different ways, taken contractually based liberal approaches while trying to contain its more deleterious effects (Habermas 1998a, 1998b; Rawls 1996, 2020). Broadly speaking, such positions posit that constitutional democracy, properly constructed, can be the basis of a functioning, integrated, and just civic society. Universal principles, based on shared civic principles, are both a viable and desirable basis for constituting society and its political rule. Building on identarian foundations like nationalism, even in its liberal variants, is in this line of argument neither viable in the long term nor desirable, especially in increasingly multicultural environments.

Conversely, as we noted in Chapter 4, liberal nationalists like David Miller (1995) dispute the viability of creating a society on abstract principles alone, even based on what Habermas called "constitutional patriotism." Liberal forms of national identity provide the foundations for a pluralistic society, Miller argues, if that form of nationalism grows to be more inclusive. An example may be the way a White Anglo-Saxon Protestant United States over time became more inclusive (in part at least) religiously, racially, and in terms of national origins. Habermas and others argue that approaches like that of the liberal nationalists would necessarily involve imposition of the majority culture on minority cultures.[3]

Let's parse the concepts of interest and identity, how they have in practice come to be juxtaposed upon one another, and then suggest how they can be unpacked to promote a more authentic civic model.

The Leitmotifs of Interest and Identity: Historical and Theoretical Foundations

In modern politics, interest and identity are two fundamental building blocks upon which, in theory, citizens can be brought together—the foundation upon which human beings associate as larger social groups (Aristotle 2009). Interest and identity, in this telling, account in different ways for relations between individuals, as well as between them and the larger associations that they form. While on the one hand these associations have been thought of as the first expression of social life (the *pactum societatis* under the "social contract" in Natural Law theory), they have also been crucial in establishing the foundations of a fully-fledged political community and its rulemaking institutions (the *pactum subjectionis* in Natural Law theory). Interest and identity consequently also account for the historical formation of government, grounded on the relationship between those who govern and those who are governed. The concepts of interest and identity came even more to the forefront in Europe with growing societal complexity from the end of the first millennium CE, well before the Renaissance or the Enlightenment (Greaves 1982; Tierney 1987).

112   CITIZENSHIP

Early on, interest and identity were claimed as the basis of human association. Starting with the prevalence of interest for nurturing social life, the Latin adage *quod omnes tangit ab omnibus approbetur* ("whatever touches all, must be approved by all") corroborated civil law under the Code of Justinian, showing that already in the passage between Ancient Rome and the early Middle Ages self-interest was embedded within a larger social concert of interests. Interest was seen more as a facilitator of selfishness—one of the sins that Enlightenment thinkers would grapple with and transform into a kind of virtue. The "selfishness" was viewed through the prism of an Augustinian view of postlapsarian man as morally corrupted (Deane 1963; Bejczy 2011; Hirschman 1977). Yet, interest was later resurrected and brought into modern politics in the Renaissance with Machiavelli's and Guicciardini's conceptualizations of "state interest" (Pocock 1978, Viroli 1992). This combined push of secular and religious forces brought interest to the core of action by individuals. However, interest could be portrayed in both "egoistic" and "social" ways, and so left wide room in terms of how interest could be articulated in governing human relations.

Following developments in French Absolutism in the seventeenth century, interest fitted the image of a selfish and ambitious individual who could satisfy, even deceptively, their own egoistic needs in terms of their appetites for a joyful life. This is a common thread running across philosophers, historians, and literary figures, such as Descartes, Corneille, La Rochefoucauld, Pascal, Molière, and La Bruyère (Kuhn 1976; Krailsheimer 1962). From this viewpoint, interest meant self-interest, characterizing a position where individuals stand within an atomized world with little in the way of affective relations among them.

On the other hand, following developments of Scottish moral thought, interest was social—the main substance nurturing social life through growing interactions among individuals. By arguing that individuals are moved by "benevolent affections" for the happiness of others and not just by their self-interested desires, works by Shaftesbury, Hutcheson, Butler, and "Christian Stoicism" in general established that, through social interest, individuals can promote the public good (Sher 1985; Cooper the 3rd Earl of Shaftesbury 2001, Hutcheson 2003). Even if some differences remained in the way these different works combined self-interest and social interest for the promotion of public social life, the prevalent view was that God pushes humans toward virtue; hence, human nature is sociable and even particularistic appetites are a first step for bringing individuals closer among themselves (Butler 2018; Clarke 2018).

This complicated balance between self-interest and social interest for nurturing social life opened space for reflection to be focused on the specific role that politics could possibly play. Some authors argued that social life did not necessarily imply the establishment of exogenous political structures, as interest in all its forms strengthened social life and its endogenous institutional forms and thus rendered meaningless the surrendering of decisions to ad hoc rulers (Goldsmith, 1985). It was on this basis that Adam Smith (2010b) established the role of interest at the core of economic liberalism, sustained by some providential deism. The "natural" matching of self-interest and social interest stood out as a first foundation stone of social life and welfare for all (Lux 1990).

Given full equality among citizens and their purported predisposition for mutual empathy, the "invisible hand" could nurture social life and aim at the collective good with limited need for additional top-down government (Viner 1958, 1978; Teichgraeber, 1981). Most crucially, this idea that relations of interest constitute themselves suggested that the self-organization of society would have a durable life. Interest has since become associated with a purportedly spontaneous order to the advantage of whole society, as if it was the product of a non-human planner (Arrow and Hahn 1971; Hayek 1982).

Other authors, however, have given a much stronger role to the political constitution of rulemaking structures, focusing on the prevalence of interest for nurturing the political legitimacy of rulers. This attention to interest in the realm of politics developed as early as the Middle Ages through the work of canonists and early medieval thinkers. Medieval commentators drew not only on Aristotle's idea of the interest of individuals to constitute government (the *politeia*), but also on the German idea of *Genossenschaft*, which established the interest of tribal members to select their own leaders, as well as Judeo-Christian notions of autonomy (Watner 2005). Hence, the idea that rulemaking relies on individual interests opened space for the formation of representative bodies across different kingdoms, from Sicily to England. Examples include the creation of institutions such as the Great Charter and the Model Parliament of King Edward I (Cairns and Du Plessis 2010; Reid 1991; Pennington 1970; Post 1964). By the end of the Middle Ages the idea of "consent" (*quod omnes tangit*)—which established the centrality of self-interested individuals as "stakeholders" for political legitimacy of rulemaking—was evident across works of authors as varied as William of Ockham, Marsilius of Padua, Bartolus of Saxoferrato, and Nicholas of Cusa (Maiolo 2007, Oakley 1961; Sigmund 2013).

Afterward, the developments that followed from the Renaissance to the Enlightenment, until the consolidation of political liberalism in the nineteenth century, came to reinforce the idea that rulemaking is legitimate insofar as it coordinates self-interested individuals rather than nurturing deep common belongingness. Interest thus became the main ingredient for rulemaking, in the way this later would lead one way or the other to the notion of a plurality of private interests. Early thinkers of modern politics made clear their belief in a society which is a composition of different interests; they differed, however, on whether to guarantee harmony between self-interest and social interest through force or deception. In fact, in Machiavelli, force and deception are both useful ways for guaranteeing the full primacy of the "Prince" and his government but these two ways soon departed from each other in the following scholarly elaborations (Machiavelli 2014 [1514]).

Hobbes represents the apparent necessity of a top-down political force forcing individuals into social life: without political coercion, the disruptive character of self-interest would push individuals to fight each other in an endless state of war. In the Hobbesian argument, it is true that the first initiative of collaboration came from individuals themselves as they decided to join in the "social contract": yet the sole thing that they could really agree on was that the forceful rulemaking under the guardianship of the Leviathan was needed to compel them to collaborate (Hobbes 2020a).

As regards the use of deception, Mandeville (1988) put it at the core of his argument for building social order upon private vice: this is possible by manipulating the human predisposition for "self-liking," as each individual regards himself to be better than any other individual. Accordingly, social interest is not guaranteed by allegedly natural social affections, but rather, by the political manipulation of self-overevaluation hiding behind self-interest. Rulemaking is about manipulation of self-liking to avoid the negative outcome of competitive self-interests among individuals: for example, politicians can introduce rules of honor for flattering one's own self-liking together with rules of politeness for flattering the self-liking of others.

Therefore, whatever the way to fulfill harmony between self- and social interest, the primary view on politics emerging from the Renaissance was that rulemaking was about satisfying everybody's self-interest (Hume 1982). The Enlightenment furthered the ultimate promotion of self-interest, freedom,

INTERESTS AND IDENTITIES   115

and self-determination, yet with no overarching reference to shared beliefs and belongingness. So, it follows that the raison-d'être of liberal constitutionalism since its nascent state has been consisting of political pluralism for the safeguard of self-interested individuals. In this spirit, the growing wealth of post-revolution North America, in its most famous account by Tocqueville (2000), was the result of this pluralist political defense of interest.

This way of thinking has left a long-lasting legacy for Western politics in which interest has been claimed to be a cornerstone in the transition from "traditional" societies to modernity (Hollinger 1983; Giddens 1991). Many scholars have argued that even the key role of welfare and social rights in the wake of World War II was grounded in interest. Thus, the argument that the promotion of welfare is best achieved through the pursuit of self-interest in a market-like public sphere, as self-interest needs no governmental intervention for producing, albeit unintentionally, social well-being for all (Shand 1990; Poole 1991). This, in turn, leads to the notion that the market should be left in its "natural" state, largely free of government intervention—and, as such, beyond democratic accountability.

Interest is, almost by definition, a cornerstone also of utilitarians, notably Bentham. Under this perspective, interest is crucial for rulemaking, but based on a shared belief in human happiness to be pursued in turn by a "felicific calculus" for pleasing the majority interest (Bentham, 1988; Mitchell, 1918). This "natural" belief in human happiness thus brings together the political calculus made by the government on the one hand and, on the other, a similar calculus which individuals themselves "naturally" make when considering the interest of others. Thus self-interest, when grounded in shared moral obligation and guided by government, coincides with the interest of society (Brunius 1958).

In the Benthamite approach, rulemaking engages with self-interest by persuading the ruled that obedience is advantageous, so that their obedience is self-chosen rather than compelled politically. Social life is no longer nurtured by atomized individuals, each of them out only for themselves, but rather in an emerging public space connecting people who share a complementary view of human happiness. Thus, citizenship is not only about sovereignty and self-determination, but it comes to be attached to a normative vision that brings people together with similar values, and hence, the possibility to develop a sense of common belonging and shared trust. This is a first crucial step to root human action in a social, holistic perspective that dovetails with assumed human desires. In so doing, Bentham engaged with

116 CITIZENSHIP

the radical politics of his time, whether that was about sustaining public instruction and the free press or bringing forth laws to account for the depredations of the Industrial Revolution.

What of Identity?

The emphasis on interest does not have a monopoly on explanations for what drives collective action. The role of identity has also been acknowledged since classical politics. Just as for interest, identity was brought into the core of modern politics through the combined push of secular and religious forces. Machiavelli and Guicciardini argued that the existence of a same Italian identity could sustain the formation of national institutions spanning across regional differences. In the same vein, the emergence of the Lutheran Church provided a chance for socially embedding a "German" culture in opposition to the Catholic Church and other nations in Europe (Rosa 2019; Dewhurst 2013).

It is among the legal advisers of the two principal Lutheran electors—Philip of Hesse and John of Saxony—that constitutionalist theories were first used to justify the resistance of the Protestant princes against the Catholic emperor (see Rupp [2006] for the doctrine of Philip Melanchthon and Martin Bucer). Here, the duty and right to resist unjust political authorities was also grounded in deep religious convictions. Writing in the aftermath of the massacre of the night of St. Bartholomew, the Huguenot theorists of resistance transformed a contractual conception, based on interest, into a doctrine of resistance against rulers without legitimacy, based on identity (Manetsch 2000).

At the same time, when theories over the social contract were widespread, the notion of *animorum unio* ("union of minds") by Spinoza (2019), writing in the seventeenth century, marked a fundamental shift from conflict to agreement based on common understandings and beliefs, in turn establishing the foundations for a legitimate and commonly acknowledged authority.

In British moral philosophy in the eighteenth century, we can detect further substantive developments in terms of identity, especially in the concern for the building of social structures. Samuel Clarke and Francis Hutcheson argued that the common good was to be built upon a shared vision of happiness among individuals. This process of identification transforms self-interest into a morally virtuous push, which in turn guides the individual toward the happiness of others (Harris 2008; Stewart 1982). Archibald Campbell developed the same argument by saying that the common good lies in the fit between self-love and love for others within a shared desire for common well-being. Even trivial appetites may thus be instances of loving ourselves in others (Maurer 2013).

Identity can also provide the substance for transforming rulemaking into a mutual and even symbiotic public sphere. This is certainly reflected in the writing of Rousseau, from whom German Idealism and Marxism would later borrow expansively in their search for an ethical state (Coutinho 2000). Taking inspiration from earlier thinkers dealing with the divine will, Rousseau argued that society is just when the "general will" guarantees that individuals' interest is in the public good, thereby achieving full agreement out of contrasting interests (Riley 2014). The crucial point here is in the projection of a state as a "moral person," drawing not only on the duties that each citizen must perform to enjoy full rights, but also as an embodiment of the citizens' constitution of a cohesive cultural community (Barnard 1983; Canivez 2004). It is in this context that civic education becomes so central (Gomes 2020). Rousseauian politics is no longer the realm for governing the life conditions of people (as in contractual understandings), but rather a dynamic political sphere where citizens constitute a shared understanding of the "general will."

No doubt all these developments signal a great distance from the primacy of self-interest in Hobbes and Mandeville, who relied on force and manipulation for twisting immoral human selfishness to the advantage of all. That distance is also sizable in Adam Smith, despite his acknowledgment of sympathy and natural social affections. Smith's theorization of the ability to place ourselves in others' shoes does not follow real experience but only a process of imagination (Smith 2010a). By contrast, natural sociability in Hutcheson's approach provides individuals with a human predisposition to identify and associate among themselves. This process of identification is given a further epistemological twist in Gay and Hartley, as they consider empathy to be rooted in childhood experiences, transforming personal pains and pleasures of a lower kind into higher social concern. It is in this same fashion that self-interest can be transformed into shared benevolence (Allen 1999; Harris 2005).

Contemporary scholarship is all too aware of processes of cultural constructions and identifications when dealing with the definitions of goals,

118 CITIZENSHIP

the sharing of motivations, and the identification of "legitimate" strategies and their implementation (Melucci 1985; Offe 1985; Touraine 1981; see also Snow 2004; Snow et al. 1986). Identity has been taken as socially rooted within the psychological field (Tajfel 1982; for reviews, see Reicher, Spears, and Haslam 2010; Postmes and Branscombe 2010). This is evident in a large variety of studies on self-esteem, cooperation, belongingness, reciprocity, the sense of eternal life beyond personal death, and the capacity to shape one's own history. The importance of identity is such that interest alone has been insufficient for individual self-regard (Baumeister and Leary 1995; Yamagishi and Kiyonary 2000).

The role of identity has been at the core of post-World War II politics, for political persuasion, regarding ideas of what is just or authentic. Put simply, *certain dominant identities and frames must be widespread to combine the different interests at stake*. In turn, interests do not impact politics directly (as in, for example, Marxism), but rather via the interpretation that they are shared within the social body. It is in this passage that a catharsis is established in the transition from centrality of selfish economic interests to the centrality of ethical-political hegemony based on shared culture and identity (Gramsci 2011; Jones 2007).

Democracy and the Entanglement of Interest and Identity

What is surprising is that these two primary building blocks of interest and identity have rarely been engaged in terms of their mutual synergies—how they become conjoined. Rather, they have misleadingly been taken as mutually independent. We noted, in Chapter 4, how Enlightenment thinkers naturalized categories, making them "essential attributes" of what became the constituent elements of modern democracies: the individual, the nation, ethnic group, and race. Such primordial understandings became entangled with democracy. Such purportedly primordial attributes were associated with preferences, which is to say that interest and identity were juxtaposed. The idea of interest—self-interest, interest group, and national interest— arose from and reinforced such primordialist assumptions. Contemporary identity politics, of both the Right and the Left, are imbued with such associations.

From such a basis the individual associates with a group to pursue their interest, and the group relies on the associated individual's advancement.

INTERESTS AND IDENTITIES   119

By fusing interest and attribute, notions of ingroupness and outgroupness are accentuated. That understanding (reinforced by much of economics and the social sciences) deviates from the fundamental logic of citizenship. Put simply, where identities and interests fully intersect as constituent parts of the same foundation stone, boundaries are more sharply defined. As a result, relations become transactional or, potentially conflictual—whether in traditional context (e.g., between tribes) or in the present-day domestic politics. Capitalism (and this, too, goes back to Enlightenment thinkers) reflects and reinforces this phenomenon in the "commodification" of people, groups, cultures, and identities. Sharply defined actors—individual, tribe, corporation, and nation—are more likely to see themselves as *sui generis*, with intrinsic interests and in a state of competition, or worse, with other such actors.

The state has reinforced this process through legal mechanisms, not least in defining the nation-state as a sharply bordered entity, sovereign in its authority. Consequently, the "matching" of identity arises—how does a potential immigrant "fit" in terms of national identity? This has led to the abiding concern with "integration," and an extensive corpus of social science engaging the topic for many decades now. Similarly, the constituent parts of nations—however defined, such as racially, religiously, or ethnically—start competing over narratives as to what the national identity is or should be (multicultural, "universalist," ethnonationalist, and the like). Such will be especially challenging in times of heightened tensions and, in such circumstances, boundaries (internal social groupings or international borders) will increasingly harden. Hardened boundaries in turn favor elites purporting to represent different groups, and the actual space for individuals to engage civically is narrowed. The complexity of human identity—and the human as a *social* and *political* being—is lost in this light.

A long tradition of scholarship has argued that interest and identity simply cannot be amalgamated. Marxists, for example, rejected the idea that humanity is self-interested. Rather, self-interest is a false ideology reflecting the greed of a small, bourgeois clique that owns capital and private property. Communism is thus seen as a programmatic framework to restore full belongingness of humans first based on social class, and then within the "true nature" of a shared classless society (Campbell 2010; Roemer 1988). This classless society stops the insatiable self-interested accumulation of the few, by which all other citizens are severed from their shared communal belonging (Veblen 1994).

120   CITIZENSHIP

Well beyond the Marxist camp, other scholars have argued that interest is part of a culturally bounded choice rather than human nature, suggesting that the idea of self-interest is hardly a salient notion of human life in non-Western society (Canterbery 1987; Mauss 1990; Polanyi 2001). In fact, the same market is considered, in this light, exogenous to citizens, consisting of economic forces that distort their otherwise natural motives. Citizens are thus transformed into lonely consumers no longer embedded into their community ties (Wicksteed 2016).

Another argument is that self-interest breaks the "natural" continuity of our human species with the natural environment, while at the same time preventing living individuals from considering the well-being of their children (Ikerd 2005). Simply put, self-interest seems to work on a completely different basis than the principle of identity. In the latter case, individuals can purportedly move their regard toward the future, to defend the well-being of their earth and of their offspring (Handy 1998).

Borders and Boundaries

Borders and boundaries, both in their institutional and cultural significations, prove how interest and identity interact.[4] In fact, they can become fused, embedding the individual into larger communities (social classes, ethnic factions, religions, or nation-states). While promoting co-operation, reciprocity, and belongingness endogenously within any given community, borders and boundaries keep the community apart from other communities, thereby moving conflict from an inter-individual to an inter-community level. Accordingly, interest and identity become fused together, such as when a tightly bounded community provides the only reassuring environment for its members, who consider other communities beyond their boundaries as a danger for their own resources, values, or safety (Castano et al. 2002; McDaniel, Nooruddin, and Shortle 2011).

Cooperation flourishes endogenously within borders (whether this is about social class, an ethnic group, or a nation). On the other hand, the fusion of interest and identity substantiates, exogenously, a zero-sum game by which positioning in one's community also means to be against another. Across such boundaries and borders, where interest and identity have been juxtaposed, relations will lean more to the transactional. Hence, borders and boundaries of different kinds are likely to be linked to a conflictual style of exchanges by which cohesive communities move against each other. Primordialist and essentialist understandings of identity are amalgamated, and thus its subjects are unable to see how interests can be malleable and tied in more polyvalent ways with different identities.

The standard idea of democracy as a count of heads, each of them with its own interest and vision, and as an expression of adversarial politics, with its dramatization of a purportedly permanent group cleavage between challengers and insiders, has well served the purpose of building sophisticated theories to analyze social movements (McAdam 1999; McAdam, Tarrow, and Tilly 2001; Tilly 2004). Those theories, which have informed the tactics of social movements themselves, reinforce these dynamics of highly bounded, transactional, and adversarial politics. The fusion of interests and identities has contributed to the digging of trenches everywhere, not only between different countries, as in the shocking revival of war foisted upon Ukraine, but also fragmenting a shared social body, such as between migrants and nationals, labor workers and employers, different parties' constituencies, and the like.

At the same time, "normal politics" increasingly includes leaders and representatives who pick up on divisive issues in the public sphere to increase supporters' loyalty. Their concern is for maintaining and patrolling the boundaries of "their" own constituencies, seeking to freeze votes and support so that each constituency is insulated and thrown into a permanent competition. Ultimately, tightly overlapping interests and identities can threaten even the most established democracies, transforming them into spaces for strife between majorities and minorities, and for strengthening cleavages. The effect is the nurturing of normative justifications that draw on sectional legacies, including the identification of divisive issues. Polarization in the body politic ensues, thus diluting the legitimacy of political authority.

In particular, the potential juxtaposition of interest and identity have been at the core of much research on contentiousness between the "ingroup" and the "outgroup" (Brewer 2017; Gaertner and Insko 2000). While interest is crucial for individuals who gather instrumentally into different groups, emphasis has also been put on mutually shared cognitive schemata and emotional meanings at the core of any experience of community (Rabbie 1991). This means that cognitive understanding and emotions are crucial for linking the self into a grouping, accounting for the human tendency to exaggerate differences between different groups based on emotional stereotypes (Tropp and Pettigrew 2005; Brown and Hewstone 2005).

122   CITIZENSHIP

The development of contentious processes such as in social movements draws on material resources and on the appropriation of cognitive schemata (and, within the group, the sharing of mutual affections). A continuous fusion of interests and identities partition groups from the broader social body around them (Gamson 1992; Goffman 1959; Snow 2004). Such interests and identities can be maliciously manipulated by extreme political agents for gaining power (David and Turner 1996; Reicher 1996). History is replete with examples, such as in the case of marginalizing Jews in the Middle Ages or in the conflicts between Hindus and Muslims in South Asia, Serbs and Croatians in the 1990s, and Palestinians and Israelis (Kakar 1996; Ludden 1996; Bar-Tal 2004).

Universal norms can buckle when faced with the borders and boundaries of overlapping interests and identities. Take, for example, the understanding of fairness: the more a community considers the distribution of resources or the application of rules to be fair, the more this is supposed to strengthen its internal cohesion, self-esteem, legitimacy of rules, and personal involvement of individuals within (Tyler and Degoey 1995; Smith and Tyler 1997; Blader and Tyler 2003). Yet fairness is usually applied within the boundaries of a community by which members consider themselves worthier than non-members. Accordingly, fairness loses its universal reference and can be applied with a double standard, such as we saw in uneven distribution of COVID-19 vaccinations that democracies oversaw for underdeveloped countries to the advantage of their own citizens. In fact, fairness may be applied within the ingroup as in the case of decisions by referees or in the International Court of Justice (Mohr and Larsen 1998; Posner and Figueiredo 2005).

By collapsing interest and identity in a way that one perfectly fits the other, borders and boundaries become an omnipresent obstacle to a richly varied social life, and they pose political challenges as well. Where individuals identify just with their own interest, or alternatively identity becomes their only interest, this leads to a bounded community that is less adaptable to shifting challenges. For example, during a pandemic young people may not join a vaccination plan as soon as they are convinced that it is much less beneficial to them than for other, more fragile, cohorts. Another example can be seen in an international conflict driven by nationalist narratives, such as that of Putinist Russian nationalists claiming Ukraine has no cultural salience outside of a "greater Russia."

Interests and identities are crucial: they tell us who we are, how we relate to each other, how to be active members rather than passive subjects, what's important and what's not, and how we should act; that is to say, citizenship has hardly any meaning without them. The main question is, therefore, how interest and identity can work as inclusive tools for detecting the potentially abundant intersections across boundaries, nurturing more inclusive social processes by which individuals understand and feel themselves as a part of a larger collective whole?

Creating Just Civil Societies: The Limits of Rawls and Habermas

So, how to foster more virtuous dynamics? Interest can be approached in different ways, alternatively as a divisive force among humans, or otherwise as a pivot to keep them together. A touchstone text in these centuries-long reflections over interest is John Rawls (2020) on the "veil of ignorance." Rawls, more than anybody, was aware of the constructive and at the same time destructive force of interest. A crucial part of his normative vision is thus dedicated to eliciting the most propitious conditions for making it work inclusively. In particular, he argues that individuals can break through the destructive potential of interest when they choose rationally and justly by adopting the "original position." When we place ourselves behind a veil of ignorance, we keep ourselves from being misguided by our own limited views on the surrounding world. We can better consider how society should function. From this follows the constructive force of interest, insofar as humans come to agree on the assignment of fundamental rights and the rejection of social and economic inequalities, especially of the least advantaged (Rawls 2020).

Certain ideas, such as slavery, are clearly unjust, yet they were not so unjust to many of our antecedents—so much so that it took millennia for its almost global sanction. In addition, morally questionable beliefs may be misguided by limited information that is based on more immediate interest (it is my interest to better my economic conditions) to the detriment of more distant interests that are even more fundamental (it is my interest to avoid economic profit that destroys the environment where I live). This is why Rawls recommended continuously rechecking all our convictions against the point

124 CITIZENSHIP

of view of the original position. This is the point where direct self-interest connects with the interest of everybody else. This is crucial for rethinking interest in a way that can produce cooperation across social divisions. So taken, interest no longer produces zero-sum games (De Lazari-Radek and Singer 2014; Nakano-Okuno 2011).

However, the condition of the original position may be at odds with the way that people think and act within contemporary democracies. A true revolution of information has taken place in the last forty years and in a world where knowledge has become the most praised asset, the recommendation to make decisions in a condition of "ignorance" sounds paradoxical, if not incredulous (Castells 1996). Everywhere, across democracies citizens crave an exchange of knowledge before making decisions, so the veil risks being considered as a mischievous (at best) tool for hiding from people their felt right to know. Although Rawls wants to free the notion of interest from its limitations, he refrains from engaging in a clear critique of how these limitations can be overcome *consciously* and collectively.

Insofar as interest remains veiled, Rawls cannot provide a satisfactory answer vis-à-vis democratic claims for knowledge and public scrutiny. His liberal conception remains too abstract and individualistic. As such, the veil can really suit only spirited liberals who decide autonomously and—thanks to their considered judgments, sincere desire for truth, and their reflections on attaining equity between the advantaged and disadvantaged—see things through internal reason better than through their eyes. Ultimately, Rawls fails to provide a compelling account of what brings people together beyond abstract principles that are individually conceived, and that are more appropriate to a courtroom than to the lived human world (Sandel 1984).

Rawls does not deny self-interest but seeks to veil it, so we preempt the strong dominating the weak. But the predicament is self-interest itself. Rawls is not intuitive—why would someone not want the veiled information? The veil here is as effective as the analogous act of "veiling" women, from a cloistered nun to a burqa-covered woman, or enforcing celibacy on monks, and believing sexual desire itself can thus be banished. The problem is, we argue, self-interest's fusion with primordialist identities.

Compared to Rawls, Habermas makes a crucial step forward. His objective is not to hide self-interest but to unveil that self-interest, as the interest is (in Habermas' rendering) often unknown to individuals. Just as with Rawls, Habermas wants to transform interest into a virtuous force by helping people to get rid of their limited view on the surrounding world.

In contrast to Rawls, however, he contests the ideological nature of an individually conceived notion of interest—this is as a normative notion that assumes an atomized political community. The individual is only conscious of interest just from their own perspective. The individual also remains disconnected from others, and their interests, with little room to exchange and unite their interests. In so doing, Habermas engages with interest in its most fundamental sense.

Given that the individual may be unaware of their best interest, Habermas suggests instead relying on extensive communication in the public sphere. This, allegedly, allows for mutual connection among all self-interested individuals, and thus can be the basis of a broader normative vision that promotes conscious and collective consensus-building. The notion of interest thus loses its inactive and ego-centric substance because it is only through deliberate collective engagement within a shared public space that each learns of their own interest, and how this fits in a process of consensus-building.

Yet the problem in such a scenario is mostly about its feasibility. Consensus-building relies, in principle, on never-ending exchanges within a public sphere that considers every voice. However, when agreeing on universal norms, these may equally work to ignite division between mutually bounded communities, whatever the nature of those divisions (Boldizar and Messick 1988). Absent a never-ending public deliberation, the risk is always that exchanges may have to stop somewhere, consequently marking off boundaries and transforming consensus-building into the very basis for contention. Furthermore, Habermas conjures up a rule-based, abstract citizen in which everyone is an abstract agent. But humans are not abstractions, nor do they all have uniform qualities.

Walking through a field of beautiful flowers, the veil of ignorance would prevent an individual from knowing whether they are the first or not to walk through that field; whether they live far away or nearby; or whether they have children. From the viewpoint of the original position, they will likely agree that a ban on flower-picking is in the collective interest. Yet the point is that whatever that individual's position is in real life, it is in "everybody's interest" to leave the flowers where they are: unpicked flowers will be longer lived and will be of greater benefit for humans and nature altogether. At the same time, "everybody's interest" has the power to be understandable just as self-interest: there is no need to call for a virtually infinite number of deliberative exchanges to discuss flower picking in a cumulative process involving people from more-and-more distant valleys.

126 CITIZENSHIP

Both self-interest and "collective interest" are culturally bounded. We can see this in the way public spaces, some with flower beds, get treated—in some contexts with respect (even by the resident acting unseen), in others with indifference (even by the resident acting openly). Those differences come down to how "interest" is culturally framed. Our argument is that the inclusive force of interest, transformed into everybody's interest, can be there even when people are not spirited liberals who can see without their eyes, or "even" when everyone cannot take part in consensus-building or have somebody speaking on their behalf. "Everybody's interest" is about freeing the individual from a primordialist, egocentric pleasure in the appropriation of flowers. It is about understanding that unpicked flowers serve both individual and collective interest. More crucially, everybody's individual interest allows for embracing the lives of all others, opening space for their perspectives, lives, and actions. In such environments, they can defuse the zero-sum game that a strict individual, ego-based notion of interest would otherwise command. The issue is, in part, about generating social and institutional structures that make shared civic goals possible.

Neither Rawls nor Habermas consider the intrinsic human depth of social cognition and passions, and in so doing, they disregard the importance of identity for nurturing a civic community or a legitimate political authority. Their solutions for collective action, in ways that would serve a just, civil society, are consequently epistemologically blinkered. They do not consider that identity, just as interest, can be transformed from an exclusionary force to one that can reach across multivalent boundaries and intersections. Identity, freed of its identification with primordialist and essentialist bases, can overcome mutually exclusive ingrouping and outgrouping (Buhrmester et al. 2018; Gómez, Macías, and de la Mata Benitez 2013). That in turn demands eliciting, in thought and institutionally, the underlying grammar of citizenship.

An Ever-Changing Community

The juxtaposition of interest and identity, even in present circumstances, does not completely define our contemporary moment. Nor is the world made up of communities that are fixed once and for all. Boundaries between different types of groups are continuously reshaped and, for example, many people of migrant origins—once termed foreign and alien, if not worse—are today fully part of autochthonous populations. In fact,

INTERESTS AND IDENTITIES   127

there may not be stable differences between self-interest and interest by others, nor are there universal representations and identities by which people define themselves (Staerklé, Clémence, and Spini 2011). To take a case in point, on occasion of successive phases of electioneering, from primaries to general elections, the same leader moves in a matter of weeks from the outgroup to the ingroup, while good leadership is often about creating an ever-changing community rather than seeking to reflect it (Haslam, Reicher, and Platow 2020).

Our argument doesn't suggest interests or identarian attributes don't exist. But they can be (in the right institutional contexts) treated as more multifaceted, cross-cutting, more fluid, and in a manner less reinforcing of one another. Interest does not necessarily need to be identified with some supposedly singular attribute like ethnicity, class, gender, or race. Identity (and interest) are not necessarily *ex ante*, and thus permanent "first principles" that must organize social and political life. Instead, the civic social and political environment can lend itself to seamed, multivalent associations and dynamic framing of issues. Civic engagement does not supersede ingroupness and outgroupness as such, but disaggregates the Matryoshka doll-like, singular ingroupness and outgroupness imposed by the fusion of identity and interest.

At its most philosophical, civic engagement across multivalent seams nurtures the capacity to live beyond looking at the other solely by their particularistic interests and their attributed identities at each point in time. Rather such engagement is characterized by seeing in the other their capacities to engage civically, socially, and politically. Citizenship—in its fundamentally creative qualities—sees what is not immediately there. We have seen this capacity for imagining the unseen historically, in various social movements that saw nations, religious communities, and political projects before they existed. Citizenship opens the possibility of imagining "unled lives," of a "self with inner depths, alive at once to its uniqueness and its commonness," moving from that imaginative capacity held by all individuals to a collective imagining (quotation from Miller 2020, 101). It does so precisely because citizenship, in its root sense, is not about attributes of time immemorial, animated by the past. Citizenship, grammatically, does not start with the notion that we "know" our self-interest, rooted in assumptions of *ex-ante* identities and attributes. The *ex-ante*, primordialist attributes have been naturalized and imposed, creating old and new forms of enclosure in the civic imagination. That, in turn, created a repertoire of ongoing contentious politics that haunt us to this day.

128 CITIZENSHIP

Citizenship, instead, recognizes the profundity of the observation of the individual as ontologically a *social* being. Making the ego primary, which is frequently also identified with primordialist categories such as ethnicity, tribe, or nation, has involved exceptional violence. This is also true in the context of unfettered capitalism. In different ways, collectivist ideologies of both the far Left and the far Right have extinguished individual "sociality" by imposing *ex-ante* ideological blueprints and attributes of, for example, class or ethnic nationalism (Scott 1998). Citizenship privileges the social ontology of the human being over the relatively static epistemologies that undergird our prevailing ideologies. The *promise* of citizenship puts the *practice* of citizenship back on its feet.

Notes

1. The literature on collective action is extensive. In terms of interest, the literature considers acting in concert as a function of citizens' capacity to give shape to their interests through organization and optimal allocation of resources (Obershall 1973; McCarthy and Zald 1977, 2001; see treatment of ethnic capital in Fennema and Tillie 1999, 2001). Other scholars consider the sharing of a system of mutual identities and values as key (Inglehart 1977; Melucci 1985, 1989; Offe 1986; Touraine 1981) as well as in constructing common beliefs and interpretations (Gamson 1992; Snow 2004; Snow et al. 1986). An earlier generation of work on "collective behaviorism" was based on notions of "structural tensions" (Gurr 2015; Kornhauser 1959; Smelser 1962). These approaches about why citizens get together are still employed (Bauman 2011; Zizeck 2011; Ball and Drury 2012; Reicher and Stott 2011). In this line of argument, citizens resort to violent disruption as their ultimate resource (Bagguley 1991, 1992; Katz 1992; Piven and Cloward 1977; Richards 2002).
2. The relationship of the *demos* and the *ethnos* has been a matter of much discussion in recent years, the earlier assumptions under criticism. See, for example, Pogonyi (2022), Lucka (2019), Reeskens and Hooghe (2010), and Kuzio (2002). For earlier applications see Brubaker (1992) and Kohn (2017 [1944]).
3. On Habermas and Rawls, see section "Creating Just Civil Societies: The Limits of Rawls and Habermas," in this chapter. See also overview by Leydet (2017).
4. By borders we are referring to geographic borders, such as those of a nation-state. Boundaries can include borders but also designate nonterritorial social boundaries— which could be the "territorialities of the self," in Goffman's terms, or the various ways we see bounded communities, such as racially, ethnically, religiously, and in gendered groups (Goffman 1959; Zerubavel 1991).

7

From Borders to Seams

The English writer Nick Hornby, in his book *Fever Pitch* (2014), described the experience of being a football fan, in this case a fan of Arsenal:

> I fell in love with football as I was later to fall in love with women: suddenly, inexplicably, uncritically, giving no thought to the pain or disruption it would bring with it . . .
>
> I had discovered . . . that loyalty, at least in football terms, was not a moral choice like bravery or kindness; it was more . . . something you were stuck with . . .
>
> Few of us have chosen our clubs, they have simply been presented to us; and so as they slip from Second Division to the Third, or sell their best players, or buy players who you know can't play . . . we simply curse, go home, worry for a fortnight, and then come back to suffer all over again.

Football fans of the same team have an extraordinary comradery. It is simultaneously individual and collective commitment. The fans' experience is deeply emotional and aesthetic. It is a commitment that transcends the failures of the team—even shared commiseration becomes a form of community (as is evident in the diehard fans of Sunderland, as it dropped two tiers from the Premier League in rapid succession). The team's "goals" unite fans who span every race, ethnicity, religion, and global region, albeit mostly male. It is a *felt* community, literally feeling the same range of emotions with the team as a source of endless deliberation.

We do not think of the team supporters as a "society," yet it is a form of association that demands a high level of civic commitment with clear, shared goals. It is an association that is built around a set of rules that are "judicially" enforced (by referees), with demands for fairness and justice (although with a certain bias). It is voluntary and democratic in that every fan can express their opinion of the team, fair or foul. It exhibits, usually, a reasonable degree of trust between fans and their team that everyone is doing their part. The commitments transcend, for the true fan, failure (and after all, most teams

Citizenship. David Jacobson and Manlio Cinalli, Oxford University Press. © Oxford University Press 2023.
DOI: 10.1093/oso/9780197669150.003.0007

130   CITIZENSHIP

"fail" in football's triumphs on a year-to-year basis—failure is the norm).[1] Most notably, the fans relate to one another as part of the same project, their very selves synergistically felt—the relationship, for the fan, is not primarily transactional, contractual, or instrumental. The relationship among fans is relational and seamed (of which more in a moment). The fans have a *socially embedded* relationship, a civic society writ small. Football fandom is telling in a larger sense: it can be nationalistic, clearly, in international games. Racism is a continuing problem in the stands. And yet it also provides examples of football as a civic project, an identity which goes beyond such primordialist politics.

Could it be that the intense, involved, almost unconditional fan following of sports teams reflect profound desires, simultaneously individual and collective, for how community "should" be experienced—in its darker primordialist forms, but also in its more promising civic forms as well?

Borders, Boundaries, and Citizenship

The language of alienation, of the "alien-other," characterizes discourse of important constituencies on both the Right and the Left. This is a consequence of the respective "first principles" involved, that human motivation derives from hard attributes and interests. Adversarial politics, in this context, are seen as the *fuel* of economic and political life (Tilly 2008). On the Right, the alien-other is built into an understanding of the marketplace, of a world of self-interested competitors and adversaries, a view of the world that is extended beyond the market to politics. For parts of the Right, the alien-other can be the foreigner. On the Left, the language of alien-other can be represented in class enemies and in the dynamics of identity politics. Conflict and "contestation" are purportedly the engines for societal change. The alien-other is also endogenous to nationalism, from the mild forms of liberal nationalism to the eliminationist practices of the fascist varieties. The alien-other is not necessarily just the foreigner but can also be directed at marginal parties domestically. The language of conflict and "resistance," whether this is violent or non-violent, is, internationally and domestically, endemic (see, e.g., Gills 2000; Roberts and Ash 2009).

The language of the alien-other is engendered by the understanding of actors as self-contained and clearly bounded—be it an individual or corporate actor in the marketplace, ethnic groups, or the nation itself. Such "hard"

FROM BORDERS TO SEAMS   131

borders, geographically, and hard boundaries, socially, provide the grounding for binary distinction between inside and outside, citizen and alien, and self and other. Such borders and boundaries have been "naturalized," as if they are an invariant part of nature, even genetic. Even outsiders who fulfill the process of becoming citizens need to be "naturalized." The process of naturalization has been made "second nature" through a steady accretion of ideology and institution-building. In terms of modern history, we can find the ideas from the *homo economicus* to the allegedly *sui generis* categories of race and nation. The nation-state aggregates geographical, national, communal, and political boundaries as singular—historically reinforcing its boundedness—which was a sharp departure from the mishmash of boundaries and authorities in medieval Europe, or in historical India, Japan, and beyond.

In a world of pervasive global flows, transnational identities, and dual citizenships, we can rethink the monopoly of hard borders and boundaries. Such boundedness never had complete dominion, even in the twentieth century, but it is even less the case today. But to truly reimagine social and political institutions—to rethink prevailing ideas of boundedness—requires getting to the root meaning of citizenship itself. Domestically, institutions have also been thought of as clearly bounded and even naturalized. The market, as noted earlier, has also been treated as something to be protected from robust intervention (Polanyi 2001; Somers 2021). Hard borders and hard social boundaries were clearly the creation of the human hand, and not natural at all.

Much as the way in tribal societies, the threat of violence is paradoxically the basis of order (what anthropologists call "balanced opposition"), so contentiousness is institutionally contrived. For example, in the constitutional system, opposing parties and institutional "checks and balances" are built into government. Likewise, the international system mimics the tribal form, captured in the language of "balance of power" and deterrence. But as in tribal societies, and so in our democracies, if in different ways, such "balanced" systems are fragile and can slip into dysfunction of increasing severity (Salzman 2008).

When pivoting away from claims of primordialist categories, social and political relations must perforce be engaged and constructed. It must be, in such circumstances, relational—there are no *a priori* essentialized social categories for automatic "sorting." The bordered notions on which we base citizenship today—the self-contained individual, the ethnic group, the

132   CITIZENSHIP

interest group, and the nation—obscure the underlying anthropological and sociological foundations of citizenship. Citizenship, in this light is *seamed* and *relational*, involving a tissued network of ties, and the production and reproduction of the civic fabric. The root meaning of "primordial" is "from the beginning (of time), unchanging, predetermined, immemorial." The intertwining of civic and kinship-like threads through the history of citizenship has blunted (but not completely compromised) the underlying relational process of citizenship. This is only partly, at best, comprehended.

Seams

The concept of seams—analytically of present practice and as a prescriptive approach—is key. Boundary and inclusion issues have quite evidently become among the most vexatious in our democracies.

Seams, in the sartorial metaphor, are both connectors and dividers. Seams are a line of delineation *and* of bringing together. Civic life, in its authentic sense, is "seamed"—it is not relying on assumed, *a priori*, primordialist or essentialist attributions. In this regard, seams are an extension of the self as a social process. Self and Other, rather than in a state of alienation and with hard boundaries, are (in the civic context) seamed—delineated and connected. Unlike boundaries per se, the concept of seams better captures the relationship, mutual dependence, and opposition of connected parties. Such parties are mutually constitutive and dependent, yet in opposition. Seams at the dyadic level—boss and employee, master and servant, governor and citizen, wife and husband, or friends—is a nexus of demarcation and of suturing. Seams also capture the mutual enmeshment of interpersonal relationships and institutions—notions of privacy, for example, thread together the personal and the institutional (Jacobson and Goodwin-White 2018).

When we have hard borders or boundaries—for example, between states or ethnic groups—relations are not only more transactional but are also more vulnerable to violence. One party is generally trying to claim authority to "write the script" politically and economically. State behavior reveals this. In highly patriarchal environments, in a dyadic context, husbands rule the household; not coincidentally, wife-beating is much more common (Jacobson 2013). In a civic environment, where the rule of law has more traction, dyadic ties, as well as institutional arrangements, tend to be more relational rather than transactional or coercive.

Citizenship is rooted in and, to operate, must assume a significant level of civility, of nonviolence, and of a *civilian*ized environment. Citizenship and democratization are associated with rapid declines in homicide, overall (Elias 1994; Eisner 2014).[2] It is in such civil and civilianized environments we can imagine civic compacts and contractual ties. It is in such circumstances that ties could develop in full their relational potential—where, consequently, more relationships can also develop *ex post*. By contrast, in the context of primordialist identities, relationships will only lean into, almost by definition, the *ex-ante*.

What is striking about social distance and proximity on the personal level is that it is intricately related to the shape and form of society as a whole. As the sociologist Georg Simmel (1950, 322) wrote, a "circle" surrounds the individual, encompassing their characteristics; "[to] penetrate [this] circle ... constitutes a violation of [their] personality ... The question where this boundary lies [around the individual] cannot be answered in terms of a simple principle; it leads into the finest ramifications of societal formation." Moral distancing and closeness are the very warp-and-woof off the social fabric. As Simmel (1950, 315) further noted: "Concord, harmony co-efficacy, which are unquestionably held to be socializing forces, must nevertheless be interspersed with distance, competition, repulsion, to yield the actual configuration of society. In Émile Durkheim's (1984, 172) terms, the "individual depends upon [others] to the very extent he is distinguished from them." Marriage, friendship, comradeship, kinship, conflict, work, play, and notions of private and public indicate varying forms of association and social spacing. The "social order" is implicitly about spacing, the *seaming*, of social relations.[3]

Thus, the seam is also operative institutionally: for example, public and private are mutually constitutive and in a dialectical relationship. Seams also capture the mutual enmeshment of interpersonal relationships and institutions—it is in this regard notions of privacy thread together the personal and the institutional. Thus, a society that prides itself on the rights of privacy of the individual will limit the public reach of government. Conversely, in Maoist China, particularly during the cultural revolution, the self was (officially) subsumed under the collective interest. Even friendship was a threat; it implied a particularistic world closed to outsiders. "Comradeship" came to be the imposed mode of personal relations in place of friendship. Comradeship implied a universal morality wherein all are equal (Vogel 1969). Thus, relations at the dyadic level

134 CITIZENSHIP

are invariably caught up in the larger configuration of institutions, and vice versa.

The metaphor of seams reflects the dialectical character of relationships more acutely than that of boundaries. The seam, however, is not just a descriptor of a static relationship. The seam is kinetic and animative, a catalyst, and thus also expressive of a diachronic process. The seam is the "engine" for engagement—politically, socially, economically, and psychologically— whether dyadically or across countries. Thus, seams do not only facilitate human engagement, but they *generate* political, economic, and affective relationships, discourse, and networks. On the dyadic level, think of desires and tensions across gendered seams. Or, economically, the seams between adjacent poor and rich countries. The seam activates, drives, and provides fuel for relationships, and for their transformation. Thus, seams are distinctly different from borders, which are about protecting, regulating, and limiting the forms of flows and interactions.[4]

Citizenship as a Relational Act

In contexts where seams are facilitated, where we move from hard borders to more seamed ties, we begin to move beyond static "insiders and outsiders." In such circumstances, the possibility of backgrounding categories of ethnicities, class, and caste in favor of collective, civic projects becomes conceivable. Seams are—being relational—logically associated with the *ex-post* (rather than *ex-ante*) character of citizenship, of the civic project. Thus, *the making* of a civic community—a dynamic, ongoing, and at times fragile process—is as significant as the goals and objectives of that community.

In the civic, relational context, the key animating concern is *where are we going* rather than the *ex-ante* basis of primordialist attributions which ask, explicitly and implicitly, *where do we come from*. For culturalist, primordialist (which is, remember, definitionally about "first in time") approaches, notably in nationalism, the question "where do we come from" is the *sine qua non* of identity. The narratives in such cases, defining that primordial moment, can be the basis of unifying "a people" in national movements, which can root their purported origins in the mists of time, such as for certain streams of German and French nationalism evoking Germanic tribes or the Gauls. Clashing claims of "where we have come from" have been the basis of countless bloody conflicts from the Balkans to Rwanda.

Citizenship, in its underlying logic, creates a basis for a new form of social connectivity based on that of a shared project. As such, it can connect across the usual ways we divide humanity (race, nation, gender, tribe, religion, and national origins). Citizenship in the nation-state is and has been, in its formal and legal sense, binary, but that is a historical and ideational artifact. The underlying grammar of citizenship is not binary but is relational and scalar.

The character of seams is such that they are first and foremost anthropological and sociological—and as such, at heart, *quotidian*. Citizenship cannot be, solely, abstract, formal, or legal. It is an act or, better, an ongoing series of acts. Nor is the concern simply "the citizen" and their individual rights and duties. Citizen*ship* is (in principle) a social, connected, and collective act as well; it is not simply about the conduct of the individual citizen. It is a "social reality" in Polanyi's (2001) terms. This is at the heart of "relational."

The relational approach recognizes that the individual has (or is) a "self" that is enmeshed in a broader social fabric. The mind is not simply an element of the organic brain, but it is an integral part of a dynamic social environment. This is not a matter of altruism. Rather, in the self we see a dialectic of the self as both socially scripted and as script writer. Seams are expressive of that dynamic and dialectical relationship, in contrast to constructions of bounded, independent actors. This springs from the understanding that, in George Herbert Mead's (2015 [1934]) phrasing, *the self is itself a "social process."* Mead recognized that individuals (or, by extension, corporate bodies) are a product of their (pre-existing) society. But the "self" and the "other" are in an ongoing dialogue in ways that transcend the individual *qua* individual: we are "objects" to other people, but equally we are objects to ourselves by viewing ourselves through the perspectives of others. When we "talk" to ourselves, in our minds, much of that internal dialogue involves the back-and-forth (a kind of negotiation or navigation) between, simultaneously, our self as object *and* our self as subject. Our self-understanding is, in part, built by others and vice versa, a process which can be quite stressful. This has also been called the "looking glass self" (Cooley 1902). Language is key: there is no mind or thought without language (Mead 2015). Language represents individual articulation, but that articulation depends on a social construct—the language itself, and what it socially represents.

In social life, to put it in the philosopher Alex Honneth's (2020) terms, we come to understand ourselves "instinctively" through shared meanings and solidarities. "Subjectivity" is contingent on "intersubjectivity." The social bond is "woven from the fabric of mutual recognition." We thrive when

136 CITIZENSHIP

institutions allow us to mutually realize who we are—in Hegel's words, of "being with oneself in another." The law thus embodies (or should embody) the civic community.[5] Relieved of the primordial, recognition mutually arrived at is the only means to be, as an individual and as a (civic) collectivity. Citizenship is, at its core, about recognition—recognition by others and our recognition of them in a shared sociality.

Where borders and boundaries are presented as "hard" and sharply delineated, this will—to put it a little simply—suggest fixed interests, invariant conditionality, and largely ahistorical assumptions. Market actions, for example, may change but the nature of the actors and rules of engagement remain the same. Engagement in that light is transactional rather than relational.

In sum, to put it in its most emphatic sense, *seamed ties are relational, process-oriented, kinetic, and dynamic.* Conversely, *bordered, and bounded relationships are static and transactional.* The latter, when actors are highly bounded, are more easily conceptualized in mechanical, quantitative, and formulaic ways. It is no surprise, then, that the social sciences in the main lean toward theories like rational choice, neorealism in international relations, game theory, and many other structured approaches that presume bounded actors (individual, corporate or institutional). In some circumstances, where such bounded presuppositions reflect the character of the actors themselves, such social science approaches may work well. But where ties become more seamed and less bounded—and thus less predictable—these kinds of models begin to fail us. We always need to match our epistemological assumptions with the social reality, rather than shoehorning "reality" into our models. (The very word "model" implies a more static and structured, even mechanical, approach, implying that the subject of analysis is also static and structured.)[6]

No social environment is solely bordered or, alternatively, seamed. It is clear, on reflection, even in contexts in which we assume economic and political relations are based on bounded actors engaged in transactional exchanges, there are adjacent social worlds which are seamed and relational: friends, lovers, religious congregations, and sports fans, for example. Seamed ties can be evident *within* bounded corporate actors, such as the cooperation based on trust within co-ethnics and affiliated religious groups in a banking system like *hawala.* Note, too, seamed ties are also vulnerable to breakdown for reasons ranging from divorce to religious schism. Historically, Baptists—a voluntary, mostly egalitarian, relationally minded religious denomination—have been notoriously prone to schisms, again and again. These examples highlight the kinetic quality of seamed ties.

If a community, on whatever scale, is to be based on civic, voluntary principles, that community requires "engagement"—deliberation, exchange, conversation, consent, and dissent. We can witness that transition from the hierarchical, medieval church with the priest "above" facing his congregation while conveying received wisdom (the Catechism) to, in the Reformation, the Quakers, who meet in a literal circle. For the Quakers, no congregant is above another, and the Bible is open to interpretation and debate. The Quakers are an early example, in modern history, of a relational approach to human association.

A relational approach recognizes that, at its heart, civic organization demands voluntarism and engagement. This relational approach is the antithesis of kinship or primordialist assumptions, where status is ascribed—and as such, in which status and practices—cultural and political—are presumed. In such kinship and primordialist environments, roles are more defined and relations are more scripted. Distinctions such as "male and female" will be more sharply delineated, not least in dress, body language, and speech. The civic is in contra-distinction to pre-existing or presumed kinship ties, including "fictive kinship" assumptions. Similarly, the civic (in its unadulterated form) does not assume fixed (or genetically predetermined) qualities as endogenous to human association, be it ethnic, religious, caste, gender, or even class.

Civic association is an act of social creation and re-creation—rules are not experienced as handed down and pre-determined through birth. So, conversely, the *civitas* per force demands engagement. Engagement is thus, by necessity, relational. The civic sphere is inherently an act of construction—a project. The system of formal law (as opposed to customary law, in its origins) is expressive of that process. The law is an act of "construction" and reconstruction, in the creation, interpretation, and adjudication of law.

The relational approach, as such, can facilitate engagement based on reasoning rather than interest-based contention and calculation. This springs from the understanding that the self is, in Mead's words, a "social process." Civic goals are set, and the process becomes one of determining the best pathway forward (to be discussed further in Chapter 8). In a more authentically civic environment, decision making is not based on, at least initially, the "majority," but is instead based on "the better argument" in reaching

138   CITIZENSHIP

enunciated civic goals. In a system based on imputed attributes of discrete, self-interested individuals and factions, the objective is to end up with the most rewards—resources, bureaucratic control, and political aggrandizement, for example. That, in turn, reinforces the contentious process. Majority-rule becomes a means to cope with the limits of representation as it now works.

Multivalent Ties and Seams

Formalistic and legalistic approaches to citizenship are, of course, extremely important. They impact the (highly uneven) life quality and opportunities of humans everywhere (Kochenov 2019; Spiro 2019). But the question remains: do these formal and legal arrangements—including how rights are construed—reflect the underlying "grammar" of citizenship, or do such legal arrangements compromise those principles?

The way citizenship has evolved—and the assumptions about, say, the individual, race, nation, and the way the rules of politics are subsequently construed—is not natural as such, but is a function of political choices. The assumptions and political structures are the accretion of historical decisions over centuries which have come to feel as innate—indeed, consciously naturalized in the case of Enlightenment thinkers. We have noted how Polanyi talks of this at length regarding the market, as do Margaret Somers and Fred Block. Institutional rules, including the law, sediment such assumptions and over time can become detached from underlying social developments. In democracies, institutions can adapt—through judicial case law, for example—but institutional evolution and reform invariably lags societal evolution.

The seamed, anthropological approach can reveal how formal and legalistic categories can, in fact, compromise the civic process. Take undocumented migrants, who can have genuine ties with their "host" community that, say, an American with a deceased Irish grandparent does not have vis-à-vis Ireland—and, despite this, that American will be eligible for Irish citizenship (on "genuine links" see Bauböck [2019a]; see also Vink and Bauböck [2013] and Shachar [2009]).[7] Different scholars have revealed how civic ties emerge anthropologically and sociologically in ways that are not apparent at the formal level. For example, the geographer Jamie Goodwin-White's (2020) observes regarding the American case:

> Asylum claimants, DACA recipients, and others, who build lives whilst in immigration limbo are deferred from full inclusion certainly, but are sociologically, at least, still more inside than out.[8] In negotiating claims of physical belonging, with its *in situ* social and economic relations, undocumented residents hold locally varying assemblages of rights unavailable to non-residents . . . The critical bordering literature have often not acknowledged the consummate "insider-ness" of even illegal long-term residents, and the quotidian constitution of nation-states by those within their borders and well-beyond them . . .
>
> [Early on] the quintessential "American-ness" of the Dreamers was evident. [The Dreamers] spoke little or no Spanish, and had little knowledge of Mexico . . . [They were] stalled in their attempts to gain employment, join the military, or attend university. And more importantly, the Dreamers themselves, citing civil rights leaders and the ideals of the country that had reared them, became politically active . . . They have been, in a sense, the consummate citizens, needing no integration but the legal status of a country that had both made them and that they increasingly constituted . . . [9]

Where ties develop organically, in direct and seamed ways, social trust is more marked. Indeed, Messing and Ságvári (2018, 2021) show in their studies of European countries that the proportion of population that is of migrant origin is not so critical in levels of stated trust in institutions and in general (see also Jeannet et al. 2020). Rather, where that trust is high, fear of migration is lower. Notably, countries with a negligible level of migrants are likely to show the most hostility to migrants.

The presumption of fixed identities and attributes—and the associated concepts of "hard selves"—is of course itself a social understanding. But it is one that reduces transaction costs as such static understandings short-circuit the level of "negotiation" involved between people. A kind of demographic reductionism takes place in which factors like ethnicity, tribe, race, and sex are essentialized and become, in effect, a sorting mechanism. One could also refer to it as, metaphorically speaking, an algorithm that simplifies the calculations of everyday interaction. Prejudice works the same way; it is "pre-judgment" which minimizes the need for relational navigation. George Herbert Mead in his work was talking about all societies, and saw in his discussion of self, mind, and society a universal quality. He did not make this distinction regarding kinship-based or civil societies. However, in social contexts where essentialized attributes are in play, the "roles of the self" are

140 CITIZENSHIP

circumscribed, relatively static, and routinized. Selves are more structured and constrained—notably in gender roles.

The main challenge is to open spaces for inclusion in polyvalent directions, whether this is across football fans, party members, race, class, religion, or members of different ethnic groups. Seams allow for multifaceted connections between different ingroups and outgroups, even if this cannot fully nullify opposition between them. Accordingly, seamed connections can allow opposing groups to have different but complementary roles: in this way interdependence between groups can be transformed from opposition to cooperation (Van Oudenhoven, Groenewoud, and Hewstone 1996). The seamed approach makes possible, and even induces, crisscrossing identities.

The state, for example, has enormous challenges, and significantly fails in controlling access across the (unofficially) seamed borders. The state is limited in its capacity vis-à-vis economic differences that drive migration across borders, or the supply and demand forces that facilitate the seamed ties of transnational criminal networks. Much of the literature on state border control depicts it as if it is highly efficient, of the state as omnipresent, a "panopticon," but this is overstated. Millions upon millions of undocumented or otherwise irregular residents in the United States and in Europe are evidence of a now only partially controlled border. Seamed ties, however, also take place mostly licitly, through a much denser set of transnational connections, from family relationships and business ties to medical research.[10]

Seams are not simply a line in the sand; they are not like borders, which are inert and need to be protected and patrolled. This is where they are distinguished, in part, by their kinetic quality. As we noted, the seam is animative, a catalyst, and an engine for engagement—politically, socially, economically, and psychologically. They generate political, economic, and affective relationships, discourse, and networks. This is critical because if we soften the desire to patrol boundaries (e.g., the careful marking of ethnic and racial politics that characterizes our present moment), the polyvalent ties will follow. This illustrates the diametrically different character of boundaries and borders compared to seams; *boundaries are designed to limit pathways of interaction* (just like borders between states). *Seams, when such patrolling is more nuanced, open the scope for—and induce—polyvalent relationships and ties.*

By allowing for continuous connections to occur across boundaries, crisscrossing ties will develop, disaggregating the juxtaposition of interests and identities. This will occur without undermining "original" identities or interests—of, say, Latino, African, Jewish, or Indian groups—but other, civic forms of association can then weave a cross-cutting lattice of relationships. Such a lattice of relationships can ameliorate sectional conflicts and induce a healthier democracy (see, in a different context, Dovidio, Gaertner, and Kafati 2000; Hornsey and Hogg 2000). Such circumstances are more propitious (although not guaranteed) for enabling individuals to combine, collaborate, and work together through shared projects. Ultimately, multifold, intersecting groupings can nurture collective norms and shared purposes. By contrast, when social and political spaces become mutually exclusive, relationships can become more adversarial and polarized. The darkest outcomes are reflected in war, terrorism, or in mob violence, when to be on the one side means to be unequivocally against the other.

Interests and identities do not need to conjure up widespread, endemic contentiousness. Ingroupings and outgroupings, representing a cross-cutting plurality, can themselves continually evolve over time into new ingroups and outgroups. To return to our football example, fans of different, competing teams unite on the occasion of international competitions (Levine et al. 2005). This reshuffling may take place even when the football metaphor is applied to much more divisive contexts, such as deeply divided societies. The national question in Scotland or in Northern Ireland, the construction of a post-Apartheid democracy in South Africa, as well as the many experiences of national independence throughout the nineteenth and twentieth centuries, highlight (directly or indirectly) the role of seams in bottom-up collaboration.[11] Adversarial contentiousness can be diffused and ameliorated (although not removed) through superordinate, shared civic goals.

Transnational Ties: From International Borders to Global Seams

Borders, we observed, conjure sharp breaks, politically, economically, culturally, and even morally. Those on "the inside" of the border are (in principle) felt to be morally proximate. "We," the insiders, purportedly share a legal system, normative codes, and understandings that shape our moral conduct. For those on the outside, well, they are strangers and aliens. We all know that binary break of borders is now highly diluted. Citizenship, formally, has

142   CITIZENSHIP

reflected that binary distinction. Although the border's role as a line of sharp demarcation has been diluted, *legally* citizenship remains binary.

However, citizenship in a seamed environment is scalar in the sense that we have various forms and levels of civic engagement that are taking place. Sociologically, if not legally, this is indeed what is happening. Transnational ties are a case in point. This is evident in the plethora of statuses that are no longer marginal in numbers of people or in their at least tacit legitimacy. If citizenship is viewed through the formal and legal lens, we lose sight of the scalar quality of civic participation. Seams are more gradual, more fluid, more dynamic, and expressive of a dynamic process and that is true across borders. Cross-border activity can be a nexus of what we can call "global seams."

The political sociologist and theorist Rainer Bauböck (1994, 2017b) introduced the concept of "transnational citizenship" which we suggest is expressive of a more seamed environment. Bauböck states that transnational citizenship reflects how citizenship status, rights, and practices—while remaining anchored in the nation-state—reaches beyond a state's territory and is grounded in the relationship (by nationality or residence) of individuals to a particular state. States, in turn, remain grounded in a special relationship with individuals of a particular polity (of residence or nationality). Bauböck sees the three main expressions of transnational citizenship as "denizenship" (or noncitizen residents), extraterritorial citizenship (or citizen nonresidents), and dual or multiple citizenship. These are, he suggests, the three primary manifestations of transnational citizenship. Relatedly, Bauböck (2013) also points to emerging "citizenship constellations." Such constellations capture not only denizens, nonresident citizens, and dual citizens, but also membership rules for cities, regions, and supranational regions, notably the EU. Thus, in practice, citizenship can be "differentiated and generate forms of multiple, quasi, and semi-citizenships."[12] We argue that postnational citizenship and transnational citizenship are partly interconnected—human rights, the basis of the postnational argument, provided the legal and normative grounding for these categories which go beyond traditional notions of citizenship. The growing normative impact provided the ballast for dual citizenship and various statuses that fell outside the citizen–alien duality of singular loyalties.[13]

Be this as it may, the larger point is that under the impact of postnational and transnational developments citizenship has—in sociological and anthropological terms—become scalar. It represents the kind of seamed phenomena noted here, with all kinds of cross-border relationships. This demands a more nuanced understanding of borders. In some respects, the border remains conventional, a line to control flows and promote national interests. This includes military self-defense, as in the case of Ukraine. But, especially among democracies, we can see the emergence and growth of distinctly seamed ties. This is not only regarding the movements and residencies of people. The COVID-19 pandemic was telling; medical research for vaccines was largely seamed, with cross-border collaboration across academic institutions, pharmaceutical companies, and government agencies to develop the vaccine. Other government agencies, especially at the executive level, were seeking to get advantageous access to those vaccines, hurting developing countries and staggering access to vaccines among developed democratic states. The COVID-19 case illustrates how "bordered" and seamed processes can coexist and conflict.

We noted previously that while borders and boundaries are designed to limit pathways of interaction, seams open the scope for—and induce—polyvalent relationships and ties. This is notable at the international level. Curiously, the sharper the contrasts across the seam, the more kinetic it becomes. For example, across the Mediterranean seam, with its stark economic, cultural, and political differences, all kinds of connections and flows are engendered. Cases in point: the trade and business between the developing and developed economies, from small entrepreneurs to corporations; immigrant communities sending remittances South, and migrants flowing North; diaspora activists in Europe supporting refugees, or human rights activists in the Middle East and North Africa; and the opportunities for supposedly "exotic" travel. The seam activates, animates, and provides fuel for seamed networks and discourse (Jacobson and Goodwin-White 2018).

The Civic Project

The civic project is potentially any association, on any scale from a cooperative to a sports club to the state itself, that is characterized by shared civic goals and leans to relational rather than transactional forms of engagement. At the nation-state level, we witness this more as an exception than as the rule, and the seamed, relational ties may be expressed domestically, not internationally. Ukraine, in its fight against the Russian invasion, has demonstrated this quality domestically with displays of enormous civic self-sacrifice. At a smaller scale, the cooperative—for example, the Mondragon

144 CITIZENSHIP

Corporation, the world's largest cooperative—is a civic project (cooperatives and other such endeavors will be briefly discussed in the next chapter). But any civic project must be renewed again and again, and any such project runs the risk of becoming routinized, bureaucratic, overtaken by interest-group politics, or simply expiring. But, historically, many forms of civic and voluntary associations have also proved extraordinarily resilient, from religious denominations to charities to environmental movements.

Civic projects are *socially embedded*, a function of their seamed, relational character driven by shared civic goals. As such, civic projects embody and respond to fundamental human qualities—their overall, innate sociality, and the emotional and psychological foundations of self. In this context "social" and "psychological" are artificial distinctions; these elements are of the same cloth. It is also the experience of being of the whole, of a shared civic *telos*, that has emotional resonance on the individual and collective levels. Here we can think of football fans acting as one in the stands, sharing the emotions of exhilaration and loss (although football is a more concentrated expression of that civic dynamic).

Glen Loury (2021) articulates what we are calling "socially embedded" forms of human society this way:

> Business investments are transactional. Human investments are essentially relational . . . [T]he development of human beings occurs inside of social institutions. It takes place between people, by way of human interactions. The family, community, school, peer group—these cultural institutions of human association are where development is achieved. Resources essential to human development, the attention that a parent gives to her child for instance—are not alienable . . . . Developmental resources, for the most part, are not "commodities." The development of human beings is not up for sale. Rather, structured connections between individuals create the context within which developmental resources come to be allocated to individual persons.

As Margaret Somers (1994, 628) puts it, "people are guided to act by the structural and cultural relationships in which they are embedded and by the stories through which they constitute their identities—and less because of the interests that we impute to them."

The symphony orchestra is a useful metaphor for showing why socially embedded environments animate—and are a source of vitality—individually and socially. The individual musicians transcend themselves by acting in *concert*. The "concert" is more than a group of individual musicians. In a palpable sense, acting in concert transcends the individuals as a collective group of people. The concert captures a "relational" reality, a symphonic (civic) goal, which is more than the sum of the parts. It is telling that the experience for the musician and for the listener can be unusually emotional, felt to be highly personal while inherently a function of a relationship to others, of a kind of "mutuality." These examples—football fans and a symphony orchestra—are particularly heightened compared to most civic engagements. But they capture the underlying meaningfulness of the social and civic enmeshment at different scales. Socially embedded associations are, in other words, of profound ontological importance. The orchestra is, furthermore, not only of metaphoric import but is itself a civic endeavor.

Of course, this sense of the psychological-social resonance will be true for a fascist rally, Maoist Red Guards, white supremacist movements, and Islamist militant groups. This is part of the challenge. The draw for primordialist ideologies and groups that can create essentialized outgroups to be persecuted and even eliminated have, in certain circumstances, been a particular fascination. More typically, the attraction to revert to primordialist categories in milder forms of nationalism, racial identity, and religious affiliation, especially in times when institutions are being tested, is all too evident. But we ignore the importance of identity at our peril—the peril just noted—and the challenge is rather to find *civic* forms of identity that have an emotional resonance. Contractual models of society, notably civic constitutionalist approaches and the postnational citizenship arguments, bypassed the question of identity except at the sectional level. It is in that vacuum that primordialist arguments threaten to win the day, whether in the form of right-wing neo-nationalism or with a different form of identity politics on the left-wing.

In the nation-state framing, expressed in the very term nation-state itself, policy and public debate has tended to focus on the *attributes* of citizenship—nationhood itself is projected in this context as an attribute, such as French, Japanese, Nigerian, or Brazilian. Framed this way, the question becomes about the matching of nation and state. Membership is foregrounded as the primary concern. This, in turn, has generated debates about who is to be considered a "welcome" immigrant. Such debates turn to matters of integration and assimilation. Even as states went beyond explicitly racial and other attributional criteria (e.g., dropping policies regarding "White Australia" or

146 CITIZENSHIP

ethnic quotas in the United States) the role of race, ethnicity, and religious affiliation remained key. This has been the case, over time, across the political spectrum. Challenges to the monocultural views of the nation did not so much unwind this essentializing approach as they did valorize it in other ways, such as in multicultural policies and discourse.

Focusing on membership so centrally has not only turned citizenship into an extraordinarily feudal-like privilege globally (Kochenov 2019; Spiro 2019; Fitzgerald 2014; Shachar 2009). In isolation, the attention to membership matters reproduces and reinforces a constant loop of contention, structurally generating an invitation for conflict. The nation-state as an organizing frame institutionalized a transactional, zero-sum conflict between insiders and outsiders, Left and Right, ethnic groups, and social classes.

Historical contingencies explain well the regular legal shifts which alter the rules governing nationality and re-form the boundaries of a country's national community. For example, policies regulating the acquisition of nationality—the most emblematic way of declaring who belongs to the national community—have changed significantly in many countries over time. They have changed to such an extent that today there is still no conclusive scholarly consensus whether, for example, France should be considered a country of civic or of ethnic citizenship, or the United States should be considered a universalist or multiculturalist country (Weil 2008). The only individuals who bypass such concerns are those who are highly privileged through being able to buy residence and, ultimately, citizenship through schemes like Portugal's Golden Visa. Rather than replacing primordialist criteria, such a transparently transactional approach contributes to what some have called "citizenship light" (Joppke 2010; Džankić 2019; Harpaz and Mateos 2019). But these developments do not engage the conundrum of nurturing a civic identity that reflects a more porous global environment with communities that cut across borders. Nor do they engage the material developments, as Peter Spiro (2017) observes, which challenge the binary quality of formal citizenship. Rather, Spiro argues, social attachments are increasingly scalar, something that citizenship in its (legally) in/out form has difficulty processing. (Spiro's error is, in our view, to take the present legal rendering of citizenship as binary as characterizing citizenship itself, including its sociological qualities.)

The seamed and relational approach demands a rather radical reorientation. Rather than focus almost solely on the horizontal question of membership, with the associated focus on issues such as ethnicity, race, and culture, whether in its neonationalist or identity politics formulations, attention turns to engagement as a civic project on different scales from the local and urban to the state itself. Rather than the framing of nation and state, the organizing frame becomes one of civic politics and of the civic project. Projects, in principle, generate civic purposes, a *telos*, and can fuse the politics of rights with the politics of consent. Further, civic projects, from the local to the national to the transnational, serve, in principle, as socially embedded civic communities. The state is still bordered but the character and forms of regulation change. Transnational ties themselves are drawn into the relational, seamed forms of civic engagement.

In the longer term, civic trust is built based on mutual engagement on the *telos* of citizenship—in other words, project driven—rather than reproducing categories of immigrant status, class, ethnicity, or even Left and Right. Too deterministic an account of the construction of "us" can harm any purposeful, civic endeavor.[14] Civic projects allow for harnessing the rich cognitive and emotional content of identity without sharpening identarian borders within a bordered, primordial-like community.

Defeating a pandemic, moving on from fossil-based to recycled forms of energies, setting up an institution of regional governance, building a cross-country alliance against common external aggressors, financing a new hospital in the city or a new bridge connecting two villages across a river, all can be examples of projects that foster processes by which the self and the other, writ large, are mutually constitutive and reflected in one other. In fact, the strongly socially embedded character of projects does not necessarily guarantee any particular outcome as such. But through shared civic goals, through the creation of common visions, the civic outcomes live well beyond any immediate objective. Uniting in a view of a civic objective, even without achieving it, can provide the same kind of meaning-production and emotions that lie behind primordialist processes of strictly bounded identity. In this case, however, the identarian experience is linked through the future of a project ("where we are, together, going") rather than being rigidly grounded on a fixed legacy from the past ("where do we come from").

Concepts, ideas, and visions have no practical effect, however, without some form of institutionalization. Institutionalization—the rules, laws, and organizations that regulate society—will not happen if promising social, economic, and political developments to provide the foundations for such institutionalization are not there. Further, the severe challenges facing

148   CITIZENSHIP

democracies demand an imaginative response as its present-day institutions become more fragile. In this light, we turn to the "twenty-first century guild."

Notes

1. Similarly, supporters of a sports team will unite behind it through different matches, tournaments, victories, or defeats. The team is, in effect, a transcendent project. In fact, fans' support for their team is likely to be even stronger during recurrent losses (Branscombe and Wann 1990; Wann and Grieve 2005). "Failure" can thus lead to even more involvement and cohesion by supporters. By extension, it demonstrates that civic projects can be effective in developing a belongingness that goes beyond temporary failure (Turner et al. 1987).
2. The term "civilianization" was introduced in academic literature by Arévalo (2018).
3. The discussion in this and the following paragraph draws from Jacobson (1997).
4. See discussion on seams in Jacobson and Goodwin-White (2018) and in Cinalli and Jacobson (2020).
5. See Gordon (2022), the source of the quotations by Honneth and Hegel, respectively.
6. See Ronald Coase's (2012) criticism of the dominant formal economics—what he called "blackboard economics." Hayek (2013) had a related comment: "The curious task of economics is to demonstrate to men how little they really know about what they imagine they can design." See also Jacobson and Wang (2008).
7. The legal roots of the "genuine links" concept goes back to a case well known among international law scholars, the *Nottebohm* case. In that judgment the court argued that "[n]ationality is a legal bond having as its basis a social fact of attachment, a genuine connection of existence, interests, and sentiments, together with the existence of reciprocal rights and duties. It may be said to constitute the juridical expression of the fact that the individual . . . is in fact more closely connected with the population of the State conferring nationality than with that of any other State" (*Nottebohm Case* [Liech. v. Guat.] [Second Phase], 1955 ICJ, rep. 4, 23 [Apr. 6]). See discussion in Macklin (2017).
8. President Obama initiated the Deferred Action for Childhood Arrivals program, better known as DACA, in 2012. The program temporarily protected from deportation, and made available work permits, for certain undocumented immigrants who arrived as children. To qualify, immigrants had to have been under the age of thirty-one when the program was announced, had to have arrived in the United States before reaching their sixteenth birthday, and had to have lived in the United States continuously since June 15, 2007. They also had to be in school, have a diploma, or be an honorably discharged veteran. They could not have a criminal record or multiple misdemeanors.
9. The public seems to recognize such undocumented residents are part of the civic fabric. Goodwin-White (2020) notes in this light that surveys show that "nearly 90% of registered voters express support for allowing undocumented adults who arrived

as children to remain in the United States, so long as they are high school graduates who have not committed a serious crime. Among Republicans, nearly 80% express this same support."

10. The literature on borders is extensive, indeed. Much of the literature on borders, while recognizing changes in the proliferation of scales in which the border is encountered and the use of various technologies for border control, are tied to the notion of a sovereign state boundary, and a mistaken assumption of overwhelming state control. See, for example, Balibar (1998), Kofman (2002), Rajaram and Grundy-Warr (2007), Paasi and Prokkola (2008), Darling (2009), Mountz (2010), Mezzadra and Neilson (2012), Brambilla (2015), and Shachar (2020).

11. On Scotland, see Reicher and Hopkins (2001); on Northern Ireland, see Cinalli (2002) and Cinalli (2003); on South Africa, see Salazar (2002); and on discussion regarding bottom-up collaboration, see Cinalli (2003) and Diani and McAdam (2003).

12. Personal communication with Rainer Bauböck, April 13, 2022.

13. Bauböck (1994) argues otherwise, that postnational citizenship and transnational citizenship are discrete phenomena.

14. See the case of the "iron law of oligarchy" within political parties (Michels 2019 [1911]); see also, for example, Conger (1999) and Jetten, Postmes, and McAuliffe (2002).

8

A Twenty-First Century Guild

In a 1926 essay, "The End of Laissez Faire," John Maynard Keynes mocked the "idea [that capitalism represents] a divine harmony between private advantage and the public good," and he further scoffed at the notion the economists supposedly gave the publicly minded marketplace "a good scientific basis." He also observed:

> For my part I think that capitalism, wisely managed, can probably be made more efficient for attaining economic ends than any alternative system yet in sight, but that in itself is in many ways extremely objectionable. *Our problem is to work out a social organization which shall be as efficient as possible without offending our notions of a satisfactory way of life.* (emphasis added)

Keynes (2010, 288) was anticipating a different kind of "system," one that eschewed state control per se—as in some forms of communism—as well as one largely unfettered by capitalism. In broad strokes, he was arguing for a form of the guild, if not fully articulated or developed:

> I believe that in many cases the ideal size for the unit of control and organization lies somewhere between the individual and the modern State. I suggest, therefore, that progress lies in the growth and the recognition of semi-autonomous bodies within the State—bodies *whose criterion of action within their own field is solely the public good as they understand it . . .* bodies which in the ordinary course of affairs are mainly autonomous within their prescribed limitations but are subject in the last resort to the sovereignty of the democracy expressed through Parliament.
>
> *I propose a return, it may be said, towards medieval conceptions of separate autonomies.* But, in England at any rate, corporations are a mode of government which has never ceased to be important and is sympathetic to our institutions. It is easy to give examples, from what already exists, of separate autonomies which have attained or are approaching the mode

Citizenship. David Jacobson and Manlio Cinalli, Oxford University Press. © Oxford University Press 2023.
DOI: 10.1093/oso/9780197669150.003.0008

A TWENTY-FIRST CENTURY GUILD 151

I designate—the universities, the Bank of England, the Port of London Authority. (emphasis added)

Keynes was writing well before the human rights revolution of the post-war era and well before the progress of environmental, social and governance (ESG) principles this century, so his essay was, in a certain sense, prophetic. Here we talk of a "twenty-first century guild," which builds on the quality of medieval guilds, such as citizenship and self-governance, civic objectives of the larger community, the integration of social concerns with economic prosperity, and an association of "brotherhood"—what we may now talk about as solidarity or civic community.

But in our present environment, the guild, while purportedly absorbing such civic qualities, needs to answer to and address other major challenges in democracies. So why propose the guild form today? In our contemporary context, we can learn from these medieval guilds in both positive and negative respects. Building on ESG developments and adjusting for the twenty-first century, a prescriptive guild form can address several concerns. The nexus of the guild with the corporation is opportune in our contemporary context. The corporation, especially now, is so extraordinarily important in shaping people's lives and the world itself from the environment to human rights to human wellbeing. The guild model can also help address the damaging effects of high-tech industries and artificial intelligence (AI) on citizenship and democracy. That damage derives from the technocratic and "depoliticizing" role of high-tech companies and AI, on the one hand, and as a catalyst for populist forces (and polarizing society) on the other. Thinking prescriptively, but grounded in empirical developments, we propose the following:

The guild can provide an alternative pathway to political engagement by confronting the democratic distrust and deficit and shoring up the legitimacy of the state. The civic demands on corporations have been growing, through pressure from primary and secondary stakeholders, government, and the broader public, on issues from climate to punishing Russia for the invasion of Ukraine. Civic goals must include, and be balanced with, the requirement for profit and competitiveness, which is essential for the sustainability of the guild itself.

By developing mechanisms of employee governance (e.g., through innovative board structures and stakeholder engagement), the

152 CITIZENSHIP

democratically unaccountable structure of corporations is confronted. This is especially critical in confronting the diluted ability of states (and local authorities) to regulate corporations for the public gain in recent decades.

Critically, the guild can be a nexus of citizenship. In the medieval model, citizenship in communes and cities was alternately dependent on guild membership and vice versa. In a moderated version, we propose how this may be applied in our contemporary context. Universities and corporations do this already, indirectly, through their hiring practices, but right now this favors the privileged and the elite rather than the broader society.

Paradoxically, through the intersection with the place of work, the new guild can put forward civic *practice* as a core expression of citizenship. Rights are not simply "enjoyed." Democracy is not simply a spectator sport.[1] Rights are *enacted*. This includes choosing members, including those who are not yet citizens or who are not engaging politically. In this regard, the guild is republican in a lived way. As the workplace includes a mix of citizens and noncitizens, the guild effects a seamed republicanism, without the sharp binaries of insider and outsider. This has implications for secondary stakeholders, including across borders.

By asserting juridically required civic goals, combined with democratic participation, the guild functions as a civic project, and thus engenders civic and social "embeddedness." The civic goals stimulate a relational and seamed form of engagement, rather than interest-driven transactional politics (which has weighed on attempts at employee engagement at companies like Google).

The guild model can be a direct measure of stakeholder engagement (beyond stockholders) at both the primary and secondary level and extending to the broader community. Equally, the guild approach provides an institutional nexus for gauging the "genuineness" of the civic connection to a country and can do so in a scalar manner (see Bauböck 2019a; Shachar 2009).

The guild also can provide the "localness" in which stakeholder commitment and solidarity is most palpable. This accords with theories of democracy and republican community in writings from Rousseau to Jefferson. Local, often urban, citizenship (which has been the subject of much literature of late) is where both material interests and affective loyalties come into play, where the civic dimensions are of critical importance to populations—from public squares to education to police to parks to football teams to city government.[2] It is at the local level that governance is more tangible and can be more readily held accountable, and voices can be heard. It is at the local level, even at the neighborhood level, that social trust and political legitimacy can be engaged in a more direct way, where the social fabric of citizenship can be woven.

Note, in addition, how the "bordering" of cities is less clear, and more fluid; even long-time residents have a hard time defining exactly where the city "ends." This point is parallel to the observation of where cities find themselves in the spectrum from highly sedentary to mobile to nomadic—the urban population mix is, in part at least, liquid. People arrive and leave, and the idea of the city "citizen" is, to a degree, more malleable (Bauböck and Orgad 2020). Thus, the city is seamed, more than bordered, both geographically and sociologically. The stakeholder is more apparent, the connection more genuine, and the socialization more immediate. But in the openness of the cities, the broader, even transnational, fabric of ties is also more felt (notably for immigrant communities).

But we also argue that the guild takes us beyond the urban citizenship approach, while still incorporating it. The guild has certain advantages.

The locus of guilds is not urban writ large but is tied to actual associations of people. Citizenship is not simply a legal status, but it is a participation in a self-governing entity that shapes and is shaped by the membership of a broader community, by civic life, and by political engagement. Ironically, the guild goes beyond the formal, at times hollow, character of prescribed citizenship, by including people of a variety of statuses, including noncitizens and even undocumented residents. Already, for some decades now, people of all kinds of legal statuses have had, in the context of the workplace, rights protections (with local, national, regional, and international legal grounding), even for noncitizens. Under the guild proposal, the democratic inclusion will be even more palpable. The self-government gets closer to republican practice. Urban populations who do not have the vote, but are in the workforce, can more formally participate in civic society.

The guild is, furthermore, civically much richer than simply extending voting rights. Voting at the urban level (or national, for that matter) is important but we should not overstate its significance, even when extended to noncitizens. So many powers of government are administrative and judicial, and thus beyond the reach of the voter (a frequently overlooked issue in citizenship scholarship). Nor does voting generate much in the way of

154   CITIZENSHIP

actual civic association beyond party activists comprising a tiny percentage of the urban population. Nor does voting, as such, impact the power of corporations and other bodies over its workers and employees—essentially undemocratic entities. The percentage of eligible voters who vote can also be rather small and it is a very occasional civic act.

The guild approach is more promising in terms of citizenship practice in that businesses and public bodies usually represent a cross-section of the geography of the city and of class, ethnicity, and of legal statuses. As such, the guild creates a gateway for a more seamed approach—it provides the space for genuine engagement and the development of social trust. As such, the approach addresses a key lacuna in contemporary scholarly discussion on citizenship—*how to get buy-in of the current citizenry*? Scholars agree, by-and-large, on their concerns about populism and its risks for democracy. But populism is a symptom of a deep alienation from societal and political institutions, and the perception of the lack of accountability of authorities of different kinds. Relying on more coercive measures to institutionalize, say, extending the civic standing of noncitizens through the courts, risks a backlash (already realized) that undermines the otherwise virtuous motivation.

Conversely, we have examples where, in workplace contexts and in places like churches, quotidian relationships have developed a strong civic fabric, even when undocumented migrants are concerned. Jamie Goodwin-White (2020) writes, noting a case in rural Morristown, Tennessee, after a US Immigration and Enforcement (ICE) raid on undocumented workers in a meatpacking plant in 2018:

> The supposedly "white working class" red-state base of neo-nationalism has turned out to protest, often bodily, the deportations of brown "alien" parents of local children, and to provide intensive community support to those who remain. The invading threats in heavily Republican and only recently pro-immigrant Tennessee were the ICE agents taking parents from their children, parents who were also neighbors, workers, and parishioners . . . [S]hared identity can result from weeks of school drop-offs and daily breakroom chats rather than primordial [relations]. They are also, notably, not Marxist, global, or cosmopolitan. In rural Tennessee, Trump supporters and avowed Republicans criticize how difficult US immigration policy has become for hard-working families like their own, how they had not known this before it affected their neighbors, how "we all get a little bit

smarter as the issue gets more personal," all while keening for their missing schoolchildren.[3]

Their relationships had grown from their mutual work in a meatpacking plant to shared participation in local churches and schools—in actual, face-to-face relational associations. Cities do not generate trust in some intrinsic way. Indeed, they can be anonymous and alienating spaces (Park 1952; Simmel 1964). The institutional mechanisms of civic engagement must be thought through.

Relatedly, while urban citizenship may address specific and contextual concerns, such as cities and regional authorities responding to irregular migration, they do not address the core challenges of citizenship today. Urban citizenship cannot unwind the larger problems of state legitimacy or the withering of the relationship between the governors and the governed. City governments do not have the wherewithal to respond to a range of civil challenges and citizen demands on scale, such as the novel coronavirus epidemic or, in more extreme cases, invasions as in the case of Ukrainian cities. Cities also do not have sufficient networks and institutional ties internationally in the way larger corporations do; cities are unable to respond in a nimble fashion to the fabric of citizenship concerns or the seamed relationships and civil ties across borders.

The guild creates primary stakeholders, but this extends to secondary stakeholders as well—churches, schools, and community groups, for example. In the ESG study, the growing recognition of secondary stakeholders, in the general shift from "stockholders to stakeholders," is increasingly evident (see Jacobson et al. 2022). Depending on location, the kind of corporation (e.g., local, national, or international), and other factors, the secondary stakeholders' concern can extend well beyond the locality. Sometimes it will be intra-urban, such as a neighborhood, and other times it will be international or global, such as when human rights and environmental considerations come into play.

The Corporate Nexus

The modern corporation, as Satyajit Bose and his colleagues (2019, 48) note, is ubiquitous. The size and scale of resources under the control of corporations make their operations of existential importance to civic society. Employment,

156 CITIZENSHIP

goods and services, contributions to government revenue through taxes, investment returns for pension funds, and their foundational role for research and innovation mean that the "scale and power of corporations dwarfs the resources available to the governments of most countries to regulate the societal impact of corporate activity." Corporations, for better or worse, shape the quality of life in civil societies. Referring specifically to environmental concerns (but applicable more broadly), Bose, Dong, and Simpson observe that the "relative impotence of the vast majority of governments in the face of the power of large corporations renders ineffective any effort at sustainable development that does not include the corporate sector as a driving force."

Based on Global Justice Now data from 2015, of the one hundred largest world economic entities, sixty-nine are corporations rather than countries. The world's top ten corporations—which include Walmart, Shell, and Apple—have a combined revenue of more than the 180 "poorest" countries *together*. Those countries include Ireland, Indonesia, Israel, Colombia, Greece, South Africa, Iraq, and Vietnam. These numbers compared government revenues (drawing from the *CIA World Factbook*) to corporate turnover (Fortune Global 500).[4]

Herein lies a paradox. Corporations have a critical role for civil society and democracy. Yet, particularly in the last four decades of a globalizing economy, their deleterious impact on democracies has been unmistakable—on the growing class and socio-economic inequalities; the apparent detachment of economic and other elites from the working classes and civic concerns; and the growing polarization of democracies given significant ballast by Internet and social media platforms of companies, such as Google and Twitter (Lasch 1996; Piketty 2014).

Furthermore, corporations are powerful entities that are singularly undemocratic in the form of their accountability. This, as T. H. Marshall (1950) famously argued, could be ameliorated through regulation by the state, for example, in enforcing collective bargaining and trade union rights (although still weak in the United States). But that capability of the state has diluted precisely under the same forces of globalization that has empowered corporations.

It is in this light that the "corporate nexus" deserves close examination from the perspective of citizenship and democracy, and it is in this context that a guild model deserves scrutiny. The co-mingling of public and private has always been a feature of large corporations. The corporation was always a creature of statute and not of "nature" (Charkham and Simpson 1999).

But the state has shielded the corporation from robust regulation in recent decades under a neoliberal ideology driven by growth—let alone promoted civic commitments and accountability—until it came under pressure from both the progressive Left and the populist Right (Gerstle 2022). This moment is also reflected in the gradual maturation of ESG principles.

We propose an approach which can address several contemporary civic challenges. And rather than a *de novo* institutional form, an adapted guild system builds on ESG developments in the corporate and private sector of some decades—albeit not sufficiently matured, partial, and insufficiently articulated.

ESG and the "Second Wave" of Human Rights

The cascading of human and civil rights into the workplace, most noticeable from the 1970s, was primarily judicial. Such rights are even more accentuated today. However, we have noted the frequently damaging effects these developments have had on civic society and democracy. This has included the declining faith in political, economic, and civic institutions and elites; the reinforcement of interest-driven politics, with "identities" generally understood in essentialist ways (on both the Right and the Left); and severe polarization.

Yet one factor of these cascading of rights into the workplace is overlooked. Quasi-judicial bodies abound in both private and public sector organizations and corporations. The gains of those developments have been considerable, from confronting racial discrimination to sexual harassment. What is critical to note is that those rights, among others, also began to fence off the assumptions that the workplace is solely market driven (even if economic goals have still been privileged). The concerns of profit could not override, in principle, certain fundamental rights—and, over time, concerns about the environment or issues of governance (Jacobson et al. 2022).

In one sense, this is a continuation of the progressive changes from the turn of the twentieth century, such as collective bargaining rights and the statutory limits as to how many hours workers could work each day. However, the newer rights went beyond the strictly economic concerns of, say, trade unions, to engaging issues of, especially, race and gender. Furthermore, in a country like the United States, where trade unions have been less pervasive than in Western Europe and less united across economic sectors (such as the

158   CITIZENSHIP

coal miner union supporting the striking electrical workers in the United Kingdom), such rights were even more of an advance (Matthews 2017). Finally, the quasi-judicial mechanisms were a categorical change, as opposed to bargaining committees and the like—which, in turn, benefited noncitizens in a way that was novel. The political scientist Galya Ruffer (2003) calls the effect of such rights on non-citizens as a "virtual citizenship," in the old-fashioned sense of virtual.

What we can call "second wave" human rights, in terms of the corporate sector as well as public organizations, comes under the rubric of ESG. This second wave is partly rooted in the first wave; that is, in the cascading of human rights norms and quasi-judicial bodies within the private sector and public bodies. Although ESG practice can be seen (under different names) as early as the 1960s environmentally, and in pressure on corporations in the anti-Apartheid movement, it takes on an increasing salience after the turn of the twenty-first century. ESG has different components—from the use of ESG criteria to guide socially conscious investors (e.g., through ESG targeted index funds) to local, national, regional, and global compacts to advance human rights and employee governance. Examples include:[5]

- The UK Modern Slavery Act of 2015 aims to prohibit slavery or trafficking in a company's supply chains.
- By 2018, legislation intended to minimize the impact of modern slavery on supply chains had been passed by seven of the G20 countries and Australia (Lewis, Sullivan, and Warren 2019).
- Independent commitments have been made by numerous corporations to eradicate human rights violations in their commercial relationships.
- Bans on illegal logging of forests and endangered mammal, flora, and fauna species through the US Lacey Act of 2008 (amended) have been enacted. Other countries have similar bans.[6]
- International treaties, such as the Convention on International Trade in Endangered Species of Wild Fauna and Flora (known as CITES), have been ratified. Signers pledged to make the trade of listed endangered species prohibited and they can impose sanctions on those who disobey, such as prohibiting trade in listed species (CITES 1973).
- The International Tropical Timber Agreement (ITTA) is the only multilateral treaty that deals with illegal logging. It calls for strengthening "the capacity of members to improve forest law enforcement and

governance and address illegal logging and related trade in tropical timber" ("International Tropical Timber Agreement" 2006).

- The United Nations Global Compact, formed in 2000, is a "call to companies to align strategies and operations with universal principles on human rights, labor, environment, and anti-corruption, and take actions that advance societal goal."[7]
- MSCI reports 890 ESG-relevant regulations globally between 2010 and 2020 (MSCI 2021). In the United States, the Securities and Exchange Commission (SEC) has announced a task force related to ESG standards and disclosure, part of what is perceived as a priority shift under the Biden administration (SEC 2021; Smetana 2021).[8] Additionally, recent MSCI research analyzes funds that fall under the European Union's Sustainable Finance Disclosure Regulation (SFDR), including a metric for emissions risk (i.e., carbon intensity).[9]
- Some four thousand ESG regulatory initiatives—mandatory and advisory—are now on the books. In 2019, MSCI, a major provider of equity and other stock market indexes, noted that as many regulations concerning ESG were proposed in 2018 as were passed in the prior six years.
- The number of signatories to the United Nations' Principles for Responsible Investment (PRI) has grown significantly. Some three thousand organizations have signed on since 2006 (PRI 2021).
- ESG assets became a third of the total global assets under management in 2020, surpassing $35 trillion, up from $30.6 trillion in 2018 and $22.8 trillion in 2016. Assuming 15 percent growth, a third of the pace of the prior five years, ESG assets could exceed $50 trillion by 2025 (Bloomberg 2022).
- The Business Roundtable, a large network of the most prominent CEOs in the United States, announced in late 2019 a shift in emphasis on "stakeholder" interests, including employees and local communities— rather than a singular focus on shareholder interests.[10]
- There is an increasing presence of entire supply chain requirements (e.g., commodity specific roundtables, supplier codes of conduct, Walmart's Project Gigaton, and AIM-Progress),
- Activists are applying pressure through shareholder resolutions related to climate, governance, lobbying, and the like.
- Public facing coalitions and corporate commitments are increasingly evident (e.g., CDP, Science Based Targets, RE100, The Climate Pledge).

160 CITIZENSHIP

Reputational risk has, in many cases, outrun regulatory risk. Alison Taylor (2019) notes that American corporations are ahead of the policymakers in the United States in a number of areas of concern in ESG, such as on the climate crisis, gender issues, and even labor rights. The Europeans have been even more aggressive than the United States, demanding more comprehensive ESG reporting by the private sector. Most of Asia has been relatively weak in promoting ESG but stock markets in Taiwan, Singapore, Hong Kong, and India have more recently increased ESG disclosure requirements. European countries, such as Germany and the Scandinavian countries, have historically embraced stakeholder models more so than the United States (Pillay 2013; Jacobson et al. 2022).

The ESG developments underway, even if partial and uneven, provide the context for proposing a guild model adapted for the twenty-first century. The developments have been defined in terms of a gradual shift to "stakeholder" (as opposed to the stockholder) principles and corporate social responsibility. Others have noted the growing significance, in certain sectors, of employee activism. Commentators note the "exponential" increase in transparency, in good part due to the digital world. Local conflicts can turn into global crises for corporations and their reputations. If once the issues of corporate social responsibility were driven by the CEO, and frequently a public relations exercise, now concerns about reconciling profit motive with social concerns is increasingly "bottom up" and driven by employees (see Alison 2019).

The curious thing about this second wave of human rights is that it parallels the first in the following sense: in the first wave, as we noted in Chapter 5, we see international human rights instruments initially (from 1948) largely ignored in practice through what has been called "organized hypocrisy." Due to various structural pressures—migration being key—from the 1970s we observe a distinct change across the democratic world, when judicial bodies began to take human rights seriously (Jacobson 1996). In other words, we see what can be called an "on-ramp" toward significant human rights practice from the 1970s, but one which depended on the development of a prior, extensive development of a human rights' legal regime. The same pattern is evident regarding ESG, as revealed in an extensive statistical study by Jacobson and colleagues (2022). In that study, based on a two-way, fixed-effects analysis of over thirty-six hundred US-based corporations from 1991 to 2016, we observed a period of "organized hypocrisy" that is, ironically, the prerequisite for normative change—if there are triggering structural pressures for institutions to take the norms in question into their modes of operation. In ESG such a transition, the "on-ramp"—from organized hypocrisy to a progressively expansive normative practice—is evident from about 2009 to 2012—an inflection point in ESG practice.

Several factors are driving the upward trajectory of commitment to ESG among some corporations, albeit in selective ways depending on the corporation. The growing role of human rights law forces corporate response, including in areas of human slavery, supply chain management, and local community consent for extractive and infrastructure industries (wherever in the world). A growing body of investors is driven by concerns beyond profit. On environmental issues, corporations face public concern, in particular the pressure of activist groups, regarding the climate emergency and its supply chain impacts, as well as allied corporate reputational considerations. Revelations about labor abuses—for example, regarding Apple in China—represent reputational risks for corporations. Employees are using the "tools of this hyper-transparent era," including leaks and petitions, to batter corporate reputations in the process becoming a "powerful interest group" (Taylor 2018).

The Google Case Study

High-tech companies appeared to show elements of a different model for employee governance. Google epitomized a Silicon Valley belief that it was engendering in its workplaces a radically new relationship between ownership, management, and the workers—albeit workers of a particular kind. "Silicon Valley," commented the *New York Times*, "has often held itself up as a highly evolved ecosystem that defies the usual capital–labor dichotomy—a place where investors, founders, executives, and workers are all far too dependent on one another to make anything so crass as class warfare" (Schelber and Conger 2020).

In a widely read article in *Wired*, Nitasha Tiku (2019) wrote of Google:

Larry Page and Sergey Brin, the former Montessori kids who founded Google as Stanford grad students in the late '90s, had designed their company's famously open culture to facilitate free thinking. Employees were "obligated to dissent" if they saw something they disagreed with, and they were encouraged to "bring their whole selves" to work rather

162 CITIZENSHIP

than check their politics and personal lives at the door. And the wild thing about Google was that so many employees complied. They weighed in on thousands of online mailing lists, including IndustryInfo, a mega forum with more than 30,000 members; Coffee Beans, a forum for discussing diversity; and Poly-Discuss, a list for polyamorous Googlers...On Thursdays, Google would host a company-wide meeting called TGIF, known for its no-holds-barred Q&As where employees could, and did, aggressively challenge executives.

Google leaders promoted this open culture, branding Google as a new model that had transcended corporate models in the United States and beyond. Eric Schmidt, executive chairman of Google's parent company Alphabet, and Jonathan Rosenberg wrote a book, *How Google Works*, on the need to support "divas"—the brilliant yet non-conforming employees who would be the drivers of Google's most innovative products. Such workers demanded a particular kind of work environment: "In our experience, most smart creatives have strong opinions and are itching to spout off; for them, the cultural obligation to dissent gives them the freedom to do just that," Schmidt and Rosenberg wrote (quoted in Tiku 2019). This Google culture, or at least the branding of Google's culture, became a powerful recruiting tool.

To a "remarkable extent," Tiku wrote, Google employees took the supposed slogan of Google—"Don't be evil"—seriously. And they became very active and vocal in expressing their concerns, regarding both Google's actions in the world and issues within Google. Google employees acted out this vision assertively. Early on, in 2006, employees began vociferously protesting Google's concessions to China's authoritarianism, allowing a censored version of their search engine to operate in the country. By 2010, Google management withdrew from China. Google workers, outside the Beijing office, were euphoric. "The legacy of the China decision was a giant dose of goodwill from Googlers around the world," Schmidt and Rosenberg wrote, and showed "how all tough decisions should be made" (quoted in Tiku 2019).

Yet Google, in doing so, was generating business costs. Other high-tech companies like Apple were profiting hugely from both the Chinese market and Apple's China-based manufacturing plants. Bing cooperated with the Chinese government in generating a censored search engine. In 2015, seeking a larger piece of the cloud market, and to catch up with Amazon, Google needed major clients. The Department of Defense (DOD) was such a

A TWENTY-FIRST CENTURY GUILD   163

client. Google entered a contract with the DOD on Project Maven, with the goal of using AI to recognize objects from moving or still imagery, a capability that could be used for drone strikes (Lynch 2018). Tiku noted:

> There was no consensus on Maven inside Google's fractious workforce, which includes former Defense Department researchers, military veterans, and immigrants from countries under US drone surveillance. Even the employee group for veterans was split on the project. But Maven's opponents were organized in a way that Google hadn't really seen before. Employees fanned out into different groups. Some scoured Google's open databases, where they discovered emails that appeared to contradict [a Google] statement about the size of the Pentagon contract; they also found snippets of Python code for computer-vision technology that seemed designed to track human beings and vehicles.

Supporters of the project, and the DOD, pushed back. Robert Work, former deputy secretary of defense, stated that Google employees said, "look this data could potentially, down the line, at some point, cause harm to human life. And I say 'Yeah. But it might save 500 Americans or 500 allies, or 500 innocent civilians from being attacked," adding that Google employees' shot "a blank shot," and noting the imagery must be filtered first by humans before it facilitates a strike (Lynch 2018). By June 2018, Google announced it would not renew the contract on Project Maven (Chappellet 2018).

The list of issues roiling Google metastasized. One major issue that generated wide interest, after Google released data in 2014 that showed over eighty percent of its workers were male, was the underrepresentation of women in the company (and in the industry more broadly). This, in turn, generated a response from the minority inside Google who represented conservative positions. (About ninety-five percent of Googlers donated to Democratic candidates in the 2018 midterm election, the *Wall Street Journal* noted, citing public disclosures from the Center for Responsive Politics [Copeland 2019].)

Kevin Cernekee, who had been hired in 2015, was one prominent conservative critic who questioned diversity policies. He, *inter alia*, defended a fellow Googler who argued Google should not factor in race or gender when making hires. "A bunch of people jumped on him and started cussing him out and calling him names," Cernekee said. "And then his manager

164 CITIZENSHIP

showed up in the thread and denounced him in public. I was very disturbed by that." He pressed Google to protect "banned" opinions in its employee handbook to make Google more hospitable to conservative workers. He said he was also targeted by colleagues, pointing to a post of one manager to Human Resources, saying "Can't we just fire the poisonous assholes already?" Google fired Cernekee in 2019 for what it called misuse of equipment, and of its remote-access software system. He said the firing was due to his conservative views and complained of politically biased bullying at Google (Copeland 2019).

Cernekee's accusations about the suppression of conservative speech reopened the freedom of speech debates within Google that had been first unleashed when engineer James Damore was fired in 2017, after arguing in a memo that women were biologically less adept to work in tech. CEO Pichai said of Damore's firing that suggesting some workers "have traits that make them less biologically suited to that work is offensive and not OK." Of Cernekee's firing and complaints, Google responded "We enforce our workplace policies without regard to political viewpoint. Lively debate is a hallmark of Google's workplace culture; harassment, discrimination, and the unauthorized access and theft of confidential company information is not" (Ghaffary 2019).

These cases in turn generated ongoing flak from Republicans and then-president Donald Trump. Republican politicians claimed such alleged internal biases made their way into Google's products. Trump promoted a claim of Silicon Valley investor Peter Thiel, namely that Google was collaborating in treasonous activities with the Chinese government. The problem for Google is that these accusations amounted to more than "noise," but to real risks of regulatory controls (Ghaffary 2019).

Google also faced ongoing criticism on the other side of the political spectrum. Thousands of Google workers walked out in protest after the *New York Times* revealed, in 2018, that Google had paid millions of dollars in exit packages to male executives accused of sexual harassment. Furthermore, Google had remained silent regarding their acts. The most prominent case was that of Andy Rubin, the "Father of Android," who was given a $90 million exit package and who was highly praised while keeping silent on a claim of sexual misconduct—a claim Google found credible (Wakabayashi and Benner 2018).

Sundar Pichai and Larry Page, respectively the chief executive of Google's parent company, Alphabet, and the co-founder of Google, took steps to calm the anger. Pichai said in the wake of the 2018 protests that Google had fired forty-eight people over two years regarding claims of sexual harassment and that none of them had received an exit package. Employee anger remained. A year later, Google was still struggling with the issue. Alphabet's board of directors, the *New York Times* (which had originally revealed the Andy Rubin story) reported, was "investigating allegations of sexual misconduct and inappropriate relationships by current and former executives as part of its legal defense against shareholder lawsuits over its handling of the matters" (Wakabayashi and Benner 2018).

From Google's leadership perspective, their view that Google required an open and dissenting culture and that Google's first imperative was to "don't be evil" became problematic for business and for public relations. From upturned business endeavors in China to the Department of Defense, and from public relations disasters which hurt them among regulators and politicians from Washington to Brussels, Google began to backtrack on their vaunted culture and employee empowerment.

By 2018, Google began to pull back on its weekly Town Hall, which had epitomized Google's open and transparent culture where employees could freely speak and dissent. Co-founders Brin and Page stopped attending. Videos of meetings were available online for only a week, rather than years (Tiku 2019). On November 15, 2019, CEO Pichai emailed the Google staff to say that the formerly weekly TGIF meetings would now be held monthly, focusing only "on product and business strategy" (Lecher 2019). Among other things, the email noted:

> we're unfortunately seeing a coordinated effort to share our conversations outside of the company after every TGIF . . . [This] has affected our ability to use TGIF as a forum for candid conversations on important topics . . . Of course, we still need some company-wide moments to share product and business strategy, celebrate great work, learn from our failures, and ask tough questions. So, we're going to try something different for 2020: TGIF will become a monthly meeting focused on product and business strategy, with Q&A on the topics being discussed.

Google's "community guidelines" changed as well, including a prohibition on "raging debate over politics or the latest news story" (Ghaffary 2019). The company's internal social networks quieted. Google sought to shut down workers engaging with outside groups on their labor rights. They hired a consulting firm that focused on stopping unions and unionization (Scheiber and Wakabayashi 2019). Prominent activists, on both the Left and the Right,

166 CITIZENSHIP

were fired, although Google claimed the reasons for their firing was not their activism (Conger and Scheiber 2020).

As a result, activists built up ties with external actors and media. "Dissent," writes Tiku "was no longer a family affair." The *New York Times Magazine* published "The Great Google Revolt" in 2020, which explored the most recent developments at Google. These developments show that even in the "most rarefied corners of Silicon Valley, the bosses are willing to close ranks and shut down debate when the stakes are high enough." If, the article continued, "the nation's most sought-after workers can't stop their employer from behaving in ways that they deplore, where does that leave the rest of us?" (Conger and Scheiber 2020).

Even if Google's model of employee participation had worked, it presented challenges as a model writ large. Its workers are highly capitalized—they have financial means, strong social capital in their developed networks, and the cultural capital of the highly educated. The question would remain as to how such a model would expand, for example, to blue collar workers in other industries—and indeed how to at least partially even out the enormous disparities financially and in status between tech and blue-collar workers. But ultimately Google's model failed as it (1) did not find a model to reconcile the business objectives of Google, and (2) the employee participation was an expression of a model based on interest-group politics. In sum, the purported "employee governance" was transactional, rather than civic and relational, let alone expressive of a common civic project. Google was national politics, in a sense, writ small. What can we learn from it moving forward?

What would a guild in the modern context look like? A modern guild would be an irony of sorts—a completed circle in those incorporated businesses which themselves have their roots in the guild. The concept of "joint stock," for example, is rooted in the guild. Today, the concept of joint stock is understood in its discretely economic sense. But in the guild the meaning was wider. This meaning would include what today we would consider a metaphorical meaning of having joint stock in the guild, namely having stock in social, communal, and political senses, as well as economic.

A New Approach: Juridical Democracy

In developing a prescriptive approach for a guild-like model, we can build on the charters that guild members committed to historically. These charters in effect created a juridical "framing" for guild's internal democracy. They were akin to what the political scientist Theodore Lowi (1969), called "juridical democracy," albeit in a very different context. He first broached juridical democracy as an antidote to American interest-group politics on the national level.[11] The concept generated widespread debate among political scientists, but by the turn of the twenty-first century it almost ceased to be a topic of attention. There are several reasons why, most notably that it was impossible to institute at the national level because interest-group politics at the time precluded its acceptance into federal politics. We, however, use this concept in an evolved form, and in a completely different institutional context.

Lowi argued that special-interest politics, which he dated to the New Deal, had replaced elected representation with interest groups as poor, partial, and ultimately self-interested substitutes for citizen participation (Roberts 2017). These groups paralyzed the government and undermined the popular will. Indeed, interest-group politics was at odds with the very idea and practice of citizenship. The machinery of government, particularly the process of legislation, no longer served the public and civic goals. Interest-group politics, Lowi argued, undermined democratic legitimacy. Organized groups were advantaged over the citizenry in such a framework, and public policy responded to such interest groups. Lowi argued that this took place in the administrative entities implementing policy—the legislature was not stipulating enough the rules of implementation, giving too much discretion to agencies regulating everything from agriculture to the environment. (In this Lowi's argument anticipates the democratic deficit arguments that would come later.)

In fact, interest groups work on legislators as well. Democratic citizenship is thus elided or co-opted, and it "encourages citizens to press their claims through interest-group bargaining, not through legislative representation" (Grady 1984). These tendencies bring "death to legitimacy" (Lowi 1971a, 180–181).

Interest-group politics contained "the mentality of a world [of] universalized ticket-fixing" (Lowi 1979, 297). It "destroyed conflict by yielding to it," redistributed "power by the maxim of each according to his claim," and won "support for the regime by reserving an official place for every major structure of power." Interest-group politics is inherently inegalitarian, and generates inegalitarian outcomes, as interests seek to advantage their own "sovereigns"—the more organized an interest, the more advantaged it is (Grady 1984: 417).

168 CITIZENSHIP

The question of legitimacy is institutional. In other words, institutions shape the relationships between governors and governed, and interest-group politics is driven by and upholds an institutional structure that promotes a certain kind of politics—one that disrupts the practice of citizenship and of civic purpose. To reform these dysfunctional practices, from a citizenship perspective, demands reforming institutions. Lowi never overcame the conundrum of how such a system could be reformed when the ensconced interest groups had little interest in reforming such a system that served them so well.

Lowi's response to such politics was "juridical democracy." Juridical democracy integrates the juridical ("rule of law operating in institutions") and the democratic ("majority rule democracy"). It operates so that, rather than serving largely discrete interests, juridical democracy promotes a civic interest while engaging democratically.

A working example of juridical democracy (as opposed to Lowi's aspirations for national politics) is, in the main, a jury. The judge stipulates rules, procedures, *and civic objectives*—in this case "justice"—and ideals, such as equality before the law and due process. Justice serves the citizens. The institutional impetus of the jury is to transcend the individual interests of the jurors for the higher interest of civic outcomes, but it marries that with a democratic practice, namely the votes and equal voice of each of the jurors. The jury is to be made up of "responsible citizens," and such juries—or equivalent boards or committees—reach decisions not based on "representativeness" but on "explicit standard of public decision" (Anderson 1977). The question becomes how a group (such as a jury or board) arrives at an institutional process to fairly determine an outcome that embodies the public interest. That intersection, when arrived at, represents juridical democracy. It is noteworthy, for reasons we will return to, that the process of engagement in such juries and boards is *deliberative* and *face-to-face*.

Lowi wrote, aspirationally, that this would play out on the national level of politics—focusing on the federal government in the United States but, in principle, would be true elsewhere as well. In Lowi's telling, the rule of law is not simply a procedural matter in that the rule of law "centers upon the *actual consequences* of public policies and of their forms of implementation" (Lowi 1967, 24). The rule of law is explicitly the expression of public purpose (a policy). It contains "the existence of publicly-shared values" (Grady 1984, 407). Interest-group politics "tends to regulate the environment of conduct, not conduct itself [inviting] discretion on a case-by-case basis." Juridical democracy "mobilizes citizens as citizens, not as private actors." In juridical democracy, citizens:

> are reminded that they are tied by reciprocal relationships to one another. As such, they have a stake in demanding egalitarian and equitable policies from their legislative representatives, policies that are generalizable to anyone, not limited to someone. By contrast, under [interest-group politics] citizens are encouraged to view public policy as action serving or affecting vested interests, hence, to demand dispensations of legislators according to the principle: "to each according to his claim." (Grady 1984, 409)

Lowi (1971b, 208) is asking if "the state, through a given statute, [is] directing itself to the citizen in us?" Is the state "dealing with the citizens in us in terms that we can fully understand," rather than in the language of prior interest and clientelistic relations?

Juridical democracy confronts the redistributive issues in a distinct way. Consider racial equity: from a juridical democracy perspective, racial equity measures would be treated as a matter of public concern and desire—all citizens deserve, for example, economic justice. But such an approach does not preclude a focused concern for particular groups in society, such as ethnic minorities or women. The process for arriving there, in a juridical democracy context, is different. Once economic justice, for example, is the goal, anti-racism actions derive from such civic interest, and thus, in such a process are more likely to generate consensual support (which may, thus framed, be extended to others based on class and the like). This is different from what is termed "identity politics," as the term has come to be publicly understood, namely that in different groups, or more accurately purported leaders of such groups, press for their respective "interests." In the longer term, one could argue, forms of engagement of the juridical democracy format generate stronger support for policies of, say, racial equity, than we may see today. Equity becomes one wide-ranging civic objective, and through the engagement of citizens it is applied across a range of issues.

Lowi's juridical democracy concept was criticized on the grounds that interest-group politics and clientelism have "always worked to the advantage of the organized. The stress here is on organizational stability, not upon the stabilization of a particular class or power elite. It is biased not so much in

170   CITIZENSHIP

favor of the rich as in favor of the established and the organized" and that it has, in essence, "developed its own state, its own jurisprudence, and its own capabilities for artificial perpetuation" (Anderson 1977). Lowi offers no pathway for inducing the beneficiaries of interest-group politics and clientelism to change their modus operandi.

Although Lowi did not address the issue, juridical democracy allows us to tackle the presupposition of fixed attributes. Interest-group politics is built upon assumptions of stable interests and preferences—and institutions that are shaped on the assumptions of interest-group politics reinforce the assumptions of fixed attributes. "Attributes," as we have noted previously, may be associated with ethnic, class, gender, religion, and economic characteristics. Juridical democracy—in the appropriate institutional context—can engender a more relational and reasoning approach. By putting forth a larger civic goal—for example, economic justice—and structuring the institutional mechanisms accordingly, relational reasoning can ensue. Economic justice is potentially one part of the "project" that defines the endeavor and softens the attributional and contentious dynamics of most political engagements today.

We have examples of such institutional arrangements, and so the idea (albeit labeled in different ways) is not *de novo*. In addition to juries, we have seen "corporate" arrangements in countries such as Sweden and Germany that lean in this direction. For example, historically Swedish national wage bargaining—involving the state, labor, and corporate sector—was justified not only on procedural grounds, but also that it met explicit public and civic goals. The goals included full employment, equal pay for equal work, and meeting productivity goals that were internationally competitive (Martin 1975, cited in Anderson 1977). Note that the interests of capital and capitalists were addressed as well—this was not simply a reiteration of the battles of capital and labor.

In sum, democracy is not, or should not be, just about *representation of interest groups*, broadly construed. It also needs to be about the *civic purpose*—which "juridical democracy" puts at the forefront. By stressing civic purpose (not simply public "interest"), we uncover different experimentations, different models, and, within limits, even different ways of addressing public concerns, for example, about the environment.

Importantly, it is an approach which addresses the tensions between judicial and administrative mechanisms of government vis-à-vis the "popular" legislative and democratic underpinnings of modern politics—and thus it gets at criticisms regarding the "democratic deficit." It brings together, in more harmonious fashion, the "politics of rights" and the "politics of consent." As such, it can help address the discontent driving populist movements.

The Guild and Juridical Democracy

The juridical democracy framing, where direct engagement is possible (in person or virtually), can provide the circumstances for a relational, civic project approach. The civic goals are built into the structure of the incipient guild—through its charter, board, decision-making, procedures, and assemblies. It is a form of association in which rights are not simply "enjoyed," but enacted—its relational structure engenders as such—and, by extension, is also socially embedded. To put it in the abstract terms of Polanyi, it privileges "social reality," and social connectivity. Indeed, such association also reflects a more genuinely republican form of engagement.

The juridical democracy approach, in the context of the proposed guild, is apparent in many existing organizations, such as the historical example of the Mondragon Corporation (Whyte and Whyte 1991). They contrast with a market that has been "naturalized" with rules that shield it from democratic accountability, essentially creating undemocratic entities and foreshortening citizenship (Block and Somers 2014). This is particularly severe in the context in the last forty years, during which globalization and neoliberal policies have eroded state regulatory capacities.

However, juridical democracy is also realistic—and here the charters and juridical rules are critical, too. Corporations must make a profit; they have "to keep the lights on" and to survive in competitive economies, both domestic and global. Guilds are not communist, anarchist, or autarkic experiments. Economic objectives remain core. Yet they are "civic democracies" that endeavor to go beyond narrowly interest-driven and interest-group politics. This does not mean that group concerns are not addressed—for example, regarding racism—but by folding them under shared, "universal" civic goals they can be addressed through cross-cutting engagement and support.

The "democracy" in juridical democracy is the basis for building representativeness, consensus, and legitimacy; the "juridical" recognizes the importance of expertise, civic goals, and informed leadership. Rather than the venomous discourse we have in many democracies today, with populist movements attacking experts, elites, and the like—or of an elite that is indeed unaccountable and detached—a more virtuous cycle can be induced.

172   CITIZENSHIP

Guilds as a Response to the Digital Economy and AI

It is hard to overstate the impact of the digital economy, AI, and the high-tech industry on both the global economy and on political and social life. The role of corporations in the context of the digital economy in this regard makes the guild model vital for sustaining an active citizenship and democracy. The emergence of a world of what Rogers Brubaker (2023) calls "hyperconnectivity" generates certain opportunities from the perspectives of guilds, but practically the impact hitherto of the digital economy has been severely damaging for democracies. This damage has been to the point of flirting with a veritable democratic meltdown (realized in countries like Hungary and Poland, and with India and Israel tottering on the edge). Overall, we can point to two forces: Silicon Valley promoting a "technological solutionism" that erodes civic engagement together with (relatedly yet paradoxically) the ways in which social media drives populism, with its anti-elite ethos and sense of democratic exclusion.

For the new data-driven technologies, the basis of governing is technocratic and, in Brubaker's (2023) terms, "depoliticizing." This form of governing sees administrative, social, political, and judicial problems as technical problems that can have technical solutions. Depoliticization is also reinforced because the platforms are operated by private companies—but companies that now exercise public functions. Astonishingly, these companies—indeed any corporation collecting digital information—know more about the citizen (through their abundance of data) than the citizen knows about those companies. This turns democratic ideals on their head—of governors being transparent and the citizen having a clear zone of privacy. Algorithms funnel the thoughts and actions of the individual through what Shoshanna Zuboff calls the computational "tuning" or "herding" of behavior.[12]

In a sense, we have a reversion to, in form, a Roman model of citizenship. Access to politics is more opaque, while the individual citizen or resident receives curated rights and privileges. Marion Foucade (2021, 154) argues that we have an emerging "ordinal citizenship" in which demands for "self-care and individual fitness pile up, eroding the universal and solidaristic basis upon which the expansion of citizenship historically thrived." Ordinal citizenship is "a form of social inclusion that thrives on social measurement, differentiation, and hierarchy."

However, the picture is not quite so static as suggested in these analyses, which tend to be partial about the political forces at work. Martin Gurri

(2018), in contrast, argues that the most profound conflict within democracies is the conflict between a networked public and the elites—political, corporate, cultural, and academic. Those elites, in these circumstances, are unable to control the national narrative anymore, and in that space other multitudes of storylines ensue, including conspiracy theories about the "deep state." In some respects, Gurri rejects the view that the state, together with the corporation, is digitally omniscient and that the (highly networked) public is walking in the dark. The public is aware, Gurri states, of elite falsehoods, contrived narratives, and failed policy interventions.

Populism feeds off this dynamic. As Brubaker (2023, 152) notes, "while technocracy is depoliticizing, seeking to insulate decision-making from popular and specifically populist interference, populism is generally re-politicizing; it claims to reassert political control over issues that are seen as having been illegitimately removed from the domain of democratic decision-making and entrusted to democratically unaccountable bureaucrats, experts, or courts."

Be this as it may, civic politics is buffeted at both ends—from the developments associated with the digital economy and from the populist backlash. It is in this context the guild model becomes a significant response.

Foucade and Gordan (2020, 96) ask how these technologies might be governed in such a way that they better serve the public? Tinkering with algorithms does not deal with the more fundamental issues of citizenship. Their argument is that the "state must learn to see like a citizen. Seeing like a citizen is a mode of statecraft that identifies social problems—including those problems stemming from the deployment of dataism itself—from the perspective of those affected." They cite Rahman and Gilman (2019) in an argument for informing bureaucratic decision making with participation by non-experts. Jeffrey Green (2010) notes that democracy is not just about voice but is also about ensuring the people's gaze as a form of discipline and accountability.

Foucade and Gordan are correct in their prescription (in broad strokes) but the primary target should be the corporation itself. The guild, the "citizens' trade," structured appropriately, can provide that civic nexus—a locus of citizenship, opening up the people's gaze, ensuring greater accountability in the private sector (as well as in public bodies), and, conversely, getting buy-in from primary and secondary stakeholders with an interest in shaping corporations in their impact on myriad issues of civic concern.

174   CITIZENSHIP

The Structure of the Twenty-First Century Guild

One can't have a full sense in advance of what forms fully fledged guilds could take. Their development, as with any institution, would evolve in a variety of regional, political, economic, and social contexts. But we can point to some suggestive possibilities, in broad terms, drawing on the example of some contemporary developments in the governance of corporations, in cooperatives, and in the examples of historical guilds.

The character of the global economy is such today that guilds should be, in principle, much more flexible than trade unions, and also better able to handle the networked environment. In this context, guilds could be local, national, regional, transnational, intra-corporate, or inter-corporate. The guild could be defined through discrete professions across organizations, from ride-sharing drivers to computer programmers. Guilds could also be protean, in that they cooperate through issues, if for temporary periods, such as climate. Although platform-based companies have led to extremely concentrated wealth and precarious work conditions for workers, which has by extension impacted the economy as a whole (from taxi drivers to journalists), digital platforms may, ironically, also hold a particular promise for the twenty-first century guild.

The success of Silicon Valley and the digital companies, Nathan Schneider (2021) writes, has depended on lopsided policies which have favored their ownership models. For the development of employee-owned cooperatives or representation and platformed organizing of independent gig workers (e.g., rideshare drivers) shifting policy is essential. Although challenging, the policy changes do not only have to come from the government. ESG is a promising story here as even regulatory changes by the SEC or the acts of business councils and international business trade organizations have significant, even major, impact. Yet history also shows that regulations for employee-owned cooperatives, as an example, win bipartisan support.

Schneider (2021, 14) highlights the consensus that has developed around such efforts on community ownership:

Community ownership can be uncommonly cross-partisan . . . US Republicans, who once regarded the New Deal's rural electric cooperatives as a type of "creeping communism," turned far friendlier once rural areas served by cooperatives became their electoral base. Kenya's powerful agricultural cooperatives began as a segregated institution of British imperialism, then a method for African Socialism, then a tool of capitalist structural adjustment . . . [In 2018] despite fever-pitch polarization, President Donald Trump signed the Main Street Employee Ownership Act, the most important US legislation on the issue in decades, whose sponsors were nearly down-the-middle bipartisan.[13]

The Main Street Employee Ownership Act is of note due to its recency and that it was passed under the Trump administration. The Act provides for access to capital and technical assistance to transition small businesses to employee ownership. It is estimated that thousands of small businesses that would otherwise go out of business will be saved under the Act.[14]

Guilds are more promising than trade unions. Trade unions arose in a different context, often with an adversarial relationship between labor and capital, and with an economic focus. The adversary today—especially large, transnational corporations—is so powerful and has many tools to counter such efforts. Furthermore, most union organizing will succeed at the local level, but not nationally or transnationally. Civic goals, more broadly, have not been a core concern for unions. However, clearly the structures of unions and the process of unionization (e.g., with Amazon workers in New York) can be harnessed and melded into the guild model (Scheiber 2022). Indeed, we would argue that expanding employee governance and the role of stakeholders will likely improve the conditions of labor and employees more broadly.

In more conventional corporate settings, one key focus is "charters"—essentially, building on corporate mission statements but with more profound implications for the "architecture" of corporations and public organizations. The charters are, in essence, the juridical rules—the constitution—of the guild. Another key part of this development will be in the related, changing role of corporate boards. The board is a nexus of governance of employees and other primary stakeholders and is a principal seam with secondary stakeholders (whether through representative or consultative mechanisms). Under this scenario (already realized in certain cooperatives, for example), the board is also the locus of political engagement locally and, where relevant, nationally and globally. The board, however, is also accountable to juridical rules that are embodied in charters, as well as to external judicial oversight. How accountability cascades down an organization is dependent on many factors—the size of the organization, local and national practices, and the like. But the basic model, proposed here, is one of a juridical democracy.

176   CITIZENSHIP

Charters were central for medieval guilds and they often expressed broad civic goals. The Paris hosiers, for example, proclaimed in their 1268 privileges that they would pursue both "the good and profit of the craft" and of "the commonality of the people." But as Sheilagh Ogilvie (2019) has demonstrated from her extensive studies, the ability of guilds to bridge the "profit of the craft" and the "commonality of the people" was blunted by widely followed conduct that included, economically, closed-shop practices and, socially, the exclusion of religious and other groups and the favoring of familial ties for members. Such practices are not propitious for seamed ties.

How can we avoid a repetition of the experience of many medieval and early modern guilds?

Historically, charters of corporations indicated a "corporate purpose." This "purpose," up until the twentieth century, generally recognized an explicit national or civic role. The Dutch East India Company (VOC) charter preamble, for example, noted at length the importance of the shipping and trade commerce to the "prosperity of the United Netherlands" (Gerretsen 2011). Corporations chartered before 1800, in almost their entirety concerned activity now thought of as government infrastructure projects, such as canals, turnpikes, bridges, aqueducts, and public services. According to Oscar Handlin and Mary Handlin (1945, quoted in Pollman 2021), "no grant was forthcoming without justification in terms of the interests of the state as a whole." By the turn of the twentieth century, the civic purpose became less of a focus (Pollman 2021). By the time of Milton Friedman and the rise of neoliberal approaches from the late twentieth century, the civic purpose, if considered at all, was presented as a by-product of corporations driving prosperity and employment (Friedman 1962).

Any revival of a guild approach demands the development of civic purposes (while still incorporating the importance of profit). But statements clearly will not be enough. It is in this regard that charters need development in fundamental ways that structure the proposed guilds to address governance structure (including the boards). Juridical mechanisms, both internal and external to the corporation, are critical. We now live in an environment that is, of course, a considerable distance from medieval and early modern guilds. Judicial oversight is much more robust. The blatant discrimination on religious and gender grounds in historical guilds, for example, is unthinkable now. Employees are much more connected outside their corporations and communes. Digital technology opens a new level of transparency and employee activism. Workers with less capital, of all kinds, in less vaunted industries than high-tech, will likely need to be supported through a combination of activism (e.g., unionization efforts in Amazon) and legislation at the urban, national, and regional levels.

The more promising environment now is not limited to formal organizational developments regarding boards, which have been, for example, increasingly diversified in their membership (Carino 2022). Through the guild format, stakeholders that already radiate beyond members of corporations can be more formally acknowledged. Some of these relationships will invariably draw on loose or tight networks, including cross-national networks. This is part of seamed ties, which may facilitate, for example, chain migration, job opportunities, and the like.

The question of the "genuineness" of the ties is, in such circumstances, determined by actual practice—not simply that someone is a cousin, a co-ethnic, or of a shared religion.[15] If there are genuine ties which facilitate access, such connections are *measurable*. Such an approach transcends distinctions like putative kinship or ethnic ties, or even affective or instrumental drivers. So kin and ethnic ties, for example, can be part of these seamed networks but the social organization is not organized on this basis. But, insofar as geographic mobility or life-course bringing people through "guilded" places of work, it becomes the workplace as a guild that demands a commitment that is more than instrumental, which has indeed been afflicting citizenship through various schemes to buy citizenship (Džankić 2019; Harpaz and Mateos 2019).

At its base the guild is about citizenship and, as we have observed previously, it is the mediating institution of citizenship on both questions of membership and belonging, and of political engagement. Here we can learn from the historical guilds in Europe and in China. As Maarten Prak (2018, 85) writes:

[C]itizenship and guild membership were intimately related in premodern Europe. In many towns, candidates had to be formal citizens before they could join a guild. In some places, all citizens were required to join a guild. And in still other places, guild membership automatically conferred citizenship status. To contemporaries, the connection seemed almost inalienable. Incorporated trades were also known as the "citizens' trades." This intimate connection was articulated, for example, in many guild petitions, insisting that members were entitled to support from the council—as citizens and taxpayers.

178 CITIZENSHIP

"Incorporated trades were also known as the *citizens' trades*" (emphasis added). This is the decisive test—the full measure—of a guild approach. The moment work it is identified with "citizenship," not simply in the worn talk of being a good citizen in one's workplace or of "corporate citizenship" but as the guild-corporation as a marker of citizenship and a nexus of belonging and political engagement, then a core basis of social trust and political legitimacy can ensue.

The guild provides the basis for civically and socially embedded lives. Sociability was especially prized in historical guilds. Ogilvie (2011, 8–9) writes:

> Sociability fostered the multi-stranded relationships by which guild members conveyed information about one another and penalized violations of guild norms. The importance attached to social gatherings by merchant guilds is illustrated by a conflict which arose in 1449 over guild finances between the mercer and the fishmonger factions of the English Merchant Adventurers, in which harmony was restored through corporate sociability between their local merchant guilds at home in London: ". . . for as much as that great discord and variance fell between the gatherers of the conduits of the Mercery and the wardens of the Fishmongers, therefore a supper was made at the King's Head on Cheap at the desire and request of the said wardens for continuance of good love betwixt both parties"

In the context of the historical guilds this nurtured social capital had a dark side. Economically, they used their sociability to seek monopoly profits and to reinforce a sharp boundary vis-à-vis outgroups, in religious, ethnic, and gender terms (Ogilvie 2019). This highlights the importance, in adapting for a twenty-first century guild, and of maintaining seamed ties in now more favorable social and juridical environments. Internally, however, in historical guilds' both membership and its associated rights were enacted and communal. Rights, in this context, were not simply passively "enjoyed." They were intricately related to a lived and relational solidarity—in this sense rights were *inter-se*, not *per se.* The guild was a civic project.

Guilds developed representative bodies who spoke for the guilds before communal and city councils and government. Here the evolving role of the guild, in the twenty-first century, needs to be further articulated. Alison Taylor (2019) has noted how our more contemporary employee activism reflects, in part, frustrations with the state of democracy—voter apathy, corruption among politicians and elites, and, overall, the democratic deficit in the governing institutions of democracies. Employee activism and the developments around ESG are proving an alternative pathway. The civic role of corporations has been growing through pressure from primary and secondary stakeholders, government and the broader public, and corporations to varying degrees on issues from climate to human rights. The multifaceted pressures are obviously going to be different from historic guilds, in part because stakeholders now have a variety of ways to express themselves digitally and through boycotts and the like.

The boards can evolve into a distinct role in this regard. Corporations have always been heavily immersed in politics through lobbying, industry groups, and shaping the rules of regulation and industry through international non-governmental organizations (INGOs). They have been involved in engaging public agencies and governments at every level—from cities, to provinces, to the national level, and through regional and global organizations. The key question will be how changing boards, changing charters, and growing stakeholder governance can complement the focus on profit with a more civic-minded political agenda.

A Role for Universities

Universities can provide key institutional support for the guild approach. Research universities are now globally seamed. In training students, we already hear of universities claiming to create citizens for society, even "global citizens."[16] Universities are also a nexus of the local, national, and transnational, including of "genuine" ties that are global in reach. Formal citizenship status is substantively irrelevant to employee activity. But in practice the university has been increasingly "corporatized," and the focus has been increasingly vocational, especially (but not only) in the United States (Boer 2015; Davidson 2015). Yet the foundations for fusing the workplace with guild-like objectives are in sight. Engineers are increasingly addressing the key role of the environment. Business and law schools are now considering human rights in supply chains.

Universities, in other words, can become incubators for the guild model. The irony here is that universities would, in such a vision, be coming full circle, at least in one historical tradition. The University of Bologna—considered the oldest, continuous, incorporated university in the world— was founded

180   CITIZENSHIP

by a guild of students, the *studium*, in the eleventh century. The three earliest universities, which include Paris and Oxford in addition to Bologna, were the first to use the term *universitas*. But the term originally referred to an incorporated guild of any kind. *Universitas* later acquired the meaning of a "guild of scholars." Even then it was strictly a guild, and the term did not connote a university in the sense that we now understand the word (Beckwith 2012).

One must not hide, however, from the considerable challenges in arriving at a twenty-first century guild.

What about the gig economy? What is the relationship to trade unions, and can unions evolve into guilds? What is the locus of guilds in multifaceted organizational relationships, which may involve multinational corporations and cross-cutting professional associations? What about smaller businesses? Can they be organized into confederations of some sort? How does one integrate remote workers and the digital economy? What are the parameters of stakeholders, secondary as well as primary—and what should the relationship of secondary stakeholders be vis-à-vis the guild? How exactly should the vertical relationship with different authorities be worked out—or, at least, what are the range of possibilities? In articulating and organizing the new guild, the circumstances are promising but the work has just begun.

The Role of the State

The well documented distrust of political leadership, and of elites more broadly, reveals a growing disjunction between the rulers and the ruled. On the Right, this alienation is reflected mostly in populist movements. On the Left, local governments, cities, and even universities and corporations have begun to carve their own path, sometimes at odds with national state interests. This is reflected in the United States' liberal-minded sanctuary cities, states, and localities that resist federal immigration enforcement.

Civic ties develop most palpably locally, through the workplace, schools, places of worship, and in activist groups and social movements. Such associations simultaneously foster and reflect the developing civic fabric. Parent associations at schools, for example, have had in cases an effective role in integrating immigrants in Italy (Farro and Maddanu 2022). By nurturing the twenty-first century guild as a nexus for determining and defining citizenship, as a locus for civic engagement, that local commitment is harnessed. By shifting, in part, the locus of decision-making to guild formats, the distance and alienation between governors and governed is ameliorated and the "fracturing" at different levels will be arguably less evident—for example, through the citizenry's engagement in mediating citizenship through guilds.

Citizenship is enacted in a relational way, via the guild, in its forms of inclusion (on membership) as well as in representation (politically). Citizenship itself is thus literally enacted. Governance is less felt to be simply "from above." Urban citizenship will not be a "level" of citizenship but, in the context of guilds, will be a critical element in weaving together citizens and institutions nationally and regionally (Maas 2013). The guild model can be a basis for solidarity, a civic project which transcends nationalist and other primordialist bases of affective solidarity. Empirically, social trust, political trust, and legitimacy can be nurtured. Social trust, in turn, is associated with greater tolerance, such as the readiness to accept immigrants and refugees (Messing and Ságvári 2018, 2021; Jeannet et al. 2020).

The guild approach lends itself to embracing the "felt citizenship" of quotidian life. This may include citizens and their undocumented fellow meatpackers and churchgoers in rural and conservative Morristown, Tennessee, or in the multiple points of contact of Dreamers and citizens across the United States, or in the socially engaged irregular Bangladeshi migrants in Rome, Italy (Goodwin-White 2020; Farro and Maddanu 2022). Those quotidian ties are unquestionably "genuine" in the way citizenship is imagined. This contrasts with the present practice, in which such relationships can be marginalized through the institutionalization of formalistic citizenship criteria—from raids by immigration authorities to faceless bureaucrats determining rules from the top down.

Ironically, such a quotidian basis also overcomes the binaries of formal citizenship. *Felt* citizenship involves seamed ties locally and transnationally, such as that of the undocumented meatpackers from Mexico. This felt citizenship is made up of genuine ties, seamed locally and transnationally, and involves both primary stakeholders (e.g., in the meatpacking plant) and secondary stakeholders (e.g., the schools and churches of Morristown, Tennessee or, further afield, the cross-border ties of the migrant workers).

Borders as such will not, of course, end. And the state's role in seeking to regulate borders will remain. The twenty-first century guild is not about conjuring up a neo-medieval world. The state's regulative role remains key. The issue of borders has frequently been misunderstood in the context of postnational citizenship and human rights. In the wake of COVID-19 and of the Russian invasion of Ukraine, the role of borders is even more clear.

182 CITIZENSHIP

But key elements of a seamed, global world will remain, at least in democratic countries—in the impact of the internet; the role of transnational ties; the global flow of ideas, politics, and culture; global research and knowledge production. But borders need to be understood in a more nuanced way. Just as democratic states had to adapt to human rights in shaping their actions, in essence making sovereignty more conditional, so too will states need to adapt to the seamed character of the present social condition.

The role of the state also remains central in its judicial role in such a guild proposal, albeit now in ways that do not undermine civic life. The history of guilds shows us how primordialist assumptions can quickly be adopted. The guilds, in the twenty-first century version proposed here, cannot be entirely autonomous. They must still be accountable, not only to their own members but to judicial law, such that primordialist categories are not brought back through the back door and such that other essential foundations (e.g., free speech, religious freedoms, and intellectual openness) are nurtured. Intellectual openness is particularly important given the risk of "principled" associations becoming univocal and in which minority voices are marginalized.

The legislative role of the state can also play a complementary role. For example, while the bases of the guild are increasingly evident among highly capitalized workers—in high-tech companies, academia, finance, and the like—this is much less true for blue-collar workers. If the guild format is not to become yet another moment in highly skewed class privilege, legislation will likely be necessary. Why should academics or computer scientists in high-tech companies have such an extraordinary say in who their colleagues are—and, as such, in defining future citizens? Why should agricultural or manufacturing workers not have such a say? From the perspective of citizenship, and in weaving in an authentic civic fabric, an approach that disadvantages one class over another cannot be justified. Already, and this is not sufficiently understood, human rights (and rights in general) are enjoyed differentially by class.[17] Furthermore, determining citizens and their engagement would not be, clearly, exhausted by such a guild framework; the state would need to supplement the guilds in that regard as well.

The state also serves the role of security more broadly. Given the role of the "civic" and the "civil" in the roots of citizenship, it is surprising the extent to which the issue of security is largely absent in contemporary scholarship on citizenship. To refer to a painful example, Kyiv could not, on its own, defend itself from the Russian army.

In sum, the guild does not replace the state. Indeed, they play complementary roles. The twenty-first century guild can address the core political challenges of our time in a way that cuts across most political divisions. Guilds, and in recent history cooperatives, have been thought of as within the province of the Left—a part of social democracy—but now they can also respond to concerns on the Right, particularly of the working class. It is important that moving forward we work across the divides of Left and Right, race and ethnicity, and native and migrant. Contentious politics, now so sedimented in the political systems of almost all democracies, and in social movements, is failing as a model (Snow 2013: Tilly and Wood 2019). Such adversarial models now compound polarization and engender a vicious cycle. Rather, the relational, quotidian building of social and political trust— together, the basis of a civic society—should be the touchstones. In terms of equity, such trust is best nurtured through the civic project, not on *a priori* primordialist-like solidarities, nationally or domestically. At the foundation of such efforts, a fundamental commitment to civic and democratic principles, and support for the marginalized of all kinds, must be palpable. If we are to get past the present crisis of democracies, ameliorating sectional differences will be essential.

Notes

1. The phrase "democracy as a spectator sport" appears in Schneider (2018).
2. Willem Maas (2013) has documented the extent that citizenship has not necessarily been a singular institution in modern states. Maas talks of "multilevel" citizenship, pointing to, for example, the federal, provincial, and local layers of citizenship. Others have pointed to the growing salience of cities as a locus of citizenship (see essays in Orgad and Bauböck [2020]). Oomen (2020) points to the sanctuary movement in a discussion about how cities can even confront the state.
3. Writing on the case of ICE raids in rural Morrison, Tennessee, Jamie Goodwin-White (2020) cites the works of Blitzer (2018) and Miriam (2018).
4. For more information see *Global Justice Now* (2016). For a list of the top 406 economic entities, see Green (2016).
5. We are very grateful to Alison Taylor for bringing our attention to many of these developments.
6. See the Forest Legality (2021) report on bans on illegal logging of forests, mammal, flora, and fauna species.
7. In the year 2000 the United Nations urged companies to align strategies with universal principles of human rights, environment, and anti-corruption (United Nations 2022).

184 CITIZENSHIP

8. The Securities and Exchange Commission under President Biden announced a task force regarding ESG standards and disclosures. See SEC (2021) and Smetana (2021).

9. See the analysis on the funds of the European Union's Sustainable Finance Disclosure Regulation (SFDR) in Disabato, Michael, and Ng (2021).

10. More on the recent CEO's shift from shareholder to stakeholder interests can be found at Business Roundtable (2019).

11. Lowi published the first edition of *The End of Liberalism* in 1969, and developed the concept of juridical democracy further in, *inter alia*, the second edition of the book in 1979.

12. See Brubaker (2023); Brubaker cites Zuboff (2019). See also Stalder (2018) on the "digital condition" as "post-democratic."

13. Schneider cites, respectively, Ward (1958), Tomlinson (1980), Doyle (1979), Case (2013), Wanyama (2008), Speiser (1977), and Dubb (2018).

14. See https://www.govtrack.us/congress/bills/115/hr5236.

15. On the issue of genuine ties, see Bauböck (2019a). Shachar (2009) relatedly talks of an *ius nexi*.

16. See, for example, https://www.usf.edu/news/2021/global-citizens-project-far-exce eds-goal.aspx and https://www.universityworldnews.com/post.php?story=202106 18131500550.

17. Women's rights are a case in point. Santos, Jacobson, and Georgiev (2021) illustrate this through the lens of homicide. The advance of women's rights is associated with declining homicide rates for both women and men. But women of lower socio-economic status benefit much less.

9

Completing the Third Revolution?

A Conclusion

> One of the most significant facts about humanity may . . . be that we all begin with the natural equipment to live a thousand kinds of life but . . . in the end [live] only one.
>
> Clifford Geertz

> A self with inner depths, alive at once to its uniqueness and its commonness . . . ready to see what's not . . . what, at this moment or that, would encourage someone to think of themselves like this?
>
> Andrew H. Miller

> We have to work hard with the bad language that we have inherited to arrive at that language which has never yet ruled.
>
> Ingeborg Bachmann

By reducing people to a singular demographic category such as ethnicity—in discourse and institutionally—we simplify human complexity. We flatten the array of identities and interests that characterize each individual. And in so doing we are severely limiting the multivalent ways people can associate with one another, civically, socially, and politically. As nation-states patrol their borders, we noted, so too demographic boundaries are sociologically and epistemologically patrolled, closing off a multitude of human associations and endeavors. Interests and identities are accordingly grouped together, often stated in essentialist ways and, in the process, those interests and identities become hardened. We then celebrate the language of contestation and resistance, losing sight of the importance of the varied ways interests can be advanced in a way that is civically shared (e.g., organizing by class across ethnic lines).

The institutionalization of such primordialist social framing further polarizes and splinters society. In its wake, adversarial politics is further

Citizenship. David Jacobson and Manlio Cinalli, Oxford University Press. © Oxford University Press 2023.
DOI: 10.1093/oso/9780197669150.003.0009

186 CITIZENSHIP

empowered. When the Left calls for resistance, the Right can do so as well, and vice versa. We sanction, in effect, a vicious cycle, not a virtuous cycle. Resistance and even civil disobedience are clearly sometimes appropriate—for example, in the civil rights struggle in the 1960s, or against attempts to undermine the judiciary as in Hungary or recently in Israel—but even then, it is more effective when engaged with broad movements, seamed across race, class, religion, and party.[1]

Social science by its very epistemology of breaking down society into subsets of populations (e.g., migrants, evangelicals, South Asians) is frequently reinforcing this process of demographic reductionism with profound effects on both public discourse and policy. In quantitative research, limited reflection has taken place on how such epistemological assumptions are not neutral and have enormous impact (see, e.g., Alonso and Starr 1987). On the qualitative side of research, we see commitment to particular populations, such as the poor and refugees. Although admirable, in this research ethical commitments are not necessarily separated out from what is going to serve different people best—the approach tends to be, implicitly, deontological rather than consequentialist.

We, as social scientists, need to differentiate between what may provide genuine analytical purchase and the epistemological parameters (and limits) of that analysis. Over time, we learn this again and again, in practical terms, when applied social science runs into the shoals of social change—as did the Washington consensus of economists, or the projections of a permanent Democratic party majority by political scientists—precisely because the world is not static. The "rules of the game," not just the players and the tactics, are constantly evolving. Confidently held shibboleths suddenly prove to be more liquid than solid. Democracy does not necessarily follow from free markets. A rising tide does not lift all boats. Even with growth, widening and severe inequalities are not sustainable. Latinos do not continue to vote Democratic at the same rates. Women voters are not a monolith.

The challenge of demographic reductionism is not just analytical but political. Take the response to increasing diversity in Western Europe. Migrants and their vulnerable circumstances had become a pressing item of engagement among policymakers by at least the 1990s. By then, several countries in Europe had grown more culturally diverse. The policy responses were to encourage political participation via institutional structures and mechanisms of electoral politics that favored the representation of various cultural groups—not through nurturing civic engagement as such (Cinalli and Giugni 2013).

COMPLETING THE THIRD REVOLUTION? A CONCLUSION   187

The focus on "integration"—in policy, public discourse, or scholarship—has reinforced the concern with membership, even when trying to overcome histories of racism and discrimination (Favell 2022). The net effect has been to reproduce essentialized categories of race, immigrant, and religion. This in turn gives ballast to the mutually reinforcing politics of neonationalism (in nativist backlashes) on the one hand, and ethnic and religious mobilization on the other. Paradoxically such primordialist politics reinforce elites, and they do not necessarily help the respective populations themselves. These elites nurture these divisions, because they profit from them. Marine Le Pen is a case in point. Focusing on membership in isolation reproduces a constant loop of contention, generating a structural invitation for conflict, a constant struggle over who are the "insiders" and who are the "outsiders." Migrants feel marginalized, but so, too, can the White working class. In this context rights are treated as sectional and absolute—my rights as a Frenchwoman vis-à-vis supposed interlopers, or my rights as a migrant. Invariably, the fight then becomes zero-sum and, at best, transactional. Rights thus no longer nurture a cross-sectional solidarity.

Citizenship itself is, in this context (let alone in its historical renderings), a feudal-like privilege, as many scholars have argued, its battlements to be crossed, challenged, or protected. It is exclusive, to the point of racism, and to be fought over (see, e.g., Kochenov 2019; Shachar 2009). Even well-intended efforts that seek to overcome racism and discrimination inadvertently feed into this dynamic when building on primordialist politics. Democracy itself, frayed over issues of, *inter alia*, immigration, becomes increasingly polarized and even at risk of dysfunction. Far-Right parties grow over time, as demonstrated in the sequential gains of the parties of the far Right in France, presidential election by presidential election. But condemnations of citizenship as feudal, as such, are mistaken; it is to take a particular practice of citizenship and assume that that practice reflects citizenship's underlying principles, its grammar.

Citizenship needs to be engaged more holistically.

The Civic Nation

Bernard Yack (1999, 115–116), the political theorist, argues as to the impossibility of fully separating out of the *demos* and the *ethnos*, "contract" and culture, when it comes to the nation-state:

188   CITIZENSHIP

The myth of the civic nation reflects one strategy that liberals have pursued in order to salvage their hopes for modern politics: find and preserve a form of national community that is compatible with liberal political commitments. If only there were a viable form of national community that reflected shared political principles rather than some particular cultural inheritance, then the growth of national identity need not undermine social diversity and universal human rights . . . But wishing won't make it so . . . The battle to preserve that [civic] legacy is taking place within the framework provided by such [national] communities. Within that framework we have every reason to construct and defend distinctions between more and less inclusive forms of national community. But in doing so we should not fool ourselves into thinking that what we are constructing is a freely chosen and purely civic form of national identity.

Renan got it right.[2] Two things make a nation: present day consent and a rich cultural inheritance of shared memories and practices. Without consent our cultural legacy would be our destiny, rather than a set of background constraints on our activities. But without such a legacy there would be no consent at all, since there would be no reason for people to seek agreement with any one group of individuals rather than another. Focusing exclusively on one or the other component of national identity inspires the contrasting myths of ethnonationalist and civic theories of political community, myths that exaggerate, on the one side, our inability to change, build on, and improve on the communal ties we have inherited and, on the other, our capacity to recreate ourselves in the image of our liberal theories.

Yack shows how compelling the *ethnos*, cultural, or affective sense of belonging has been in the human experience. Contemporary scholarship on citizenship does not sufficiently consider the identarian dimension, with its associated emotional sense of shared belonging and commitment. Civic constitutionalist approaches are a thin reed in this regard, with the civic commitment coming down to individual volition, essentially contractual in its understanding.

Nationalism, whether it leaned in a more republican or more ethnic direction, has served that role. Nationalism has provided that "rich cultural inheritance of shared memories and practices" hitherto essential for civic society as "without such a legacy there would be no consent at all, since there would be no reason for people to seek agreement with any one group of individuals rather than another." Nor should we be assured that, Yack argues, civic

COMPLETING THE THIRD REVOLUTION? A CONCLUSION   189

society absent some cultural binding will necessarily be tolerant. We do have examples of such intolerance, from the French Jacobins to the McCarthyite United States as to loyalty tests.[3]

The challenge now, however, is that a liberal nationalism is becoming less viable—rather, we have seen the emergence of decidedly illiberal nationalisms from Putinism in Russia to the French far-Right to those of Orban in Hungary, Modi in India, and Netanyahu in Israel. Liberal nationalism is now less sustainable because, first, it works less well in a globalized environment of dual citizenships, large noncitizen populations, and transnational associations and media; and second, even liberal nationalism has come at a price for most of those outside its borders—for which, in an age more aware of human rights, has been increasingly contested.

The eroding hold of liberal nationalist narratives is a significant problem for democracies. As the civic fabric frays, with declining social trust and increasing suspicion of governing elites, more insular, primordialist, or extreme ideologies can and do fill in the vacuum. Indeed, it is in this context, in part, that neonationalist and populist movements have been growing in strength.

That civic fraying can also, however, present an opportunity to rethink the approach to citizenship.

Citizenship as Collective Identity

Citizenship as it is lived and imagined tends to be an individual activity, whether in the popular imagination or in scholarship. To the extent citizenship is practiced as a shared act, it is in the context of social movements, voluntary organizations, and in other sectional ways—not, in other words, as part of an overarching, collective civic identity. Citizenship is associated with individual rights, sometimes extended as sectional rights based on, for example, ethnicity or indigenous status. The collective "us," to the extent it is expressed, is generally captured through the *ethnos* or cultural memories of shared belonging as Japanese, Indian, French, Ghanaian, Argentinian, etc. These respective nationalities are the collective act of being a national, but they are not expressive of citizenship as such.

In the nation-state, nationalism has thus been the basis of describing the collective identity. In so doing, nationalism has complemented civic society, the *demos*. (This is the case up until nationalism, in its extreme forms,

190　CITIZENSHIP

proactively undermines civic society and democracy.) Consequently, citizenship's transformative role in making the individual part of a collective civic identity has rarely come to the fore at the national level. Citizenship and civic identity have not been the basis for turning to a particular "people to seek agreement with any one group of individuals rather than another"—the sense of shared nationhood has. A case in point: West Germany absorbed East Germany into a reunited Germany because of a shared memory of political and cultural nationhood, not because of shared civic values. History is replete with claims of irredentism—Russia's invasion of Ukraine being a recent, painful example. Irredentist claims are legitimated, overwhelmingly, through assertions of common ethnicity, culture, or religion, and not upon shared civic values.

Many people perceive themselves to be Jewish, Black, Brazilian, or Irish, not because they do it (in the main) as a proactive, thought-out, calculating act. They do so *because they feel it*. However, the emotional sense of "feeling" that I am, say, Brazilian, is not primordial or congenital. The identity of being something, of an emotional commitment rather than a contextual calculation, is an ontological matter. Similarly, one can experience that emotion of belonging to the community of die-hard fans of Sunderland F. C. We have not given proper attention to citizenship as a collective, felt identity.

It is telling that constitutions, from the United States Constitution to today, have been mostly about the machinery of government. Constitutions address the different branches of government, degrees of federalism, checks-and-balances, and individual rights, from freedom of speech to the right to vote. Constitutions have grown in length over time, from little more than a handful of pages of the United States Constitution of 1789, to the roughly two hundred pages of the South African Constitution that came into effect in 1997. But the expansion in length mostly concerns the enlargement of stated rights and related issues of government structure. Constitutions have neither engaged the substance of citizenship nor the question of collective civic identity. The assumption has been, apparently, that either collective civic identity would emerge of its own accord, or that national, cultural, and territorial markers would serve the purpose.

To get beyond the *ethnos–demos* duality, we need to address, to find a way, to nurture, and to facilitate collective civic identity. Citizenship needs to be addressed from the identarian perspective, not only as a matter of membership and political access. By addressing that challenge, we can simultaneously engage the growing alienation of citizens vis-à-vis the governing class, and the question of belonging and membership in a globalized environment where the binary of formal citizenship does not reflect the "mismatch between borders on the map and boundaries of human community" (Spiro 2017). It demands finding a civic alternative to the *ethnos* that captures the same emotion and the same sense of "intuitive" identity. In part, a collective civic identity demands addressing the *telos*, the purposes, of citizenship. The civic *project* is, by definition, driven by a "civic purpose."

Bringing together participation and collective identity becomes necessary for "completing" the Third Revolution. The twenty-first century guild exemplar, together with the framing of the civic project, is one approach which does fuse participation with identification. The guild provides an institutional framework for doing so. Let us turn now to how, conceptually, this approach turns the nation-state policy framing on citizenship (notably regarding migrant populations) on its feet.

The Civic Polity

We have proposed a paradigmatic shift in the approach to citizenship that can provide a way forward for reinvigorating democracies. It demands a more holistic framing of citizenship, which in recent decades has been flattened and undermined by the almost singular attention to issues of membership, to harmful effect. The question of who belongs in the respective democracies has been a matter of raw discontent and polarization. Relatedly, the relationship between the rulers and the ruled, and the elites and the citizenry more broadly, has been in severe decline in recent decades and years. These trends are amply documented, as is the decline in social trust and in political legitimacy.

The focus on membership has led to questions of the "fit" of immigrants in the nation-state, and to an emphasis on "integration" and "assimilation" in the politics of identity. The politics of immigration have in the process, across the political spectrum, calloused primordialist categories. Other subsets of society get essentialized by this process. The White working class gets cast, for example, as racist and reactionary, when in fact (as characteristic in different ways with all demographic reductionism) the picture is more complex. When we turned to the vertical dimension of citizenship regarding the relationship of the governors vis-à-vis the governed, we noted how, in Europe, policy responses were to encourage political participation that favored the

192 CITIZENSHIP

representation of various cultural groups—not through nurturing civic engagement as such. Thus, the vertical issues of politics are derivative of the struggles over membership and belonging.

Although immigration brings these issues to the fore most readily, the reductionism to primordialist and essentializing social categories is not just about immigration. In the United States, African Americans have long faced challenges of exclusion and discrimination. The nation-state framing, by evoking the "character" of the nation, has the effect of creating a sociological center and periphery of belonging, even for long-term citizens and residents. Take the example of the Roma in Italy. Public housing has been made available to some of the Roma, in part to make the life of the nomadic Roma more sedentary. This has become a flashpoint of sometimes violent protest. In a recent case in Casal Bruciato, a large neighborhood in Rome, the police had to be brought in. The local residents, as well as far-Right protest groups, complained that "Italians" (the Roma being thought of as not "one of us") were not receiving public housing. Furthermore, the locals, who were themselves of modest means, felt their marginality emphasized in this context—these Roma, after all, were not being settled in affluent neighborhoods in Rome. When the housing of the Roma was then justified by the law, court orders, and even EU rules, those institutions came under attack. The alienation of government and the governing class is compounded. Currently, the government (most directly in the form of the police) is facing a real mob. The anger is directed not just at Roma families, but the law, the courts, the government, and the EU. Populist parties' benefit from the rising anger, which they are quite happy to stoke.[4]

A more holistic framing of citizenship demands pivoting from the nation-state lens to that of a civic polity, a *civitas*. It creates a different "problem-set," one that is at the intersection of civic community and civic politics. Any form of framing generates a distinct problem-set that in turn generates different responses. Thus, the nation-state has generated, for example, the language of integration and assimilation for immigrants and, politically, the concept of checks-and-balances and interest groups. Those are responses to the problem-set, the challenges, induced by the idea of the nation-state, around issues of who belongs, how to handle outsiders, how to balance different "interests," and the like. In talking of different rules of naturalization, or different constitutional structures, or centralized versus federal systems—all are responses to the particular nation-state problem-set.

COMPLETING THE THIRD REVOLUTION? A CONCLUSION   193

The civic polity framing generates its own sets of questions and possible responses. One can't anticipate the varied responses to this problemset. The twenty-first century guild is one important pathway forward, but a range of other responses are conceivable, in parallel. But in emphasizing the civic, the relational, and the concept of the civic project, the form of engagement is very different. It is about the process through which individuals become "socially embedded" into a civic community. That process is relational and seamed. Although those individuals can be classed in different ways—working class, migrant, Catholic, Muslim, Asian—it is important not to reduce people to singular demographic categories. Diversity is as much interior to the individual—people are multivalent—as diversity is exogenous to the individual. For example, on the simplest level, socio-economic privileage or marginalization can characterize, respectively, both migrants and natives. Institutionally, how rights are structured to effect a civic process is critical.

Ius Civitas

We asked earlier, "What job are rights expected to perform?" The answers can be multifold, from the narrow—protect property rights; to the broad— promote national self-determination. Rights, we noted, are a tool and not an end as such. The objective of citizenship, its underlying logic and grammar, is to promote a civic society and polity free of "primordialist" attributes that are still so evident in the nation-state. We must ask how rights, or the way rights are conceived, advance, or indeed inhibit, now and historically, civic goals?

Citizenship is more than the individual citizen and their rights and conduct; it is about *civically embedded* sets of ongoing acts. It enables a fluent interaction between rights and participation in civic and political life. It unifies to the extent possible the "politics of consent" and the "politics of rights." It does so by linking social and political dimensions of citizenship, engendering shared membership, common purpose, and mutual engagement between citizens across different cultural, political, and socio-economic cleavages. This contributes to rights *inter se*—the cascading rights reinforce civic participation and representation in different contexts and at different scales. Once we recognize that the civic sphere, socially and politically, is seamed and relational, we also recognize rights of individuals are themselves *inter se*—interdependent and seamed.

194 CITIZENSHIP

Our present formal notions of citizenship privileges the individual, juxtaposes and essentializes interests and identities and assumes fixed interests and preferences to every actor, individual and group and it treats the market of interests as the paradigm of politics and social life. This is the inverse of the underlying logic of citizenship, which recognizes the true essentialism of the human condition is that of *sociality*. "We have to accept the fact," Elena Ferrante (2022, 47–49) writes, "that no word is truly ours." Even in the solitary act of writing, "We have to give up the idea that writing miraculously releases a voice of our own, a tonality of our own ... Writing is, rather, entering an immense cemetery where every tomb is waiting to be profaned."

In this environment, one is talking less about the "integration" of outsiders into a civic polity, or about "naturalizing" an outsider. Nor is someone— citizen, noncitizen, or some status in-between—defined (in terms of the civic polity) in terms of pre-existing groups with defined preferences. It is instead about shaping institutions and legal frameworks to facilitate engagement. But it does presume what has been termed a "genuine link," although there are differences of opinion as to what constitutes a genuine link. The genuine link concept, which has a deep legal history as well, concerns cross-border issues relating to nationality. In the context of a civic polity, the issue of genuine links is potentially more wide-reaching, given the emphasis on relational ties, beyond nationality and its legal ties.[5]

Getting Buy-In

A challenge in prescriptive postulations and in policymaking is that they frequently come from "on high," both in terms of the social hierarchy and in the level of abstraction. There also tends to be an extraordinary faith in "principles," like those of human rights, having sufficient internal logic that they will *ipso facto* resolve key social and political problems. Or, worse, there is a reliance on coercive mechanisms—state agencies, the police, courts—to push through resolutions to knotty challenges (perhaps with a show of consultation with community groups). But "top-down" solutions generate wariness, affecting trust on the community level (social trust) and in authority (political legitimacy). The same problem arises when officials and judges determine what is in the "public interest" (Reich 1964). We know, from studies on immigration and refugees, the key role of social and political trust in shaping the level of welcome. On some level, prescriptive proposals are likely to come from sources like government officials, academics, think tanks, and

COMPLETING THE THIRD REVOLUTION? A CONCLUSION   195

journalists. But it is critical to consider how such proposals can be engaged and developed organically and civically.

In fact, the challenge is perhaps not even primarily about the exogenous objectives of such engagements. Citizenship is also more than the citizen's individual conduct; it is about socially embedded and collective sets of ongoing acts. It is about the ongoing re-creation of a collective civic community. But we must find ways to shape institutions, places of work, and associations to facilitate and nurture such civic engagement. The twenty-first century guild can be one key and core response. The guild model answers a number of concerns in our developing social, political, and transnational environment. That is not to say civic engagements have no parameters. This is where the courts (and the state) come in, ensuring such engagements do not take, for example, a racist direction or suppress free speech and dissent.

We face the challenge of finding the virtuous nexus between the "politics of rights" and the "politics of consent." If we have the politics of consent with limited rights, we risk veering into populism or worse—extreme nationalist politics, attacks on the judiciary, exclusion of marginalized populations, and the narrowing of democratic participation. If we have the politics of rights with narrowing parameters for popular expression and consent, we get populations that are distrustful of institutions, of elites, and of each other, and elites who themselves are increasingly detached from the public. The proposed "juridical democracy" framework regarding guilds is one response to this dilemma.

In responding to the crisis of democracy, scholars and commentators tend to look back to seek to revive what worked in the past. But democracy is the institutional machinery. Without addressing the civic foundations—citizenship and the character of rule and belonging—such efforts will fail. Trying to revive democracy based on a memory of when it worked well is likely to be of limited value. We are in a different world now. That moment is past. We need to think forward, creatively, yet build upon present opportunities.

We need a new approach for the twenty-first century.

Notes

1. Internationally, the picture can be very different, of course; even violent resistance can be necessary, as in the case of Ukraine defending itself following Putin's extraordinarily brutal invasion.

196 CITIZENSHIP

2. Yack is referring to Ernest Renan (1990 [1882]), who stated of the two characteristics of the nation: "One lies in the past, the other in the present. One is the possession in common of a rich legacy of memories, the other is present day consent, the desire to live together, the will to perpetuate the value of the heritage that one has received in an undivided form . . . The nation, like the individual, is the culmination of a long past of endeavors, sacrifice, and devotion."

3. Yack (1999, 115), writes, "Even if the myth of the civic nation were true, I doubt that voluntary associations for the expression of shared political principle would be as conducive to toleration and diversity as their supporters expect them to be. There would be plenty of room for exclusion and suspicion of difference in a political community based solely on a shared commitment to political principles. We should be willing to exclude anyone from such a community who disagrees with its basic principles. Moreover, we might be inclined to exclude anyone whom we suspect of rejecting these principles. For if it is commitment to certain principles that makes one a member of a community, then we will probably want to know whether this commitment is genuine or a mask for subversion."

4. On the incident in Casal Bruciato, which took place on May 7, 2019, see the reports in ANSA (2019) and Lakic (2019). On academic treatments of the wider phenomenon, see Farro and Maddanu (2021) and Grazioli (2021).

5. On criticism of Nottebohm, see Macklin (2017). See also Shahar (2009).

Bibliography

Abulafia, David, and Nora Berend. 2017. *Medieval Frontiers: Concepts and Practices*. London: Routledge. https://doi.org/10.4324/9781315249285.

Adams, Jonathan, and Cordelia Hess. 2018. *The Medieval Roots of Antisemitism: Continuities and Discontinuities from the Middle Ages to the Present Day*. London: Routledge.

Agamben, Giorgio. 1998. *Homo Sacer*. Stanford: Stanford University Press.

Ahir, Diwan C. 1995. *Asoka the Great*. New Delhi: BR Publishing Corporation.

Allen, Katherine R., Rosemary Blieszner, and Karen A. Roberto. 2011. "Perspectives on Extended Family and Fictive Kin in the Later Years: Strategies and Meanings of Kin Reinterpretation." *Journal of Family Issues* 32, no. 9: 1156–1177. https://doi.org/10.1177/0192513X11404335.

Allen, Richard C. 1999. *David Hartley on Human Nature*. Albany: University of New York Press.

Alonso, William, and Paul Starr, eds. 1987. *Politics of Numbers*. New York: The Russell Sage Foundation. http://www.jstor.org/stable/10.7758/9781610440028.

Alwine, Andrew T. 2018. "The Soul of Oligarchy: The Rule of the Few in Ancient Greece." *TAPA* 148, no. 2: 235–267. https://doi.org/10.1353/apa.2018.0010.

Ambrosini, Maurizio, Manlio Cinalli, and David Jacobson, eds. 2020. *Migration, Borders and Citizenship: Between Policy and Public Spheres*. London: Palgrave Macmillan.

Anderson, Benedict. 1991. *Imagined Communities: Reflections on the Origin and Spread of Nationalism*. London: Verso.

Anderson, Charles W. 1977. "Political Design and the Representation of Interests." *Comparative Political Studies* 10, no. 1: 127–152. https://doi.org/10.1177/001041407701000106.

Ando, Clifford, and Seth Richardson, eds. 2017. *Ancient States and Infrastructural Power: Europe, Asia, and America (Empire and After)*. Philadelphia: University of Pennsylvania Press. http://www.jstor.org/stable/j.ctv2t4bs8.

ANSA. 2019. "Roma Woman Gets Rape Threat Amid Protest." *ANSA*. May 7. https://www.ansa.it/english/news/general_news/2019/05/07/roma-woman-gets-rape-threat-amid-protest_032c0576-87e4-4df6-9f62-5dc6be4d5012.html.

Appelbaum, Diana Muir. 2013. "Biblical Nationalism and the Sixteenth-Century States." *National Identities* 15, no. 4: 317–332. https://doi.org/10.1080/14608944.2013.814624.

Aquinas, Thomas. 1948 [1265–1273]. *Summa Theologica*. Translated by the Fathers of the English Dominican Province. New York: Benziger Brothers. 5 vols.

Arévalo de León, Bernardo. 2018. *Del Estado Violento al Ejército Político: Violencia, Formación Estatal y Ejército en Guatemala, 1524–1963*. Guatemala City: F&G Editores.

Aristotle. 2009. *Politics*. Oxford: Oxford University Press.

Armstrong, John A. 1982. *Nations before Nationalism*. Chapel Hill: University of North Carolina Press.

Arrow, Kenneth, and Frank Hahn. 1971. *General Competitive Analysis*. San Francisco: Holden-Day.

198 BIBLIOGRAPHY

Assante, Franca. 1998. "The Prophets of Welfare: The Monti and Conservatori in Neapolitan Guilds in the Early Modern Age." In *Guilds, Markets and Work Regulations in Italy, 16th–19th Centuries*, edited by Alberto Guenzi, Paola Massa, and F. Piola Caselli, 423–435. London: Ashgate Publishing.

Bagguley, Paul. 1991. *From Protest to Acquiescence? Political Movements of the Unemployed*. London: MacMillan.

Bagguley, Paul. 1992. "Protest, Acquiescence and the Unemployed: A Comparative Analysis of the 1930s and 1980s." *British Journal of Sociology* 43: 443–461. https://doi.org/10.2307/591544.

Baker, K. M. 2001. "Enlightenment and the Institution of Society: Notes for a Conceptual History." In *Civil Society: History and Possibilities*, edited by S. Kaviraj and S. Khilnani, 84–104. Cambridge: Cambridge University Press.

Balibar, Étienne. 1998. "The Borders of Europe." In *Cosmopolitics: Thinking and Feeling Beyond the Nation*, edited by Pheng Cheah and Bruce Robbins, 216–232. Minneapolis: University of Minnesota Press.

Balibar, Étienne. 2003. *We, the People of Europe? Reflections on Transnational Citizenship*. Princeton: Princeton University Press.

Ball, Roger, and John Drury. 2012. "Representing the Riots: The (Mis)Use of Statistics to Sustain Ideological Explanation." *Radical Statistics* 106: 4–21. http://sro.sussex.ac.uk/id/eprint/41622.

Barchet, Bruno A. 2015. *A History of Western Public Law: Between Nation and State*. New York: Springer.

Barnard, Frederick M. 1983. "National Culture and Political Legitimacy: Herder and Rousseau." *Journal of the History of Ideas* 44, no. 2: 231–253. https://doi.org/10.2307/2709138.

Bar-Tal, Daniel. 2004. "The Necessity of Observing Real Life Situations: Palestinian–Israeli Violence as a Laboratory for Learning about Social Behaviour." *European Journal of Social Psychology* 34, no. 6: 677–701. https://doi.org/10.1002/ejsp.224.

Bates, Ed. 2010. *The Evolution of the European Convention on Human Rights: From its Inception to the Creation of a Permanent Court of Human Rights*. Oxford: Oxford University Press.

Bauböck, Rainer. 1994 *Transnational Citizenship: Membership and Rights in International Migration*. Cheltenham: Edward Elgar Publishing.

Bauböck, Rainer. 2007 "Stakeholder Citizenship and Transnational Political Participation: A Normative Evaluation of External Voting." *Fordham Law Review* 75, no. 5: 2393. https://ir.lawnet.fordham.edu/flr/vol75/iss5/4.

Bauböck, Rainer. 2013. "Studying Citizenship Constellations." In *Migration and Citizenship Attribution*, edited by Maarten Peter Vink, 143–156. London: Routledge.

Bauböck, Rainer, ed. 2017a. *Democratic Inclusion*. Manchester: Manchester University Press.

Bauböck, Rainer, ed. 2017b. *Transnational Citizenship and Migration*. London: Routledge.

Bauböck, Rainer. 2017c. "Political Membership and Democratic Boundaries." In *The Oxford Handbook of Citizenship*, edited by Aylet Shachar, Rainer Bauböck, Irene Bloemraad, and Maarten Vink, 60–82. Oxford: Oxford University Press. https://doi.org/10.1093/oxfordhb/9780198805854.013.3.

Bauböck, Rainer. 2019a. "Genuine Links and Useful Passports: Evaluating Strategic Uses of Citizenship." *Journal of Ethnic and Migration Studies* 45, no. 6: 1015–1026. https://doi.org/10.1080/1369183X.2018.1440495.

BIBLIOGRAPHY 199

Bauböck, Rainer. 2019b. "EU Citizens Should Have Voting Rights in National Elections, But in Which Country?" In *Debating European Citizenship*, edited by Rainer Bauböck. IMISCOE Research Series, 23–26. Cham: Springer. https://doi.org/10.1007/978-3-319-89905-3_3.

Bauböck, Rainer, and Liav Orgad, eds. 2020. "Cities vs States: Should Urban Citizenship Be Emancipated from Nationality?" *Robert Schuman Centre for Advanced Studies Research*. Paper No. RSCAS 2020/16. https://hdl.handle.net/1814/66369.

Bauman, Zygmunt. 2011. *Collateral Damage: Social Inequalities in a Global Age*. Cambridge: Polity.

Baumeister, Roy F., and Mark R. Leary. 1995. "The Need to Belong: Desire for Interpersonal Attachments as a Fundamental Human Motivation." *Psychological Bulletin* 117: 497–529. https://doi.org/10.1037/0033-2909.117.3.497.

Beckwith, Christopher. 2012. *Warriors of the Cloisters: The Central Asian Origins of Science in the Medieval World*. Princeton, NJ: Princeton University Press.

Beiner, Ronald, ed. 1999. *Theorizing Nationalism*. Albany: SUNY Press.

Bejczy, István P. 2011. *The Cardinal Virtues in the Middle Ages: A Study in Moral Thought from the Fourth to the Fourteenth Century*. Leiden: Brill.

Bell, Stuart, Donald McGillivray, Ole Pedersen, Emma Lees, and Elen Stokes. 2017. *Environmental Law*. Oxford: Oxford University Press.

Bellah, Robert N., and Phillip E. Hammond. 2013. *Varieties of Civil Religion*. Eugene: Wipf and Stock Publishers.

Bentham, Jeremy. 1988 [1789]. *The Principles of Morals and Legislation*. Buffalo: Prometheus Books.

Bently, Lionel, Brad Sherman, Dev Gangjee, and Phillip Johnson. 2021. *Intellectual Property Law*. Oxford: Oxford University Press.

Benvenisti, Eyal, and Alon Harel. 2017. "Embracing the Tension Between National and International Human Rights Law: The Case for Discordant Parity." *International Journal of Constitutional Law* 15, no. 1: 36–59. https://doi.org/10.1093/icon/mox002.

Berman, Harold J. 1983. *Law and Revolution: The Formation of the Western Legal Tradition*. Cambridge, MA: Harvard University Press.

Black, Antony. 2003. *Guild and State: European Political Thought from the Twelfth Century to the Present*. New Brunswick, NJ: Transaction Publishers. https://doi.org/10.4324/9780203790373.

Black, Antony. 2017. *Guild and State: European Political Thought from the Twelfth Century to the Present*. New York: Routledge.

Blader, Steven L., and Tom R. Tyler. 2003. "A Four-Component Model of Procedural Justice: Defining the Meaning of a 'Fair' Process." *Personality and Social Psychology Bulletin* 29, no. 6: 747–758. https://doi.org/10.1177/0146167203029006007.

Blaney, David L., and Naeem Inayatullah. 2000. "The Westphalian Deferral." *International Studies Review* 2, no. 2: 29–64. https://doi.org/10.1111/1521-9488.00204.

Blitzer, Jonathan. 2018. "In Rural Tennessee, a Big ICE Raid Makes Some Conservative Voters Rethink Trump's Immigration Agenda." *New Yorker*. April 19. https://www.newyorker.com/news/dispatch/in-rural-tennessee-a-big-ice-raid-makes-some-conservative-voters-rethink-trumps-immigration-agenda.

Block, Fred, and Margaret R. Somers. 2014. *The Power of Market Fundamentalism*. Cambridge, MA: Harvard University Press. https://doi.org/10.4159/harvard.9780674416345.

200 BIBLIOGRAPHY

Bloemraad, Irene. 2006. *Becoming a Citizen: Incorporating Immigrants and Refugees in the United States and Canada*. Berkeley: University of California Press.

Blok, Josine. 2017. *Citizenship in Classical Athens*. Cambridge: Cambridge University Press.

Bloomberg. 2022. *ESG May Surpass $41 Trillion Assets in 2022, But Not Without Challenges, Finds Bloomberg Intelligence*. [Press Release]. January 24. https://www. bloomberg.com/company/press/esg-may-surpass-41-trillion-assets-in-2022-but-not-without-challenges-finds-bloomberg-intelligence/.

Bloomberg Editors. 2021 "Big Oil Finds the Climate Has Changed." *Bloomberg Opinion*. www.bloomberg.com/opinion/articles/2021-06-11/exxon-mobil-and-shell-are-told-to-try-harder-on-climate-change.

Blundell, Susan. 1995. *Women in Ancient Greece*. Cambridge, MA: Harvard University Press.

Boesche, Roger. 2003. *The First Great Political Realist: Kautilya and his Arthashastra*. New York: Lexington Books.

Boldizar, Janet P., and David M. Messick. 1988. "Intergroup Fairness Biases: Is Ours the Fairer Sex?" *Social Justice Research* 2, no. 2: 95–111. https://doi.org/10.1007/BF0 1048501.

Bonnett, Alastair. 1998. "How the British Working Class Became White: The Symbolic (re) Formation of Racialized Capitalism." *Journal of Historical Sociology* 11, no. 3: 316–340. https://doi.org/10.1111/1467-6443.00066.

Bose, Satyajit, Guo Dong, and Anne Simpson. 2019. *The Financial Ecosystem: The Role of Finance in Achieving Sustainability*. Cham: Palgrave Macmillan. https://doi.org/ 10.1007/978-3-030-05624-7.

Bosniak, Linda. 2006. *The Citizen and the Alien: Dilemmas of Contemporary Membership*. Princeton: Princeton University Press.

Bourdieu, Pierre. 2020 [1977]. *Outline of a Theory of Practice*. Cambridge: Cambridge University Press.

Brambilla, Chiara. 2015. "Exploring the Critical Potential of the Borderscapes Concept." *Geopolitics* 20, no. 1: 14–34. https://doi.org/10.1080/14650045.2014.884561.

Branscombe, Nyla R., and Daniel L. Wann. 1991. "The Positive Social and Self-concept Consequences of Sports Team Identification." *Journal of Sport and Social Issues* 15, no. 2: 115–127. https://doi.org/10.1177/019372359101500202.

Bregman, Rutger. 2020. *Humankind: A Hopeful History*. New York: Bloomsbury.

Brekke, Torkel. 2012. "Hinduism and Security: A Hierarchy of Protection." In *Routledge Handbook of Religion and Security*, edited by Chris Seiple, Dennis R. Hoover, and Pauletta Otis, 80–94. New York: Routledge.

Brélaz, Cédric, and Els Rose. 2021. *Civic Identity and Civic Participation in Late Antiquity and the Early Middle Ages*. Turnhout: Brepols Publishers.

Breuilly, John. 1993. *Nationalism and the State*. Manchester: Manchester University Press.

Brewer, Marilynn B. 2017. "Intergroup Discrimination: Ingroup Love or Outgroup Hate?" In *The Cambridge Handbook of the Psychology of Prejudice*, edited by Chris G. Sibley, and Fiona K. Barlow, 90–110. Cambridge: Cambridge University Press. https://doi.org/ 10.1017/9781316161579.005.

Brown, Peter. 1990. *The Body and Society: Men, Women, and Sexual Renunciation in Early Christianity*. New York: Columbia University Press.

Brown, Peter. 1995. *The Rise of Western Christendom*. Oxford: Blackwell.

Brown, Rupert, and Miles Hewstone. 2005. "An Integrative Theory of Intergroup Contact." *Advances in Experimental Social Psychology*, edited by Mark P. Zanna, 255–343. Cambridge, MA: Elsevier Academic Press. https://doi.org/10.1016/S0065-2601(05)37005-5.

Brubaker, Rogers. 1992. *Citizenship and Nationhood in France and Germany*. Cambridge, MA: Harvard University Press.

Brubaker, Rogers. 2023. *Hyperconnectivity and Its Discontents*. Cambridge: Polity Press.

Brunius, Teddy. 1958. "Jeremy Bentham's Moral Calculus." *Acta Sociologica* 3, no. 1: 73–85. https://doi.org/10.1177/000169935800300107.

Buhrmester, Michael D., Dawn Burnham, Dominic D. P. Johnson, Oliver S. Curry, David W. Macdonald, and Harvey Whitehouse. 2018. "How Moments Become Movements: Shared Outrage, Group Cohesion, and the Lion that Went Viral." *Frontiers in Ecology and Evolution* 6: 54. https://doi.org/10.3389/fevo.2018.00054.

Burckhardt, Jacob. 2019 [1937]. *The Civilisation of the Renaissance in Italy*. London: Routledge.

Burgess, John Stewart. 1930. "The Guilds and Trade Associations of China." *The ANNALS of the American Academy of Political and Social Science* 152, no. 1: 72–80. https://doi.org/10.1177/000271623015200110.

Burkert, Walter. 1995. *The Orientalizing Revolution: Near Eastern Influence on Greek Culture in the Early Archaic Age*. Cambridge, MA: Harvard University Press.

Burrow, Mathew. 1986. "Mission Civilisatrice." *The Historical Journal* 29, no. 1: 109–135. http://doi.org/10.1017/S0018246X00018641.

Business Roundtable. 2019. "Business Roundtable Redefines the Purpose of Corporation to Promote an Economy that Serves all Americans." *Business Roundtable*. www.businessroundtable.org/business-roundtable-redefines-the-purpose-of-a-corporation-to-promote-an-economy-that-serves-all-americans.

Butler, Joseph. 2018 [1726]. *Fifteen Sermons Preached at the Rolls Chapel*. London: Forgotten Books.

Cairns, John W., and Paul J. Du Plessis. 2010. *The Creation of the Ius Commune: From Casus to Regula*. Edinburgh: Edinburgh University Press. https://doi.org/10.1515/9780748642922.

Calhoun, Craig. 1997. "Nationalism and the Public Sphere." In *Public and Private in Thought and Practice: Perspectives on a Grand Dichotomy*, edited by Jeff Weintraub and Krishan Kumar, 75–102. Chicago: Chicago University Press.

Calhoun, Craig J. 2002. "Imagining Solidarity: Cosmopolitanism, Constitutional Patriotism, and the Public Sphere." *Public Culture* 14, no. 1: 147–171. https://doi.org/10.1215/08992363-14-1-147.

Campbell, Al. 2010. "Marx and Engels' Vision of a Better Society." *Forum for Social Economics* 39, no. 3: 269–278. https://doi.org/10.1007/s12143-010-9075-4.

Canivez, Patrice. 2004. "Jean-Jacques Rousseau's Concept of People" *Philosophy & Social Criticism* 30, no. 4: 393–412. https://doi.org/10.1177/0191453704044025.

Canterbury, Ray E. 1987. *The Making of Economics*. Belmont: Wadsworth.

Carino, Megan. 2022. "Corporate Boards Became More Diverse in 2021." *Marketplace*. January 4. https://www.marketplace.org/2022/01/04/corporate-boards-became-more-diverse-in-2021/.

Carsten, Janet. 2000. *Cultures of Relatedness: New Approaches to the Study of Kinship*. Cambridge: Cambridge University Press.

202 BIBLIOGRAPHY

Casale, Giancarlo. 2015a. "The Islamic Empires of the Early Modern World." In *The Cambridge World History Volume VI: The Construction of a Global World, 1400–1800 CE, Part 1: Foundation*, edited by Bentley, Jerry H., Sanjay Subrahmanyam, and Merry E. Wiesner-Hanks, 323–344. Cambridge: Cambridge University Press. https://doi.org/10.1017/CBO9781139194594.014.

Casale, Giancarlo. 2015b. "Tordesillas and the Ottoman Caliphate: Early Modern Frontiers and the Renaissance of an Ancient Islamic Institution." *Journal of Early Modern History* 19, no. 6: 485–511. https://doi.org/10.1163/15700658-12342469.

Case, Anne, and Angus Deaton. 2017. "Mortality and Morbidity in the 21st Century." *Brooking Papers on Economic Activity* 17, no. 1: 397–443. https://doi.org/10.1353/eca.2017.0005.

Case, Ted. 2013. *Power Plays: The U.S. Presidency, Electric Cooperatives, and the Transformation of Rural America*. http://tedcaseauthor.com/ product/power-plays/.

Castano, Emanuele, Vincent Yzerbyt, Maria-Paola Paladino, and Simona Sacchi. 2002. "I Belong, Therefore, I Exist: Ingroup Identification, Ingroup Entitativity, and Ingroup Bias." *Personality and Social Psychology Bulletin* 28, no. 2: 135–143. https://doi.org/10.1177/0146167202282001.

Castells, Manuel. 1996. *The Rise of the Network Society*. Cambridge, MA: Blackwell.

Chadwick, Henry. 1967. *The Early Church*. Baltimore: Penguin.

Chappellet-Lanier, Tajha. 2018. "Reports: Google Backs Down from Controversial Air Force AI Project." *FedScoop*. https://www.fedscoop.com/reports-google-backs-contro versial-air-force-ai-project/.

Charakham, Jonathan, and Anne Simpson. 1999. *Fair Shares: The Future of Shareholder Power and Responsibility*. New York: Oxford University Press.

Charpin, Dominique. 2012. *Hammurabi of Babylon*. London: Bloomsbury Publishing.

Chatters, Linda M., Robert Joseph Taylor, and Rukmalie Jayakody. 1994. "Fictive Kinship Relations in Black Extended Families." *Journal of Comparative Family Studies* 25, no. 3: 297–312. https://doi.org/10.3138/jcfs.25.3.297.

Chavalas, Mark W. 2014. *Women in the Ancient Near East: A Sourcebook*. London: Routledge.

Chittolini, Giorgio. 1989. "Cities, City-States, and Regional States in North-Central Italy." *Theory and Society* 18, no. 5: 689–706.

Cicero. 2009. *The Republic and the Law*. Oxford: Oxford University Press.

Cinalli, Manlio. 2002. "Environmental Campaigns and Socio-Political Cleavages in Divided Societies." *Environmental Politics* 11, no. 1: 163–171. https://doi.org/10.1080/714000594.

Cinalli, Manlio. 2003. "Socio-Politically Polarized Contexts and Urban Mobilization: A Study of Two Campaigns of Protest in Northern Ireland." *The International Journal for Urban and Regional Research* 27, no. 1: 158–177. https://doi.org/10.1111/1468-2427.00437.

Cinalli, Manlio. 2017. *Citizenship and the Political Integration of Muslims: The Relational Field of French Islam*. London: Palgrave. https://doi.org/10.1057/978-1-137-31224-2.

Cinalli, Manlio, and David Jacobson. 2020. "From Borders to Seams: The Role of Citizenship." In *Migration, Borders, and Citizenship: Between Policy and Public Spheres*, edited by Massimo Ambrosini, Manlio Cinalli, and David Jacobson, 27–45. Basingstoke: Palgrave. https://doi.org/10.1007/978-3-030-22157-7_2.

Cinalli, Manlio, and Marco Giugni. 2013. "Public Discourses About Muslims and Islam in Europe." *Ethnicities* 13, no. 2: 131–146. https://doi.org/10.1177/1468796812470897.

BIBLIOGRAPHY 203

Cinalli, Manlio, and Marco Giugni. 2016. "Electoral Participation of Muslims in Europe: Assessing the Impact of Institutional and Discursive Opportunities." *Journal of Ethnic and Migration Studies* 42, no. 2: 309–324. https://doi.org/10.1080/13691 83X.2015.1102043.

Cinalli, Manlio, and Steven M. Van Hauwaert. 2021. "Contentious Politics and Congruence Across Policy and Public Spheres: The Case of Muslims in France." *Ethnic and Racial Studies* 44, no. 14: 2532–2550. https://doi.org/10.1080/01419870.2020.1831567.

Cinalli, Manlio, Hans-Jorg Trenz, Verena Brändle, Olga Eisele, and Christian Lahusen. 2021. *Solidarity in the Media and Public Contention over Refugees in Europe.* London: Routledge. https://doi.org/10.4324/9780367817169.

Çıpa, Erdem H., and Emine Fetvacı. 2013. *Writing History at the Ottoman Court: Editing the Past, Fashioning the Future.* Bloomington: Indiana University Press.

CITES. 1973. "What is CITES?" *Convention on International Trade in Endangered Species of Wild Fauna and Flora.* https://cites.org/eng/disc/what.php.

Clark, Colin. 2016. "The Nation-State." In *The Routledge Handbook of Ethnic Conflict,* edited by Karl Cordell and Stefan Wolff, 44–53. London: Routledge.

Clarke, John. 2018 [1726]. *The Foundation of Morality in Theory and Practice Considered.* Farmington Hills: Gale Ecco.

Coase, Ronald Harry. 2012. *The Firm, the Market, and the Law.* Chicago: University of Chicago Press.

Cobb, John, and Herman Daly. 1989. *For the Common Good, Redirecting the Economy Toward Community, the Environment, and a Sustainable Future.* Boston: Beacon Press.

Cohen, Philip N., and Suzanne M. Bianchi. 1999. "Marriage, Children, and Women's Employment: What Do We Know?" *Monthly Labor Review* 122: 22–31.

Cohn Jr., Samuel K. 2008. *Lust for Liberty: The Politics of Social Revolt in Medieval Europe, 1200–1425.* Cambridge, MA: Harvard University Press.

Cohn Jr., Samuel K. 2022. *Popular Protest and Ideals of Democracy in Late Renaissance Italy.* Oxford: Oxford University Press.

Comino, Stefano, Alberto Galasso, and Clara Graziano. 2017. "The Diffusion of New Institutions: Evidence from Renaissance Venice's Patent System." *NBER.* Working Paper No. 24118. https://www.nber.org/papers/w24118.

Comte, August. 2019 [1853]. *Système de Politique Positive: Ou, Traité de Sociologie, Instituant la Religion de L'humanité.* Madrid: Hardpress Publishing.

Conger, Jay A. 1999. "Charismatic and Transformational Leadership in Organizations: An Insider's Perspective on These Developing Streams of Research." *The Leadership Quarterly* 10, no. 2: 145–179. https://doi.org/10.1016/ S1048-9843(99)00012-0.

Conger, Kate, and Noam Scheiber. 2020. "The Great Google Revolt." *The New York Times.* February 18. https://www.nytimes.com/interactive/2020/02/18/magazine/google-rev olt.html.

Cooley, Charles H. 1902. *Human Nature and the Social Order.* New York: Scribner's.

Cooper the 3rd Earl of Shaftesbury, Anthony Ashley. 2001 [1711]. *Characteristicks of Men, Manners, Opinions, Times. Vol. 1.* Edited by Douglas den Uyl. Indianapolis: Liberty Fund. 3 vols.

Copeland, Gary. 2019. "Fired by Google, a Republican Engineer Hits Back: 'There's Been a Lot of Bullying'." *Wall Street Journal.* August 1. https://www.wsj.com/articles/fired-by-google-a-republican-engineer-hits-back-theres-been-a-lot-of-bullying-11564651801.

204 BIBLIOGRAPHY

Cornell, Stephen. 1990. *The Return of the Native: American Indian Political Resurgence*. New York: Oxford University Press.

Coutinho, Carlos Nelson. 2000. "General Will and Democracy in Rousseau, Hegel, and Gramsci." *Rethinking Marxism* 12, no. 2: 1–17. https://doi.org/10.1080/0893569000 9358998.

Cowdrey, Herbert E. John. 1998. *Pope Gregory VII, 1073–1085*. Oxford: Clarendon Press.

Croxton, Derek. 1999. "The Peace of Westphalia of 1648 and the Origins of Sovereignty." *The International History Review* 21, no. 3: 569–591. https://doi.org/10.1080/07075 332.1999.9640869.

Cushing, Kathleen G. 2021. *Reform and Papacy in the Eleventh Century: Spirituality and Social Change*. Manchester: Manchester University Press.

Darling, Jonathan. 2008. "Domopolitics, Governmentality and the Regulation of Asylum Accommodation." *Political Geography* 30, no. 5: 263–271. https://doi.org/10.1016/j.pol geo.2011.04.011.

David, Barbara, and John C. Turner. 1996. "Studies in Self-categorization and Minority Conversion: Is Being a Member of the Out-group an Advantage?" *British Journal of Social Psychology* 35, no. 1: 179–199. https://doi.org/10.1111/j.2044-8309.1996.tb01 091.x.

Davidson, Cliff. 2015. "The University Corporatization Shift: A Longitudinal Analysis of University Admission Handbooks from 1980–2010." *Canadian Journal of Higher Education* 45, no. 2: 193–213. https://doi.org/10.47678/cjhe.v45i2.184441.

Davies, John K. 1993. *Democracy and Classical Greece*. Cambridge, MA: Harvard University Press.

Davies, Matthew. 2018. "Citizens and 'Foreyns': Crafts, Guilds and Regulation in Late Medieval London." In *Between Regulation and Freedom: Work and Manufactures in the European Cities, 14th–18th Centuries*, edited by Andrew Caracausi, Matthew Davies, and Luca Mocarelli, 1–22. Newcastle Upon Tyne: Cambridge Scholars.

Davis, Deborah, and Ezra Vogel, eds. 2020. *Chinese Society on the Eve of Tiananmen*. New York: Brill.

DeBoer, Frederick. 2015. "Why We Should Fear University, Inc." *The New York Times*. September 13. https://www.nytimes.com/2015/09/13/magazine/why-we-should-fear-university-inc.html?_r=1.

Deane, Herbert A. 1963. *The Political and Social Ideas of St. Augustine*. New York: Columbia University Press.

De la Croix, David, Matthias Doepke, and Joel Mokyr. 2018. "Clans, Guilds, and Markets: Apprenticeship Institutions and Growth in the Preindustrial Economy." *The Quarterly Journal of Economics* 133, no. 1: 1–70. https://doi.org/10.1093/qje/qjx026.

De Lazari-Radek, Katarzyna, and Peter Singer 2014. *The Point of View of the Universe: Sidgwick and Contemporary Ethics*. Oxford: Oxford University Press.

Della Porta, Donatella, and Massimiliano Andretta. 2002. "Changing Forms of Environmentalism in Italy: The Protest Campaign on the High-Speed Railway System." *Mobilization: An International Journal* 7, no. 1: 59–77. https://doi.org/10.17813/ maiq.7.1.j5248k8559158165.

Delli Carpini, Michael X., Fay Lomax Cook and Lawrence R. Jacobs. 2004. "Public Deliberation, Discursive Participation and Citizen Engagement: A Review of The Empirical Literature." *Annual Review of Political Science* 7: 315–344. https://doi.org/ 10.1146/annurev.polisci.7.121003.091630.

Dewhurst, Ruth L. 2013. "The Legacy of Luther: National Identity and State-Building in Early Nineteenth-Century Germany." PhD diss., Georgia State University.

BIBLIOGRAPHY 205

Diani, Mario, and Doug McAdam, eds. 2003. *Social Movements and Networks: Relational Approaches to Collective Action*. Oxford: Oxford University Press.

Diner, Hasia R., ed. 2021. *The Oxford Handbook of the Jewish Diaspora*. Oxford: Oxford University Press.

Disabato, Michael, and Katherine Ng. 2021. "The SFDR's Articles 8 and 9: The Funds Behind the Labels." *MSCI Report*. https://www.msci.com/www/research-paper/the-sfdr-s-articles-8-and-9-the/02612741814.

Dixon, Vernon. 1976. "Worldviews and Research Methodology." In *African Philosophy: Assumptions and Paradigms for Research and Black Persons*, edited by Lewis M. King, Vernon Dixon, and Wade W. Nobles, 51–102. Los Angeles: Fanon Centre Publication.

Douthat, Ross. 2020. *The Decadent Society: How We Became the Victims of Our Own Success*. New York: Simon and Schuster.

Dovidio, John F., Samuel L. Gaertner, and Gladys Kafati. 2000. "Group Identity and Intergroup Relations: The Common In-group Identity Model." *Advances in Group Processes*, edited by Shane R. Thye and Edward J. Lawler, 1–35. New York: Emerald Group Publishing Limited. https://doi.org/10.1016/S0882-6145(00)17002-X.

Doyle, Jack. 1979. "Lines Across the Land: Rural Electric Cooperatives, the Changing Politics of Energy in Rural America." The Rural Land & Energy Project, Environmental Policy Institute. Washington.

Dubb, Steve. 2018. "Historic Federal Law Gives Employee-Owned Businesses Access to SBA Loans." *Nonprofit Quarterly*. https://nonprofitquarterly.org/employee-owned-bus inesses-sbaloans/.

Durkheim, Émile. 1984 [1893]. *The Division of Labor in Society*. New York: Free Press.

Durkheim, Émile. 2005 [1897]. *Suicide: A Study in Sociology*. London: Routledge.

Džankić, Jelena. 2019. *The Global Market for Investor Citizenship*. Cham: Palgrave Macmillan.

Eavis, Peter. 2022. "Board Diversity Increased in 2021. Some Ask What Took So Long." *The New York Times*. January 3. https://www.nytimes.com/2022/01/03/business/corporate-board-diversity.html.

Ebaugh, Helen Rose, and Mary Curry. 2000. "Fictive Kin as Social Capital in New Immigrant Communities." *Sociological Perspectives* 43, no. 2: 189–209. https://doi.org/10.2307/1389793.

Eckstein, Nicholas A., and Nicholas Terpstra, eds. 2010. *Sociability and Its Discontents: Civil Society, Social Capital, and Their Alternatives in Late Medieval and Early Modern Europe*. Turnhout: Brepols Publishers.

Eder, Christina, Ingvill C. Mochmann, and Markus Quandt. 2014. *Political Trust and Disenchantment with Politics: International Perspectives*. Leiden: Brill.

Eisenstein, Hester. 2015. *Feminism Seduced: How Global Elites Use Women's Labor and Ideas to Exploit the World*. London: Routledge.

Eisner, Manuel P. 2014. "From Swords to Words: Does Macro-Level Change in Self-Control Predict Long-Term Variation in Levels of Homicide?" *Crime and Justice* 43, no. 1: 65–134. https://doi.org/10.1086/677662.

Ekelund, Robert B., Robert F. Hébert, Robert D. Tollison, Gary M. Anderson, and Audrey B. Davidson. 1996. *Sacred Trust: The Medieval Church as an Economic Firm*. New York: Oxford University Press.

Elazar, Daniel J. 2018. *Covenant and Polity in Biblical Israel: Biblical Foundations & Jewish Expressions*. London: Routledge.

206 BIBLIOGRAPHY

Elders, Leo J. 2019. *The Ethics of St. Thomas Aquinas: Happiness, Natural Law, and The Virtues*. Washington, DC: CUA Press. https://doi.org/10.2307/j.ctvcb5cmh.

Eliade, Mircea. 1957. *The Sacred and the Profane: The Nature of Religion*. New York: Harcourt.

Elias, Norbert. 1994 [1939]. *On the Process of Civilisation: Sociogenetic and Psychogenetic Investigations*. Oxford: Blackwell.

Elias, Norbert. 2021 [1978]. *The Civilizing Process*. Oxford: Blackwell.

Elias, Norbert, and John L. Scotson. 1994 [1965]. *The Established and the Outsiders*. London: Sage.

Eliav-Feldon, Miriam, Benjamin Isaac, and Joseph Ziegler, eds. 2009. *The Origins of Racism in the West*. Cambridge: Cambridge University Press.

England, Paula. 2010. "The Gender Revolution: Uneven and Stalled." *Gender & Society* 24, no. 2: 149–166. https://doi.org/10.1177/0891243210361475.

England, Paula, Carmen Garcia-Beaulieu, and Mary Ross. 2004. "Women's Employment among Blacks, Whites, and Three Groups of Latinas: Do More Privileged Women have Higher Employment? *Gender & Society* 18, no. 4: 494–509. https://doi.org/10.1177/0891243204265632.

Erdkamp, Paul, Koenraad Verboven, and Arjan Zuiderhoek, eds. 2015. *Ownership and Exploitation of Land and Natural Resources in the Roman World*. Oxford: Oxford University Press. https://doi.org/10.1093/acprof:oso/9780198728924.001.0001.

Espejo, Paulina Ochoa. 2020. *On Borders*. Oxford: Oxford University Press.

Esser, Raingard. 2007. "Concordia Res Parvae Crescunt'. Regional Histories and the Dutch Republic in the Seventeenth Century." In *Public Opinion and Changing Identities in the Early Modern Netherlands*, edited by Pollmann Judith and Andrew Spicer, 229–248. Leiden: Brill. https://doi.org/10.1163/ej.9789004155275.i-310.19.

European Commission. 2022. "Golden Passport' Schemes: Commission Proceeds with Infringement Case against Malta." *Europa*. https://ec.europa.eu/commission/presscorner/detail/en/IP_22_2068.

Falk, Richard. 2008 *Achieving Human Rights*. London: Routledge.

Fanon, Frantz. 2002. *The Wretched of the Earth*. London: Penguin.

Farrell, Zoe. 2020. "The Materiality of Marriage in the Artisan Community of Renaissance Verona." *The Historical Journal* 63, no. 2: 243–266. https://doi.org/10.1017/S0018246X19000335.

Farro, Antimo Luigi, and Simone Maddanu. 2022. *Restless Cities on the Edge: Collective Actions, Immigration and Populism*. Cham: Palgrave Macmillan. https://doi.org/10.1007/978-3-030-91323-6.

Favell, Adrian. 1998. *Philosophies of Integration: Immigration and the Idea of Citizenship in France and Britain*. Houndmills: Palgrave.

Favell, Adrian. 2022. *The Integration Nation: Immigration and Colonial Power in Liberal Democracies*. Cambridge: Polity.

Fennema, Meindert, and Jean Tillie. 1999. "Political Participation and Political Trust in Amsterdam: Civic Communities and Ethnic Networks." *Journal of Ethnic and Migration Studies* 25: 703–726. https://doi.org/10.1080/1369183X.1999.9976711.

Fennema, Meindert, and Jean Tillie. 2001. "Civic Community, Political Participation and Political Trust of Ethnic Groups." *Connections* 24: 26–41. https://doi.org/10.1007/978-3-322-85129-1_9.

Ferrante, Elena. 2022. *In the Margins: On the Pleasures of Reading and Writing*. New York: Europa Editions.

Fetzer, Joel S. 2012. "Public Opinion and Populism." In *Oxford Handbook of the Politics of International Migration*, edited by Marc R. Rosenblum and Daniel J. Tichenor, 301–323. Oxford: Oxford University Press.

Fewsmith, Joseph. 1983. "From Guild to Interest Group: The Transformation of Public and Private in Late Qing China." *Comparative Studies in Society and History* 25, no. 4: 617–640. https://doi.org/10.1017/S0010417500010641.

Fichte, Johann Gottlieb. 2013. *Addresses to the German Nation*. Translated by Isaac Nakhimovsky, Béla Kapossy and Keith Tribe. Indianapolis: Hackett Publishing Company.

Finkel, Caroline. 2007. *Osman's Dream: The History of the Ottoman Empire*. New York: Basic Books.

Finotelli, Claudia, and Ines Michalowski. 2012. "The Heuristic Potential of Models of Citizenship and Immigrant Integration Reviewed." *Journal of Immigrant & Refugee Studies* 10, no. 3: 231–240. https://doi.org/10.1080/15562948.2012.693033.

Fishkin, James. 1997. *The Voice of the People*. New Haven: Yale University Press.

Fishkin, James. 2009. *When the People Speak: Deliberative Democracy and Public Consultation*. Oxford: Oxford University Press. https://doi.org/10.1093/acprof:osobl/9780199604432.001.0001.

Fitzgerald, David Scott. 2014. *Culling the Masses: The Democratic Origins of Racist Immigration Policy in the Americas*. Cambridge, MA: Harvard University Press.

Fitzsimmons, Michael P. 2010. *From Artisan to Worker: Guilds, the French State, and the Organization of Labor, 1776–1821*. Cambridge: Cambridge University Press.

Føllesdal, Andreas, Birgit Peters, and Geir Ulfstein, eds. 2013. *Constituting Europe: The European Court of Human Rights in a National, European and Global Context*. New York: Cambridge University Press. https://doi.org/10.1017/CBO9781139169295.

Forest Legality. 2021. "China." *Forest Legality*. https://forestlegality.org/risk-tool/country/china.

Forsythe, Gary. 2007. "The Army and Centuriate Organization in Early Rome." In *A Companion to the Roman Army*, edited by Paul Erdkamp, 24–41. Oxford: Blackwell.

Fourcade, Marion. 2021. "Ordinal Citizenship." *British Journal of Sociology* 72, no. 2: 154–173. https://doi.org/10.1111/1468-4446.12839.

Fourcade, Marion, and Jeffrey Gordon. 2020. "Learning Like a State: Statecraft in the Digital Age." *Journal of Law and Political Economy* 1, no. 1: 78–108. http://dx.doi.org/10.5070/LP61150258.

Friedman, Lawrence M. 1985. *Total Justice*. New York: Russell Sage Foundation.

Friedman, Milton.1962. *Capitalism and Freedom*. Chicago: University of Chicago Press.

Friedrichs, Christopher R. 1990. "Anti-Jewish Politics in Early Modern Germany: The Uprising in Worms, 1613–17." *Central European History* 23, no. 2–3: 91–152. https://doi.org/10.1017/S0008938900021324.

Frith, Chris D., and Uta Frith. 2007. "Social Cognition in Humans." *Current Biology* 17, no. 16: 724–732. https://doi.org/10.1016/j.cub.2007.05.068.

Frith, Chris D., and Uta Frith. 2012. "Mechanisms of Social Cognition." *Annual Review of Psychology* 63: 287–313. https://doi.org/10.1146/annurev-psych-120710-100449.

Fritzsche, Peter. 2009. *Life and Death in the Third Reich*. Cambridge, MA: Harvard University Press.

Gaertner, Lowell, and Chester A. Insko. 2000. "Intergroup Discrimination in the Minimal Group Paradigm: Categorization, Reciprocation, or Fear?" *Journal of Personality and Social Psychology* 79, no. 1: 77.

208 BIBLIOGRAPHY

Galston, William A. 2018. *Anti-Pluralism*. New Haven, CT: Yale University Press. https://doi.org/10.12987/yale/9780300228922.001.0001.

Gamble, Sidney D., and J. S. Burgess 1921. *Peking: A Social Survey*. New York: George H. Doran.

Gamson, William A. 1992. *Talking Politics*. New York: Cambridge University Press.

Gardner, Jane F. 2002. *Being a Roman Citizen*. London: Routledge. https://doi.org/10.4324/9780203032121.

Garrard, Graeme. 1994. "Rousseau, Maistre, and the Counter-Enlightenment." *History of Political Thought* 15, no. 1: 97–120. http://www.jstor.org/stable/26214387.

Gates Jr., Henry L. 1992. *Loose Cannons: Notes on the Culture Wars*. New York: Oxford University Press.

Gates Jr., Henry L. 2022. *Who's Black and Why: A Hidden Chapter from the Eighteenth-Century Invention of Race*. Cambridge, MA: Harvard University Press.

Gavison, Ruth. 1992. "Feminism and the Public/Private Distinction." *Stanford Law Review* 45, no. 1: 1–45. https://doi.org/10.2307/1228984.

Gellner, Ernest. 1983. *Nations and Nationalism*. Oxford: Blackwell.

Gellner, Ernest. 1994. *Conditions of Liberty: Civil Society and its Rivals*. New York: Viking Penguin.

Georgescu-Roegen, Nicholas. 1971. *The Entropy Law and Economic Process*. Cambridge: Cambridge University Press.

Gerritsen, Rupert. 2011. "A Translation of the Charter of the Dutch East India Company (Verenigde e Oostindische Compagnie or VOC)." *Australia on the Map Division of the Australasian Hydrographic Society*. https://rupertgerritsen.tripod.com/pdf/published/_Labours_with_Cover.pdf.

Gerstle, Gary. 2022. *The Rise and Fall of the Neoliberal Order: America and the World in the Free Market Era*. New York: Oxford University Press.

Ghaffary, Shirin. 2019. "Political Tension at Google is Only Getting Worse." *Vox*. August 2. https://www.vox.com/recode/2019/8/2/20751822/google-employee-dissent-james-damore-cernekee-conservatives-bias.

Ghaffary, Shirin.2019a. "Google's Attempt to Shut Down a Unionization Meeting Just Riled up its Employees." *Vox*. October 21. https://www.vox.com/recode/2019/10/21/20924697/google-unionization-switzerland-zurich-syndicom-zooglers/.

Giddens, Anthony. 1987. *Social Theory and Modern Sociology*. Stanford: Stanford University Press.

Giddens, Anthony. 1991. *The Consequences of Modernity*. Stanford: Stanford University Press.

Gilbert, Felix. 1968. "The Venetian Constitution in Florentine Political Thought." In *Florentine Studies: Politics and Society in Renaissance Florence*, edited by Nicolai Rubinstein, 463–500. London: Faber and Faber.

Gills, Barry, ed. 2000. *Globalization and the Politics of Resistance*. Basingstoke: Palgrave.

Ginsberg, Benjamin, and Elizabeth E. Sanders.1990. "Theodore J. Lowi and Juridical Democracy." *Political Science & Politics* 23, no. 4: 563–566. https://doi.org/10.2307/419891.

Giugni, Marco, and Florence Passy. 2001. *Political Altruism? Solidarity Movement in International Perspective*. New York: Rowman & Littlefield.

Global Justice Now. 2016. "The 10 Biggest Corporations Make More Money than Most Countries in the World Combined." *Global Justice Now*. https://www.globaljustice.org.uk/news/10-biggest-corporations-make-more-money-most-countries-world-combined/.

Goffman, Erving. 1959. *The Presentation of Self in Everyday Life*. New York: Anchor.

Goldsmith, Maurice M. 1985. *Private Vices, Public Benefits: Bernard Mandeville's Social and Political Thought*. Cambridge: Cambridge University Press.

Gomes, Bjorn. 2020. "Rousseau on Citizenship and Education." In *The Palgrave Handbook of Citizenship and Education*, edited by Andrew Peterson, Garth Stahl, and Hannah Soong, 79–93. London: Palgrave. https://doi.org/10.1007/978-3-319-67828-3_50.

Gómez-Estern, Beatriz Macías, and Manuel L. de la Mata Benitez. 2013. "Narratives of Migration: Emotions and the Interweaving of Personal and Cultural Identity Through Narrative." *Culture & Psychology* 19, no. 3: 348–368. https://doi.org/10.1177/13540 67X13489316.

Goodhart, David. 2017. *The Road to Somewhere: The Populist Revolt and the Future of Politics*. London: Hurst.

Goodwin-White, Jamie. 2020. "Today We March, Tomorrow We Vote! Contested Denizenship, Immigration Federalism, and the Dreamers." In *Migration, Borders, and Citizenship*, edited by Maurizio Ambrosini, Manlio Cinalli, and David Jacobson, 61–88. London: Palgrave Macmillan. https://doi.org/10.1007/978-3-030-22157-7_4.

Gordon, Daniel. 1994. *Citizens without Sovereignty: Equality and Sociability in French Thought, 1670–1789*. Princeton: Princeton University Press.

Gordon, Peter E. 2022. "In Search of Recognition." *The New York Review of Books*. June 23. https://www.nybooks.com/articles/2022/06/23/in-search-of-recognition-axel-honn eth-gordon/.

Gordon, Scott. 2009. *Controlling the State: Constitutionalism from Ancient Athens to Today*. Cambridge, MA: Harvard University Press.

Goyette, John, Mark S. Latkovic, and Richard S. Myers, eds. 2004. *St. Thomas Aquinas and the Natural Law Tradition: Contemporary Perspectives*. Washington, DC: CUA Press. https://doi.org/10.2307/j.ctt285340.

Graeber, David, and David Wengrow. 2021. *The Dawn of Everything: A New History of Humanity*. London: Penguin UK.

Grady, Robert C.1984. "Juridical Democracy and Democratic Values: An Evaluation of Lowi's Alternative to Interest-Group Liberalism." *Polity* 16, no. 3: 404–422. https://doi. org/10.2307/3234557.

Gramsci, Antonio. 2011 [1929–1935]. *Prison Notebooks*. New York: Columbia University Press.

Granovetter, Mark S. 1973. "The Strength of Weak Ties." *American Journal of Sociology* 78, no. 6: 1360–1380. https://www.jstor.org/stable/2776392.

Grazioli, Margherita. 2021. *Housing, Urban Commons and the Right to the City in Post-Crisis Rome: Metropoliz, The Squatted Città Meticcia*. Cham: Springer Nature.

Greaves, Richard L. 1982. "Concepts of Political Obedience in Late Tudor England: Conflicting Perspectives." *The Journal of British Studies* 22, no. 1: 23–34. https://doi.org/10.1086/385795.

Green, Dennis. 2016. "The World's Top 100 Economies: 31 Countries; 69 Corporations." *F2P2*. https://oxfamapps.org/fp2p/the-worlds-top-100-economies-31-countries-69-corporations/.

Green, Jeffrey Edward. 2010. *The Eyes of the People: Democracy in an Age of Spectatorship*. Oxford: Oxford University Press.

Greif, Avner, and Guido Tabellini. 2017. "The Clan and the Corporation: Sustaining Cooperation in China and Europe." *Journal of Comparative Economics* 45, no. 1: 1–35. https://doi.org/10.1016/j.jce.2016.12.003.

210 BIBLIOGRAPHY

Groenhuis, Gerrit. 1981. "Calvinism and National Consciousness: The Dutch Republic as the New Israel." In *Britain and the Netherlands, Vol. VII, Church and State since the Reformation*, edited by A. C. Duke and C. A. Tamse, 118–133. The Hague: Martinus Nijhoff.

Grosby, Steven. 2002. *Biblical Ideas of Nationality, Ancient and Modern*. Philadelphia: University of Pennsylvania Press.

Grosby, Steven. 2018. "Time, Kinship, and the Nation." *Genealogy* 2, no. 2: 17. https://doi. org/10.3390/genealogy2020017.

Grosby, Steven. 2020. "Borders and States." In *A Companion to The Ancient Near East*, edited by Daniel C. Snell, 225–241. Hoboken: John Wiley & Sons.

Grosby, Steven. 2023. "Nationality and Ethnicity in the Ancient Near East." In *Cambridge History of Nationhood and Nationalism*, edited by Cathie Carmichael, Matthew D'Auria, and Aviel Roshwald, 11–30. Cambridge: Cambridge University Press.

Guenzi, Alberto, Paola Massa, and F. Piola Caselli, eds. 1998. *Guilds, Markets and Work Regulations in Italy, 16th–19th Centuries*. London: Ashgate Publishing.

Guibbory, Achsah. 2014. "Commonwealth, Chosenness and Toleration: Reconsidering the Jews' Readmission to England and the Idea of an Elect Nation." In *Religious Tolerance in the Atlantic World*, edited by Eliane Glaser, 193–213. London: Palgrave.

Gurr, Ted R. 2015. *Why Men Rebel*. Princeton, NJ: Princeton University Press. https://doi. org/10.4324/9781315631073.

Gurri, Martin. 2018. *The Revolt of the Public and the Crisis of Authority in the New Millennium*. San Francisco: Stripe Press.

Habermas, Jürgen. 1984. *The Theory of Communicative Action, Vol 1: Reason and the Rationalization of Society*. Translated by Thomas McCarthy. Boston: Beacon Press. https://doi.org/10.2307/2185595.

Habermas, Jürgen. 1989. *The Structural Transformation of the Public Sphere: An Inquiry into a Category of Bourgeois Society*. Translated by Thomas Burger. Cambridge: MIT Press.

Habermas, Jürgen. 1996. "National Unification and Popular Sovereignty." *New Left Review* 219: 3–13.

Habermas, Jürgen. 1998a. "Reconciliation through the Public Use of Reason." In *The Inclusion of the Other*, edited by Ciaran Cronin and Pablo De Greiff, 49–73. Cambridge: Polity Press.

Habermas, Jürgen. 1998b. "The European Nation-State: On the Past and Future of Sovereignty and Citizenship." *Public Culture* 10, no. 2: 397–416. https://doi.org/ 10.1215/08992363-10-2-397.

Habermas, Jürgen. 2002. *The Inclusion of the Other: Studies in Political Theory*. Edited by Ciaran Cronin and Pablo De Greiff. Cambridge: Polity.

Habermas, Jürgen. 2006. *Time of Transitions*. Cambridge: Polity.

Hall, Jonathan M. 2002. *Hellenicity: Between Ethnicity and Culture*. Chicago: University of Chicago Press.

Handlin, Oscar, and Mary F. Handlin.1945. "Origins of the American Business Corporation." *The Journal of Economic History* 5, no. 1: 1–23. https://doi.org/10.1017/ S0022050700112318.

Handy, Charles B. 1998. *The Hungry Spirit: Beyond Capitalism: A Quest for Purpose in the Modern World*. London: Random House.

Hansen, Mogens Herman. 2013. "Greek City-States." In *The Oxford Handbook of the State in the Ancient Near East and Mediterranean*, edited by Fibiger P. Bang and Walter Scheidel, 259–278. Oxford: Oxford University Press. https://doi.org/10.1093/oxfor dhb/9780195188318.013.0010.

BIBLIOGRAPHY 211

Hansen, Mogens Herman. 2015. *Political Obligation in Ancient Greece and in the Modern World*. Copenhagen: Videnskabernes Selskab.

Hansen, Randall. 2009. "The Poverty of Postnationalism: Citizenship, Immigration, and the New Europe." *Theory and Society* 38: 1–24. https://doi.org/10.1007/s11 186-008-9074-0.

Harari, Yuval Noah. 2014. *Sapiens: A Brief History of Humankind*. London: Harvill Secker.

Harpaz, Yossi, and Pablo Mateos. 2019. "Strategic Citizenship: Negotiating Membership in the Age of Dual Nationality." *Journal of Ethnic and Migration Studies* 45, no. 6: 843–857. https://doi.org/10.1080/1369183X.2018.1440482.

Harris, James. A. 2005. *Of Liberty and Necessity: The Free Will Debate in Eighteenth-Century British Philosophy*. Oxford: Oxford University Press. https://doi.org/10.1093/0199268606.001.0001.

Harris, James A. 2008. "Religion in Hutcheson's Moral Philosophy." *Journal of the History of Philosophy* 46, no. 2: 205–222. https://doi.org/10.1353/hph.0.0017.

Haslam, S. Alexander, Stephen D. Reicher, and Michael J. Platow. 2020. *The New Psychology of Leadership: Identity, Influence and Power*. London: Routledge.

Hastings, Rashdall. 1895. *The Universities of Europe in the Middle Ages*. Paris: Clarendon Press. https://doi.org/10.1017/CBO9780511722301.

Hatton, Timothy J. 2016. "Immigration, Public Opinion and the Recession in Europe." *Economic Policy* 31, no. 86: 205–246. https://doi.org/10.1093/epolic/eiw004.

Havercroft, Jonathan. 2012. "Was Westphalia 'All That'? Hobbes, Bellarmine, and the Norm of Non-Intervention." *Global Constitutionalism* 1, no. 1: 120–140. https://doi.org/10.1017/S2045381711000104.

Hayek, Friedrich. 1982. *Law, Legislation and Liberty: A New Statement of the Liberal Principles of Justice and Political Economy*. London: Routledge.

Hayek, Friedrich. 2013. *The Fatal Conceit: The Errors of Socialism*. London: Routledge.

Hayes, Graeme. 2005. *Environmental Protest and the State in France*. Basingstoke: Palgrave.

Heilbroner, Robert L. 2012. *The Making of Economic Society*. Englewood Cliffs: Prentice- Hall.

Herberg, Will.1983. *Protestant—Catholic—Jew: An Essay in American Religious Sociology*. Chicago: University of Chicago Press.

Herodotus. 2003. *The Histories*. London: Penguin.

Hetherington, Marc J. 1998. "The Political Relevance of Political Trust." *American Political Science Review* 92, no. 4: 791–808. https://doi.org/10.2307/2586304.

Hinsley, Harry. 1986. *Sovereignty*. Cambridge, UK: Cambridge University Press.

Hirschi, Caspar. 2012. *The Origins of Nationalism: An Alternative History from Ancient Rome to Early Modern Germany*. New York: Cambridge University Press.

Hirschman, Albert O. 1977. *The Passions and the Interests: Political Arguments for Capitalism before Its Triumph*. Princeton: Princeton University Press.

Hobbes, Thomas. 2020a [1651]. *The Leviathan*. Oliver: Engage.

Hobbes, Thomas. 2020b [1642]. *De Cive*. Denver: Random Shack.

Hobsbawm, Eric. 1990. *Nations and Nationalism since 1780: Programme, Myth, Reality*. Cambridge, UK: Cambridge University Press.

Hofmann, Andreas, and Daniel Naurin. 2021. "Explaining Interest Group Litigation in Europe: Evidence from the Comparative Interest Group Survey." *Governance* 34, no. 4: 1235–1253. https://doi.org/10.1111/gove.12556.

Hollinger, Dennis P. 1983. *Individualism and Social Ethics: An Evangelical Syncretism*. New York: University Press of America.

212 BIBLIOGRAPHY

Honneth, Axel. 2020. *Recognition: A Chapter in the History of European Ideas*. New York: Cambridge University Press.

Hooker, Juliet. 2020. "How Can the Democratic Party Confront Racist Backlash? White Grievance in Hemispheric Perspective." *Polity* 52, no. 3: 355–369. https://doi.org/10.1086/708946.

Hornby, Nick. 2014. *Fever Pitch*. New York: Viking Books.

Hornsey, Matthew J., and Michael A. Hogg. 2000. "Assimilation and Diversity: An Integrative Model of Subgroup Relations." *Personality and Social Psychology Review* 4, no. 2: 143–156. https://doi.org/10.1207/S15327957PSPR0402_03.

Howard, Marc Morjé. 2009. *The Politics of Citizenship in Europe*. Cambridge: Cambridge University Press.

Hume, David. 1982 [1882]. *A Treatise of Human Nature*. London: Penguin.

Hutcheson, Francis. 2003. *Preface to An Essay on the Nature and Conduct of the Passions and Affections with Illustrations on the Moral Sense*. Indianapolis: Liberty Fund.

Hutchinson, John. 1987 *Dynamics of Cultural Nationalism: The Gaelic Revival and the Creation of the Irish Nation State*. Crow's Nest: Unwin Hyman.

Iacoboni, Marco. 2009. *Mirroring People: The Science of Empathy and How We Connect with Others*. London: Picador.

Ikerd, John. 2005. *Sustainable Capitalism: A Matter of Common Sense*. Boulder: Lynne Rienner.

Ilany, Ofri. 2018. *In Search of the Hebrew People: Bible and Nation in the German Enlightenment*. Bloomington: Indiana University Press.

Inglehart, Ronald. 1977. *The Silent Revolution. Changing Values and Political Styles among Western Publics*. Princeton: Princeton University Press.

International Covenant on Civil and Political Rights. 2016. "Fifty Years of Fighting for Rights and Freedom." *ICCP*. https://2covenants.ohchr.org/.

"International Tropical Timber Agreement." 2006. Opened for signature February 1, 2006. United Nations Conference on Trade and Development TD/TIMBER.3/12 (2006), https://www.itto.int/council_committees/itta/. The noted quotation is found in Chapter 1, Article 1(n) of the treaty.

Ireland, Patrick. 1994. *The Policy Challenge of Ethnic Diversity*. Cambridge, MA: Harvard University Press.

Isaac, Benjamin. 2013. *The Invention of Racism in Classical Antiquity*. Princeton: Princeton University Press.

Isin, Engin. 2012. *Citizens without Frontiers*. London: Bloomsbury.

Israel, Jonathan I. 2002. *Radical Enlightenment: Philosophy and the Making of Modernity 1650–1750*. Oxford: Oxford University Press.

Jacobson, David. 1996. *Rights Across Borders: Immigration and the Decline of Citizenship*. Baltimore: John Hopkins University Press.

Jacobson, David. 1997. "New Frontiers: Territory, Social Spaces, and the State." *Sociological Forum* 12, no. 1: 121–133. https://doi.org/10.1023/A:1024612808184.

Jacobson, David. 2002. *Place and Belonging in America*. Baltimore: Johns Hopkins University Press.

Jacobson, David. 2003. "Europe's Post-Democracy?" *Society* 40, 2: 70–76. https://doi.org/10.1007/s12115-003-1054-4.

Jacobson, David. 2009. "When the Rights of Women Trump the Claims of Cultures." In *Citizenship, Borders, and Gender: Mobility and Immobility*, edited by Seyla Benhabib and Judith Resnik, 304–322. New York: New York University Press.

BIBLIOGRAPHY   213

Jacobson, David. 2013. *Of Virgins and Martyrs: Women and Sexuality in Global Conflict.* Baltimore: John Hopkins University Press.

Jacobson, David, and Galya Benarieh Ruffer. 2003. "Courts across Borders: The Implications of Judicial Agency for Human Rights and Democracy." *Human Rights Quarterly* 25: 74–92. https://doi.org/10.1353/hrq.2003.0005.

Jacobson, David, and Jamie Goodwin-White. 2018. "The Future of Postnational Citizenship: Human Rights and Borders in a Re-nationalizing world." *Mondi Migranti* 2: 7–26. http://digital.casalini.it/10.3280/MM2018-002001.

Jacobson, David, and Ning Wang. 2008. "What If the Model Does Not Tell the Whole Story? The Clock, the Natural Forest, and the New Global Studies." *New Global Studies* 2, no. 3: 1–24. https://doi.org/10.2202/1940-0004.1035.

Jacobson, David, Jamie Sommer, Andrew Hargrove, Georgi Georgiev, and Michele Aquino. 2022. "The ESG Onramp: From Organized Hypocrisy to Normative Practice." Unpublished manuscript, University of South Florida.

Jaspers, Karl. 2014 [1949]. *The Origin and Goal of History.* London: Routledge.

Jeannet, Anne-Marie, Esther Ademmer, Martin Ruhs, and Tobias Stöhr. 2020. *A Need for Control? Political Trust and Public Preferences for Asylum and Refugee Policy.* San Domenico di Fiesole: EUI RSCAS, Migration Policy Centre.

Jennings, Ivor. 1963 [1956]. *The Approach to Self-Government.* Cambridge: Cambridge University Press.

Jetten, Jolanda, Tom Postmes, and Brendan J. McAuliffe. 2002. "'We're All Individuals: Group Norms of Individualism and Collectivism, Levels of Identification and Identity Threat." *European Journal of Social Psychology* 32, no. 2: 189–207. https://doi.org/10.1002/ejsp.65.

Joannès, Francis, ed. 2001. *Dictionnaire de la Civilisation Mésopotamienne.* Paris: Laffont.

Johnstone, Steven. 2011. *A History of Trust in Ancient Greece.* Chicago: University of Chicago Press.

Jones, Meirav, and Yossi Shain. 2017. "Modern Sovereignty and the Non-Christian, or Westphalia's Jewish State." *Review of International Studies* 43, no. 5: 918–938. https://doi.org/10.1017/S0260210517000195.

Jones, Philip. 1997. *The Italian City-State: From Commune to Signoria.* Oxford: Clarendon Press.

Jones, Steven. 2007. *Antonio Gramsci.* London: Routledge.

Joppke, Christian. 1999. *Immigration and the Nation-State: The United States, Germany, and Great Britain.* Oxford: Clarendon Press.

Joppke, Christian. 2007. "Beyond National Models: Civic Integration Policies for Immigrants in Western Europe." *West European Politics* 30, no. 1: 1–22. https://doi.org/10.1080/01402380601019613.

Joppke, Christian. 2010. "The Inevitable Lightening of Citizenship." *European Journal of Sociology* 51, no. 1: 9–32. https://doi.org/10.1017/S0003975610000019.

Joppke, Christian. 2019. "The Instrumental Turn of Citizenship." *Journal of Ethnic and Migration Studies* 45, no. 6: 858–878. https://doi.org/10.1080/1369183X.2018.1440484.

Jordan, Miriam. 2018. "ICE Came for a Tennessee Town's Immigrants: The Town Fought Back." *The New York Times.* June 11. https://www.nytimes.com/interactive/2018/06/11/us/tennessee-immigration-trump.html.

Joshi, Shirley, and Bob Carter. 1984. "The Role of Labour in the Creation of a Racist Britain." *Race & Class* 25, no. 3: 53–70. https://doi.org/10.1177/030639688402500305.

214 BIBLIOGRAPHY

Jurdjevic, Mark. 2010. "Voluntary Associations Reconsidered: Compagnie and Arti in Florentine Politics." In *Sociability and Its Discontents: Civil Society, Social Capital, and Their Alternatives in Late Medieval and Early Modern Europe*, edited by Nicholas A. Eckstein and Nicholas Terpstra, 249–271. Turnhout: Brepols Publishers.

Kafadar, Cemal. 1996. *Between Two Worlds: The Construction of the Ottoman State*. Berkeley: University of California Press.

Kakar, Sudhir. 1996. *The Colors of Violence: Cultural Identities, Religion, and Conflict*. Chicago: University of Chicago Press.

Kamali, Masoud. 2010. *Racial Discrimination: Institutional Patterns and Politics*. London: Routledge.

Kaplan, Steven L., and Cynthia J. Koepp. 1988. *Work in France: Representations, Meaning, Organization, and Practice*. Ithaca, NY: Cornell University Press.

Karataşlı, Şahan Savaş. 2016. "From Communal Patriotism to City-state Chauvinism: Transformation of Collective Identities in Northern Italy, 1050–1500." *International Journal of Politics, Culture, and Society* 29: 73–101.

Karpat, Kemal H., and Robert W. Zens. 2004. *Ottoman Borderlands: Issues, Personalities, and Political Changes*. Madison: University of Wisconsin Press.

Katz, Marilyn. 1992. "Ideology and the Status of Women in Ancient Greece." *History and Theory* 31, no. 4: 70–97. https://doi.org/10.2307/2505416.

Katz, Marilyn. 1999. "Women and Democracy in Ancient Greece." In *Contextualizing Classics: Ideology, Performance, Dialogue*, edited by Thomas M. Falkner, Nancy Felson, and David Konstan, 41–68. Lanham: Rowman & Littlefield.

Kaufmann, Eric. 2018. *Whiteshift: Populism, Immigration, and the Future of White Majorities*. London: Penguin.

Keane, John. 2021. "David Stasavage, The Decline and Rise of Democracy: A Global History from Antiquity to Today." *Society* 58: 235–240. https://doi.org/10.1007/s12115-021-00600-z.

Keck, Margaret E., and Kathryn Sikkink. 1998. *Activists Beyond Borders: Advocacy Networks in International Politics*. Ithaca: Cornell University Press.

Keller, Helen, and Alec Stone Sweet, eds. 2008. *A Europe of Rights: The Impact of the ECHR on National Legal Systems*. Oxford: Oxford University Press.

Kelly, Luke. 2019. *Overview of Research on Far-Right Extremism in the Western Balkans*. Brighton, UK: Institute of Development Studies. https://opendocs.ids.ac.uk/opendocs/bitstream/handle/20.500.12413/14571/620_Western_Balkans_far_Right.pdf?sequence=1&isAllowed=y.

Kessler, Amalia D. 2007. *A Revolution in Commerce: The Parisian Merchant Court and the Rise of Commercial Society in Eighteenth-Century France*. New Haven: Yale University Press.

Keynes, John M. 2010 [1926]. "The End of Laissez-Faire." In *Essays in Persuasion*, 272–294. London: Palgrave Macmillan.

Kiernan, Ben. 2008. *Blood and Soil: A World History of Genocide and Extermination from Sparta to Darfur*. New Haven: Yale University Press.

Kılıç, Kutbettin. 2020. "Negotiating the Meaning of Kurdishness: The Construction of a Secular Kurdish Identity Perception by Kurdish Political and Intellectual Elites in Turkey." *Middle Eastern Studies* 56, no. 6: 811–825. https://doi.org/10.1080/00263206.2020.1768373.

BIBLIOGRAPHY   215

Kingo, Lise. 2019. "The UN Global Compact: Finding Solutions to Global Challenges." United Nations. https://www.un.org/en/un-chronicle/un-global-compact-finding-solutions-global-challenges#:~:text=The%20UN%20Global%20Compact%20is,the%20implementation%20of%20the%20SDGs.

Kirkpatrick, Jean. 1979. "Dictatorships and Double Standards." *Commentary Magazine* 68, no. 5: 34–45.

Klein, Ezra. 2021. "'David Shor Is Telling Democrats What They Don't Want to Hear." *The New York Times*. October 8. https://www.nytimes.com/2021/10/08/opinion/democrats-david-shor-education-polarization.html.

Knoppers, Gary N., and Bernard M. Levinson. 2007. *The Pentateuch as Torah: New Models for Understanding Its Promulgation and Acceptance.* Philadelphia: University of Pennsylvania Press.

Kochenov, Dimitry. 2019. *Citizenship.* Boston: MIT Press.

Kocka, Jürgen. 2010. *Civil Society and Dictatorship in Modern German History.* Waltham, MA: Brandeis University Press.

Kofman Eleonore. 2002. "Contemporary European Migrations, Civic Society, and Citizenship." *Political Geography* 21: 1035–1054.

Kohn, Hans. 1944. *The Idea of Nationalism: A Study in its Origins and Background.* New York: Macmillan.

Kohn, Hans. 1955. *Nationalism: Its Meaning and History.* New York: Van Nostrand.

Kohn, Hans. 1962. *The Age of Nationalism: The First Era of Global History.* New York: Harper and Row.

Kohn, Hans. 2017 [1944]. *The Idea of Nationalism: A Study in its Origins and Background.* New York: Routledge.

Koo, Jeong-Woo, and Francisco O. Ramirez. 2009. "National Incorporation of Global Human Rights: Worldwide Expansion of National Human Rights Institutions, 1966–2004." *Social Forces* 87, no. 3: 1321–1353. https://doi.org/10.1353/sof.0.0167.

Koopmans, Ruud, and Paul Statham. 1999. "Challenging the Liberal Nation-State? Postnationalism, Multiculturalism, and the Collective Claims Making of Migrants and Ethnic Minorities in Britain and Germany." *American Journal of Sociology* 105, no. 3: 652–696. https://doi.org/10.1086/210357.

Koopmans, Ruud, Paul Statham, Marco Giugni, and Florence Passy. 2005. *Contested Citizenship: Immigration and Cultural Diversity in Europe.* Minneapolis: University of Minnesota Press.

Kornhauser, William. 1959. *The Politics of Mass Society.* New York: Free Press.

Koselleck, Reinhart. 2002. *The Practice of Conceptual History.* Stanford: Stanford University Press.

Kott, Sandrine, and Kiran Klaus Patel. 2018. *Nazism across Borders: The Social Policies of the Third Reich and Their Global Appeal.* Oxford: Oxford University Press.

Krailsheimer, Alban J. 1962. *Studies in Self-Interest: From Descartes to La Bruyere.* Oxford: Clarendon Press.

Krasner, Stephen D. 1999. *Sovereignty: Organized Hypocrisy.* Princeton: Princeton University Press.

Kriesi, Hanspeter. 2018. "Revisiting the Populist Challenge." *Politologický Časopis—Czech Journal of Political Science* 25, no. 1: 5–27. DOI: 10.5817/PC2018-1-5.

Kuhn, Reinhard. 1976. *Demon of Noontide: Ennui in Western Literature.* Princeton: Princeton University Press.

216 BIBLIOGRAPHY

Kuhrt, Amélie. 1995. *The Ancient Near East: c. 3000–330 B.C.* London: Routledge.

Kulke, Hermann, and Dietmar Rothermund. 1990. *A History of India.* London: Routledge.

Kunda, Ziva. 1999. *Social Cognition.* Boston: MIT Press.

Kuzio, Taras. 2002. "The Myth of the Civic State: A Critical Survey of Hans Kohn's Framework for Understanding Nationalism." *Ethnic and Racial Studies* 25, no. 1: 20–39. https://doi.org/10.1080/01419870120112049.

Kyeyune, Malcolm. 2022. Why the Experts are Losing. *Unheard.* https://unherd.com/2022/02/why-the-experts-are-losing/.

Lakic, Mladen. 2019. "Pope Backs Bosnian Roma Family Against Italian Rightists." *Balkan Insight.* May 10. https://balkaninsight.com/2019/05/10/bosnian-roma-family-defy-italian-rightist-protests/.

Landau, Peter. 2022. "The Spirit of Canon Law." In *The Cambridge History of Medieval Canon Law*, edited by Anders Winroth and John C. Wei, 573–583. Cambridge: Cambridge University Press.

Landon, William J. 2005. *Politics, Patriotism and Language: Niccolò Machiavelli's "Secular Patria" and the Creation of an Italian National Identity.* Bern: Peter Lang.

Lasch, Christopher. 1995. *Haven in a Heartless World: The Family Besieged.* New York: W.W. Norton & Company.

Lasch, Christopher. 1996. *The Revolt of the Elites and the Betrayal of Democracy.* New York: W.W. Norton & Company.

Lax, Jeffrey R., and Justin H. Phillips. 2012. "The Democratic Deficit in the States." *American Journal of Political Science* 56, no. 1: 148–166. https://doi.org/10.1111/j.1540-5907.2011.00537.x.

Lebovics, Herman. 2018. *True France.* Ithaca: Cornell University Press.

Lecher, Colin. 2019. "Google is Scaling Back its Weekly All-hands Meetings After Leaks, Sundar Pichai Tells Staff." *The Verge.* November 15. https://www.theverge.com/2019/11/15/20966718/google-weekly-all-hands-tgif-staff-meeting-changes-ceo-sundar-pichai.

Levi, Margaret, and Laura Stoker. 2000. "Political Trust and Trustworthiness." *Annual Review of Political Science* 3, no. 1: 475–507. https://doi.org/10.1146/annurev.polisci.3.1.475.

Levin, Yuval. 2020. *A Time to Build: From Family and Community to Congress and the Campus, How Recommitting to Our Institutions can Revive the American Dream.* New York: Basic Books.

Levinas, Emmanuel. 2003. *Humanism of the Other.* Chicago: University of Illinois Press.

Levine, Mark, Amy Prosser, David Evans, and Stephen Reicher. 2005. "Identity and Emergency Intervention: How Social Group Membership and Inclusiveness of Group Boundaries Shape Helping Behavior." *Personality and Social Psychology Bulletin* 31, no. 4: 443–453. https://doi.org/10.1177/0146167204271651.

Levinson, Bernard M. 2002. *Deuteronomy and the Hermeneutics of Legal Innovation.* Oxford: Oxford University Press.

Levitsky, Steven, and Daniel Ziblatt. 2018. *How Democracies Die.* New York: Crown Publishers.

Lewis, Bernard. 1988. *The Political Language of Islam.* Chicago: University of Chicago Press.

Lewis, C. S. 1961. *Studies in Words.* Cambridge: Cambridge University Press.

Lewis, David M. 2018. *Greek Slave Systems in Their Eastern Mediterranean Context, c. 800–146 BC.* Oxford: Oxford University Press.

BIBLIOGRAPHY 217

Lewis, Gregory T., John F. Sullivan, and Hannah T. Warren. 2019. "Eliminating Forced Labor from Your Company's Supply Chains: Lessons Learned from 2018 and the Trends Developing for 2019." Pittsburgh: K&L Gates https://www.klgates.com/Elim inating-Forced-Labor-from-Your-Companys-Supply-Chains-Lessons-Learned-from-2018-and-the-Trends-Developing-for-2019-03-01-20191.

Lewis, Mark Edward. 2007. *The Early Chinese Empires: Qin and Han*. Cambridge, MA: Belknap.

Lewis, Mark Edward. 2012. *The Construction of Space in Early China*. Albany: SUNY Press.

Leydet, Dominique. 2017. "Citizenship." In *The Stanford Encyclopedia of Philosophy*, edited by Edward N. Zalta. Stanford: Stanford University. https://plato.stanford.edu/entr ies/citizenship/.

Liverani, Mario. 1991. *Antico Oriente: Storia, Società, Economia*. Roma: Laterza.

Liverani, Mario. 2007. *Israel's History and the History of Israel*. London: Routledge.

Lolive, Jacques.1999. *Les Contestations du TGV Méditerranée: Projet, Controverses et Espace Public*. Paris: L'Harmattan.

Loury, Glenn. 2020. "Relations Before Transactions." In *Difference Without Domination: Pursuing Justice in Diverse Democracies*, edited by Danielle Allen and Rohini Somanathan, 171–186. Chicago: University of Chicago Press.

Loury, Glenn. 2021. "The Bias Narrative Versus the Development Narrative." Testimony for U.S. Senate Banking Committee Washington, DC. https://www.banking.senate. gov/imo/media/doc/Loury%20Testimony%203-4-21.pdf.

Lowi, Theodore. 1967. "The Public Philosophy: Interest Group Liberalism." *American Political Science Review* 61: 5–24. https://doi.org/10.2307/1953872.

Lowi, Theodore. 1969. *The End of Liberalism*. New York: Knopf.

Lowi, Theodore. 1971a. *The Politics of Disorder*. New York: Norton.

Lowi, Theodore. 1971b. "Reply to Mansfield." *Public Policy* 19, no. 1: 207–211.

Lowi, Theodore. 1979. *The End of Liberalism: The Second Republic of the United States*. 2nd ed. New York: Norton.

Lowry, Heath W. 2003. *The Nature of the Early Ottoman State*. Albany: State University of New York Press.

Lucassen, Jan, Tine De Moor, and Jan Luiten van Zanden. 2008. *The Return of the Guilds*. Cambridge: Cambridge University Press.

Łucka. Daria. 2019. "Between Alien and Citizen: Denizenship in Old and New Europe." *Polish Sociological Review* 207, no. 3: 337–354. https://doi.org/10.26412/psr207.06.

Ludden, David, ed. 1996. *Contesting the Nation: Religion, Community, and the Politics of Democracy in India*. Philadelphia: University of Pennsylvania Press.

Lux, Kenneth. 1990. *Adam Smith's Mistake: How a Moral Philosopher Invented Economics and Ended Morality*. London: Shambhala.

Lynch, Justin. 2018. "Why Project Maven is a 'Moral Hazard' for Google." https://www. c4isrnet.com/it-networks/2018/06/26/why-googles-project-maven-pullout-is-a-moral-hazard/.

Maas, Willem. 2013. *Multilevel Citizenship*. Philadelphia: University of Pennsylvania Press.

Maas, Willem, ed. 2020. *Multilevel Citizenship*. Philadelphia: University of Pennsylvania Press.

Machiavelli, Niccolò. 2014 [1514]. *The Prince*. London: Penguin.

Macklin, Audrey. 2017. "Is it Time to Retire Nottebohm?" *American Journal of International Law* 111: 492–497. https://doi.org/10.1017/aju.2018.5.

Maiolo, Francesco. 2007. *Medieval Sovereignty: Marsilius of Padua and Bartolus of Saxoferrato*. Amsterdam: Eburon Delft.

218   BIBLIOGRAPHY

Malik, Kenan. 2019. "The Idea that the British Working Class is Social Conservative is Nonsense." *The Guardian*. December 22. https://www.theguardian.com/commentisf ree/2019/dec/22/idea-that-the-british-working-class-is-socially-conservative-is-a-nonsense.

Manby, Bronwen. 2023. "The Global State of Citizenship: Discrimination in Nationality Laws Increasingly Exceptional on the Surface, but Pervasive behind the Scenes." *Globalcit*, May 15. https://globalcit.eu/the-global-state-of-citizenship-discrimination-in-nationality-laws-increasingly-exceptional-on-the-surface-but-pervasive-behind-the-scenes/.

Mandeville, Bernard. 1988 [1729]. *The Fable of Bees: Or, Private Vices, Public Benefits. The Second Volume*. Indianapolis: Liberty Fund.

Manetsch, Scott M. 2000. *Theodore Beza and the Quest for Peace in France: 1572–1598*. London: Brill.

Mansell, Samuel F., and Alejo J. Sison. 2020. "Medieval Corporations, Membership and the Common Good: Rethinking the Critique of Shareholder Primacy." *Journal of Institutional Economics*, 16, no. 5: 579–595. https://doi.org/10.1017/S174413741 9000146.

Marshall, Thomas H. 1950. *Citizenship and Social Class*. Cambridge: Cambridge University Press.

Martin, Anton.1975. "Swedish Experience with Democratic Control of Unemployment and Inflation." Paper Presented to the Center for Comparative Policy Studies. Madison: University of Wisconsin.

Martines, Lauro. 2015. *Lawyers and Statecraft in Renaissance Florence*. Princeton: Princeton University Press.

Matthews, Dylan. 2017. "Europe Could Have the Secret to Saving America's Unions." *Vox*. April 17. https://www.vox.com/policy-and-politics/2017/4/17/15290674/union-labor-movement-europe-bargaining-fight-15-ghent.

Maurer, Christian. 2013. "Self-interest and Sociability." In *The Oxford Handbook of British Philosophy in the Eighteenth Century*, edited by James A. Harris, 291–314. Oxford: Oxford University Press.

Mauss, Marcel. 1990. *The Gift: The Form and Reason for Exchange in Archaic Societies*. New York: Norton.

Mayo, Ed. 2017. "A Short History of Co-Operation and Mutuality." *Co-Operatives UK*. https://www.uk.coop/sites/default/files/uploads/attachments/a-short-history-of-coop eration-and-mutuality_ed-mayoweb_english.pdf.

McAdam, Doug. 1999. *Political Process and the Development of Black Insurgency, 1930–1970*. Chicago: University of Chicago Press.

McAdam, Doug, Sidney Tarrow, and Charles Tilly. 2001. *Dynamics of Contention*. New York: Cambridge University Press.

McCarthy, John D., and Mayer N. Zald. 1977. "Resource Mobilization and Social Movements: A Partial Theory." *American Journal of Sociology* 82: 1212–1241. https://doi.org/10.1086/226464.

McCarthy, John D., and Mayer N. Zald. 2001. "The Enduring Vitality of the Resource Mobilization Theory of Social Movements." In *Handbook of Sociological Theory*, edited by Jonathan H. Turner, 533–565. Boston, MA: Springer. https://doi.org/10.1007/0-387-36274-6_25.

McDaniel, Eric Leon, Irfan Nooruddin, and Allyson Faith Shortle. 2011. "Divine Boundaries: How Religion Shapes Citizens' Attitudes Toward Immigrants." *American Politics Research* 39, no. 1: 205–233. https://doi.org/10.1177/1532673X10371300.

BIBLIOGRAPHY 219

McDonald, Sean, and Simon Moore. 2015. "Communicating Identity in the Ottoman Empire and Some Implications for Contemporary States." *Atlantic Journal of Communication* 23, no. 5: 269–283. https://doi.org/10.1080/15456870.2015.1090439.

McDougall, Walter A. 2018. "America's Machiavellian Moment: Origins of the Atlantic Republican Tradition." *Orbis* 62, no. 4: 505–517. https://doi.org/10.1016/j.orbis.2018.08.001.

McGhee, Heather. 2022. *The Sum of Us: What Racism Costs Everyone and How We Can Prosper Together*. London: One World.

Mead, George H. 2015 [1934]. *Mind, Self, and Society: From the Standpoint of a Social Behaviorist*. Chicago: University of Chicago Press.

Melucci, Alberto. 1985. "The Symbolic Challenge of Contemporary Movements." *Social Research* 52: 789–816. http://www.jstor.org/stable/40970398.

Melucci, Alberto. 1989. *Nomads of the Present*. London: Hutchinson Radius.

Menkiti, Ifeanyi A. 1984. "Person and Community in African Traditional Thought." In *African Philosophy: An Introduction*, edited by Richard Wright, 171–182. Lanham: University Press of America.

Messing, Vera, and Bence Sagvari. 2018. "Looking Behind the Culture of Fear: Cross-National Analysis of Attitudes Towards Migration." Bonn: FES-Friedrich EbertStiftung. https://cps.ceu.edu/sites/cps.ceu.edu/files/attachment/article/3014/messing-sagvari-fes-study-march-2018.pdf.

Messing, Vera, and Bence Sagvari. 2021. "Are Anti-Immigrant Attitudes the Holy Grail of Populists? A Comparative Analysis of Attitudes Towards Immigrants, Values, and Political Populism in Europe." *Intersections: East European Journal of Society and Politics* 7, no. 2: 100–127. https://doi.org/10.17356/ieejsp.v7i2.750.

Mezzadra, Sandro, and Brett Neilson. 2011. "Borderscapes of Differential Inclusion." In *The Borders of Justice*, edited by Étienne Balibar, Sandro Mezzadra, and Raṇabīra Samāddāra, 181–203. Philadelphia: Temple University Press.

Miaotai, Liang, and Ming Qing Jingdezhen. 1991. *Chengshi Jingji Vanjiu*. (Study on Urban Economics of Jingdezhen in the Ming and Qing Periods). Nanchang: Jiangxi Renmin Chubanshe.

Michels, Robert. 2019 [1911]. "The Iron Law of Oligarchy." In *Power in Modern Societies*, edited by Marvin E. Olsen, Martin N. Marger, and Valencia Fonseca, 111–124. London: Routledge.

Milgrom, Jacob. 2000. *Leviticus*. New Haven: Yale University Press.

Millar, Fergus. 1998. *The Crowd in Rome in the Late Republic*. Ann Arbor: University of Michigan Press.

Miller, Andrew H. 2020. *On Not Being Someone Else: Tales of Our Unled Lives*. Cambridge, MA: Harvard University Press.

Miller, David. 1995. *On Nationality*. Oxford: Clarendon Press.

Miller, David. 2000. *Citizenship and National Identity*. Cambridge: Polity Press.

Miller, David, and Ali Sundas. 2014. "Testing the National Identity Argument." *European Political Science Review* 6, no. 2: 237–259. https://doi.org/10.1017/S1755773913000088.

Mitchell, Nic. 2021. "Creating Global Citizens 'Is Back' for Higher Education." *University World News*. https://www.universityworldnews.com/post.php?story=2021061813 1500550.

Mitchell, Wesley C. 1918. "Bentham's Felicific Calculus." *Political Science Quarterly* 33, no. 2: 161–183. https://doi.org/10.2307/2141580.

220 BIBLIOGRAPHY

Mohr, Philip B., and Kerry Larsen. 1998. "Ingroup Favoritism in Umpiring Decisions in Australian Football." *The Journal of Social Psychology* 138, no. 4: 495–504. https://doi.org/10.1080/00224549809600403.

Molho, Anthony, Kurt A. Raaflaub, and Julia Emlen. 2018. *City States in Classical Antiquity and Medieval Italy*. Ann Arbor: University of Michigan Press.

Moll-Murata, Christine. 2008. "Chinese Guilds from the Seventeenth to the Twentieth Centuries: An Overview." *International Review of Social History* 53, no. S16: 213–247. https://doi.org/10.1017/S0020859008003672.

Moll-Murata, Christine. 2013. "Guilds and Apprenticeship in China and Europe: The Jingdezhen and European Ceramics Industries." In *Technology, Skills and the Pre-Modern Economy in the East and the West*, edited by Maarten R. Prak and Jan Luiten Van Zanden, 225–257. Leiden: Brill. https://doi.org/10.1163/9789004251571_009.

Moll-Murata, Christine. 2018. *State and Crafts in the Qing Dynasty (1644–1911)*. Amsterdam: Amsterdam University Press.

Moll-Murata, Christine. 2020. "Citizenship in Early Modern China. A Commentary to Maarten Prak, Citizens Without Nations." *TSEG-The Low Countries Journal of Social and Economic History* 17, no. 3: 101–108. https://doi.org/10.18352/tseg.1173.

Montesquieu.1989 [1748]. *The Spirit of Law*. Cambridge: Cambridge University Press.

More, St. Thomas. *Treatise on the Passion; Treatise on the Blessed Body; Instructions and Prayers*. Edited by Garry E. Haupt. New Haven: Yale University Press, 1976.

Morgan, Catherine. 2003. *Early Greek States Beyond the Polis*. London: Routledge.

Morris, Colin. 1989. *The Papal Monarchy: The Western Church from 1050 to 1250*. Oxford: Oxford University Press.

Morse, Hosea Ballou. 1909. *The Gilds of China: with an Account of the Gild Merchant or Co-hong of Canton*. London: Longmans.

Moses, John A. 2010. "Church and State in Post-Reformation Germany, 1530–1914." In *Church and State in Old and New Worlds*, edited by Hillary M. Carey, and John Gascoigne, 77–97. New York: Brill.

Mosse, George L.1990. *Fallen Soldiers: Reshaping the Memory of the World Wars*. Oxford: Oxford University Press.

Mosse, George L. 2021. *The Crisis of German Ideology: Intellectual Origins of the Third Reich*. Madison: University of Wisconsin Press.

Mounk, Yascha. 2018. *The People vs. Democracy: Why Our Freedom Is in Danger and How to Save It*. Cambridge: Harvard University Press.

Mountz, Alison, and Nancy Hiemstra. 2014. "Chaos and Crisis: Dissecting the Spatiotemporal Logics of Contemporary Migrations and State Practices." *Annals of the Association of American Geographers* 104, no. 2: 382–390. https://doi.org/10.1080/00045608.2013.857547.

Mouritsen, Henrik. 2001. *Plebs and Politics in the late Roman Republic*. Cambridge: Cambridge University Press.

MSCI. 2021. "Who Will Regulate ESG?" *MSCI Report*. www.msci.com/who-will-regulate-esg#:~:text=Using%20our%20interactive%20chart%2C%20we,to%20investors%20have%20risen%20sharply.

Muller, Jan-Werner. 2009. *Constitutional Patriotism*. Princeton: Princeton University Press.

Murove, Felix M. 2004. "An African Commitment to Ecological Conservation: The Shona Concepts of Ukama and Ubuntu." *The Mankind Quarterly* 45, no. 2: 195–215. 10.46469/mq.2004.45.2.3.

BIBLIOGRAPHY 221

Nadelmann, E. 1990. "Global Prohibition Regimes: The Evolution of Norms in International Society." *International Organization* 44, no. 4: 479–526. doi:10.1017/S0020818300035384.

Najemy, John M. 1979. "Guild Republicanism in Trecento Florence: The Successes and Ultimate Failure of Corporate Politics" *The American Historical Review* 84, no. 1: 53–71. https://doi.org/10.2307/1855659.

Najemy, John M. 2006. *A History of Florence, 1200–1575*. Oxford: Blackwell.

Nakano-Okuno, Mariko. 2011. *Sidgwick and Contemporary Utilitarianism*. New York: Palgrave.

Nansheng, Peng. 2003. *Hanghui Zhidu de Jindai Mingyun* [The Fate of the Guilds in the Modern Era]. Beijing: Ren Min Chu Ban She.

Nash, Catherine. 2003. "Cultural Geography: Anti-Racist Geographies." *Progress in Human Geography* 27, no. 5: 637–648. https://doi.org/10.1191/0309132503ph454pr.

Nelson, Margaret K. 2013. "Fictive Kin, Families we Choose, and Voluntary Kin: What Does the Discourse Tell Us?" *Journal of Family Theory & Review* 5, no. 4: 259–281. https://doi.org/10.1111/jftr.12019.

Nelson, Margaret K. 2014a. "Whither Fictive Kin? Or, What's in a Name?" *Journal of Family Issues* 35, no. 2: 201–222. https://doi.org/10.1177/0192513X12470621.

Nicolet, Claude. 1980. *The World of the Citizen in Republican Rome*. Berkeley: University of California Press.

Nikam, Appurao N., and Richard P. McKeon, eds. 1978. *Edicts of Asoka*. Chicago: University of Chicago Press.

Noegel, Scott B. 2007. "Greek Religion and the Ancient Near East." In *A Companion to Greek Religion*, edited by Daniel Ogden, 21–37. Oxford: Blackwell. https://doi.org/10.1002/9780470996911.ch2.

Norris, Pippa. 2011. *Democratic Deficit: Critical Citizens Revisited*. New York: Cambridge University Press.

Oakley, Francis. 1961. "Medieval Theories of Natural Law: William of Ockham and the Significance of the Voluntarist Tradition." *The American Journal of Jurisprudence* 6, no. 1: 65–83. http://scholarship.law.nd.edu/nd_naturallaw_forum/60.

Obershall, Anthony. 1973. *Social Conflict and Social Movements*. Englewood Cliffs: Prentice-Hall.

O'Brien, Karen. 1997. *Narratives of Enlightenment: Cosmopolitan History from Voltaire to Gibbon*. Cambridge: Cambridge University Press.

OECD. 2015. "How's Life? Measuring Well-being." Paris: OECD Publishing. https://www.oecd-ilibrary.org/economics/how-s-life-2015_how_life-2015-en.

Offe, Claus. 1985. "New Social Movements: Changing Boundaries of the Political." *Social Research* 52: 817–868.

Ogilvie, Sheilagh. 2011. *Institutions and European Trade: Merchant Guilds, 1000–1800*. Cambridge Studies in Economic History—Second Series. Cambridge: Cambridge University Press.

Ogilvie, Sheilagh. 2019. *The European Guilds: An Economic Analysis*. Princeton: Princeton University Press.

Ogilvie, Sheilagh. 2020. "Guilds and the Economy." In *Oxford Research Encyclopedia of Economics and Finance*, edited by Jonathan H. Hamilton. New York: Oxford University Press. https://oxfordre.com/economics/view/10.1093/acrefore/9780190625979.001.0001/acrefore-9780190625979-e-538.

BIBLIOGRAPHY

Ogilvie, Sheilagh. 2021. "Thinking Carefully about Inclusiveness: Evidence from European Guilds." *Journal of Institutional Economics* 17, no. 2: 185–200. https://doi.org/10.1017/S1744137420000508.

O'Loughlin, Thomas. 1995. "Celibacy in the Catholic Church: A Brief History." *History Ireland* 3, no. 4: 41–44.

Onnekink, David, ed. 2016. *War and Religion after Westphalia, 1648–1713.* London: Routledge.

Onuf, Peter S. 2019. *Statehood and Union: A History of the Northwest Ordinance.* Notre Dame: University of Notre Dame Press.

Oomen, Barbara.2020. "Decoupling and Teaming Up: The Rise and Proliferation of Transnational Municipal Networks in the Field of Migration." *International Migration Review* 54, no. 3: 913–939. https://doi.org/10.1177/0197918319881118.

Osiander, Andreas. 2001. "Sovereignty, International Relations, and the Westphalian Myth." *International Organization* 55, no. 2: 251–287. https://doi.org/10.1162/002081 80151140577.

Paasi, Anssi, and Eeva-Kaisa Prokkola. 2008. "Territorial Dynamics, Cross-Border Work and Everyday Life in the Finnish–Swedish Border Area." *Space and Polity* 12, no. 1: 13–29. https://doi.org/10.1080/13562570801969366.

Packer, George. 2019. *The Unwinding: Thirty years of American Decline.* New York: Vintage.

Park, Robert. 1952. *Human Communities: The City and Human Ecology.* New York: Free Press.

Peacock, Andrew C. S. 2009. *Frontiers of the Ottoman World.* Oxford: Oxford University Press.

Pennington, Kenneth J. 1970. "Bartolome de las Casas and the Tradition of Medieval Law." *Church History* 39, no. 2: 149–161. https://doi.org/10.2307/3163383.

Pentzien, Jonas. 2020. "Political and Legislative Drivers and Obstacles for Platform Cooperativism in the United States, Germany, and France." Working Paper. Institute for the Cooperative Digital Economy. https://www.ioew.de/en/publication/die_politik_des_plattform_kooperativismus.

Pew Research Center. 2020. "Global Attitudes Survey." https://www.pewresearch.org/global/2020/02/27/democratic-rights-popular-globally-but-commitment-to-them-not-always-strong/.

Pew Research Center. 2022. "Religious Landscape Study." https://www.pewresearch.org/religious-landscape-study/.

Piketty, Thomas. 2014. *Capital in the Twenty-First Century.* Cambridge: Belknap Press.

Pillay, Renginee G. 2013. "Anglo-American Model Versus Continental European Model." In *Encyclopedia of Corporate Social Responsibility*, edited by Samuel O. Idowu, Nicholas Capaldi, Lianrong Zu, and Ananda Das Gupta, 100–105. Berlin: Springer.

Piven, Frances F., and Richard A. Cloward. 1977. *Poor People's Movements: Why They Succeed, How They Fail.* New York: Pantheon Books.

Plato. 2007. *The Republic.* London: Penguin.

Pocock, J. G. A. 1978. "Machiavelli and Guicciardini: Ancients and Moderns." *Canadian Journal of Political Theory* 2, no. 3: 93–109.

Pocock, J. G. A. 1993. "The Ideal of Citizenship since Classical Times." In *Theorizing Citizenship*, edited by Ronald Beiner, 29–52. Albany: State University of New York Press.

Pogonyi, Szabolcs. 2022. "The Right of Blood: Ethnically Selective Citizenship Policies in Europe." *National Identities* 24, no. 5: 523–538. https://doi.org/10.1080/14608 944.2021.2013185.

BIBLIOGRAPHY   223

Polanyi, Karl. 2001 [1968]. *The Great Transformation: The Political and Economic Origins of our Time*. Boston: Beacon Press.

Pollock, Sheldon. 2006. *The Language of the Gods in the World of Men: Sanskrit, Culture, and Power in Premodern India*. Berkeley: University of California Press.

Pollock, Susan. 1999. *Ancient Mesopotamia: The Eden that Never Was*. Cambridge: Cambridge University Press.

Pollman, Elizabeth. 2021. "The History and Revival of the Corporate Purpose Clause." *Texas Law Review* no. 7. https://texaslawreview.org/the-history-and-revival-of-the-corporate-purpose-clause.

Poloni, Alma. 2022. "Politics, Institutions, and Society in Pisa during the Communal Era: Late Eleventh to Late Fourteenth Century." In *A Companion to Medieval Pisa*, edited by Karen Rose Mathews, Silvia Orvietani Busch, and Stefano Bruni, 139–162. Leiden: Brill.

Poole, Ross. 1991. *Morality and Modernity*. London: Routledge.

Portes, Alejandro. 1997. *Globalization from Below: The Rise of Transnational Communities*. Volume 98, Issue 8 of CMD Working Paper. Princeton: Princeton University.

Posner, Eric A., and Miguel F. P. De Figueiredo. 2005. "Is the International Court of Justice Biased?" *The Journal of Legal Studies* 34, no. 2: 599–630. https://doi.org/10.1086/430765.

Post, Gaines. 1964. *Studies in Medieval Legal Thought*. Princeton: Princeton University Press.

Postgate, John Nicholas. 2017. *Early Mesopotamia: Society and Economy at the Dawn of History*. London: Routledge.

Postmes, Tom, and Nyla R. Branscombe. 2010. *Rediscovering Social Identity*. London: Psychology Press.

Prak, Maarten. 2018. *Citizens without Nations: Urban Citizenship in Europe and the World, ca. 1000–1789*. Cambridge: Cambridge University Press.

PRI. 2021. "About the PRI." *Principle Responsible Investment*. http//:www.unpri.org/about-the-pri.

Prozesky, Martin H. 1995. "The Philosophical Anthropology of Alfred North Whitehead." *South African Journal of Philosophy* 14, no. 2: 54–59. http://pascal-francis.inist.fr/vibad/index.php?action=getRecordDetail&idt=3713615.

Putnam, Robert D., Robert Leonardi, and Raffaella Y. Nanetti. 1994. *Making Democracy Work: Civic Traditions in Modern Italy*. Princeton: Princeton University Press, 1994.

Putnam, Robert D. 2000. "Bowling Alone: America's Declining Social Capital." In *Culture and Politics: A Reader*, edited by Lane Crothers and Charles Lockhart, 223–234. New York: Palgrave Macmillan.

Raaflaub, Kurt. 2004. *The Discovery of Freedom in Ancient Greece*. Chicago: University of Chicago Press.

Rabbie, Jacob M. 1991. "A Behavioral Interaction Model: Toward a Social-Psychological Framework for Studying Terrorism." *Terrorism and Political Violence* 3, no. 4: 134–163. https://doi.org/10.1080/09546559108427130.

Rahman, K. Sabeel, and Hollie Russon Gilman. 2019. *Civic Power: Rebuilding American Democracy in an Era of Crisis*. Cambridge: Cambridge University Press.

Rainie, Lee, and Andrew Perrin. 2019. "Key Findings about Americans' Declining Trust in Government and Each Other." *Pew Research*. www.pewresearch.org/fact-tank/2019/07/22/key-findings-about-americans-declining-trust-in-government-and-each-other.

224 BIBLIOGRAPHY

Rajaram, Prem Kumar, and Carl Grundy-Warr. 2007. "Introduction" In *Borderscapes: Hidden Geographies and Politics at Territory's Edge, Vol. 29*, edited by Prem Kumar Rajaram and Carl Grundy-Warr, ix–xl. Minneapolis: University of Minnesota Press.

Ramaswamy, Narasimhiah T. 1994. *Essentials of Indian Statecraft: Kautilya's Arthasastra for Contemporary Readers*. London: South Asia Books.

Ramose, Mogobe B. 1999. *African Philosophy Through Ubuntu*. Kadoma: Mond Books.

Rawls, John. 1996. *Political Liberalism*. New York: Columbia University Press.

Rawls, John. 1997. "The Idea of Public Reason Revisited." *The University of Chicago Law Review* 64, no. 3: 765–807. https://doi.org/10.2307/1600311.

Rawls, John. 2020 [1971]. *A Theory of Justice*. Cambridge, MA: Harvard University Press.

Reeskens, Tim, and Marc Hooghe. 2010. "Beyond the Civic–Ethnic Dichotomy: Investigating the Structure of Citizenship Concepts Across Thirty-Three Countries." *Nations and Nationalism* 16, no. 4: 579–597. https://doi.org/10.1111/j.1469-8129.2010.00446.x.

Reich, Charles. 1964. "The New Property." *Yale Law Journal*. 73, no. 5: 733–787.

Reicher, Stephen. 1996. "The Battle of Westminster: Developing the Social Identity Model of Crowd Behaviour in Order to Explain the Initiation and Development of Collective Conflict." *European Journal of Social Psychology* 26, no. 1: 115–134. https://doi.org/10.1002/(SICI)1099-0992(199601)26:13.0.CO;2-Z.

Reicher, Stephen, and Clifford Stott. 2011. *Mad Mobs and Englishmen? Myths and Realities of the 2011 Riots*. London: Hachette.

Reicher, Stephen, and Nick Hopkins. 2001. *Self and Nation: Categorization, Contestation and Mobilization*. London: Sage.

Reicher, Stephen, Russell Spears, and S. Alexander Haslam. 2010. "The Social Identity Approach in Social Psychology." In *The SAGE Handbook of Identities*, edited by Margaret Wetherell and Chandra Talpade Mohanty, 45–62. New York: Sage.

Reid Jr., Charles J. 1991. "The Canonistic Contribution to the Western Rights Tradition: An Historical Inquiry." *Boston College Law Review* 33, no. 1: 37–92.

Reisman, David A. 2005. *Democracy and Exchange: Schumpeter, Galbraith, TH Marshall, Titmuss and Adam Smith*. Cheltenham: Edward Elgar Publishing.

Renan, Ernest. 1990 [1882]. "What Is a Nation?" In *Nation and Narration*, edited by Homi Bhabha, 8–22. London: Routledge.

Rennó Santos, Mateus, David Jacobson, and Georgi Georgiev. 2021. "The Cross-National Relationship Between Women's Autonomy and Long-Term Homicide Trends." *International Criminology* 1, no. 4: 299–314. https://doi.org/10.1007/s43576-021-00025-y.

Rhodes, Peter John. 1993. *A Commentary on the Aristotelian Athenaion Politeia*. Oxford: Oxford University Press.

Rhodes, Peter John. 2014. "The Congruence of Power: Ruling and Being Ruled in Greek Participatory Communities." In *A Companion to Greek Democracy and the Roman Republic*, edited by Dean Hammer, 129–145. Chichester: Wiley and Sons.

Richards, Andrew. 2002. "Mobilizing the Powerless: Collective Protest Action of the Unemployed in the Interwar Period." Working Paper 175. Madrid: Juan March Institute.

Richter, Paul J. 1890 "The Guilds of the Early Italian Painters." *The Nineteenth Century and After: A Monthly Review* 28: 786–800.

Riley, Patrick. 2014. *The General Will Before Rousseau*. Princeton: Princeton University Press.

BIBLIOGRAPHY 225

Risse, Thomas, Stephen C. Ropp, and Kathryn Sikkink, eds. 2013. *The Persistent Power of Human Rights: From Commitment to Compliance*. Cambridge: Cambridge University Press.

Roberts, Adam, and Timothy Garton Ash, eds. 2009. *Civil Resistance and Power Politics: The Experience of Non-Violent Action from Gandhi to the Present*. Oxford: Oxford University Press.

Roberts, Sam. 2017. "Theodore Lowi, Zealous Scholar of Presidents and Liberalism, Dies at 85." *The New York Times*. February 24. www.nytimes.com/2017/02/24/us/theodore-lowi/dead/html.

Robertson, Henry A., and John G. Merrills. 1996. *Human Rights in the World: An Introduction to the Study of the International Protection of Human Rights*. Manchester: Manchester University Press.

Roemer, John E. 1988. *Free to Lose*. Cambridge, MA: Harvard University Press.

Rooduijn, Matthijs, Sarah L. De Lange, and Wouter Van Der Brug. 2014. "A Populist Zeitgeist? Programmatic Contagion by Populist Parties in Western Europe." *Party Politics* 20, no. 4: 563–575. https://doi.org/10.1177/1354068811436065.

Rosa, Asor A. 2019. *Machiavelli e l'Italia. Resoconto di Una Disfatta*. Torino: Einaudi.

Roth, Martha T. 1995. *Law Collections from Mesopotamia and Asia Minor*. Atlanta, GA: Scholars Press.

Rousseau, Jean-Jacques. 1994. *Discourse on Political Economy and The Social Contract*. Oxford: Oxford University Press.

Rousseau, Jean-Jacques. 2004 [1762]. *The Social Contract*. London: Penguin.

Rowe, William T. 1984. *Hankow: Commerce and Society in a Chinese City, 1796–1889*. Stanford: Stanford University Press.

Rowe, William T. 1989. *Hankow: Commerce and Society in a Chinese City, 1796–1895*. Stanford: Stanford University Press.

Rowe, William T. 1993. "The Problem of 'Civil Society' in Late Imperial China." *Modern China* 19, no. 2: 139–157.

Rubinstein, Nicolai. 1968. *Florentine Studies: Politics and Society in Renaissance Florence*. London: Faber and Faber.

Ruffer, Galya Benarieh. 2003. "Virtual Citizenship: Migrants and the Constitutional Polity." PhD diss., University of Pennsylvania.

Rupp, E. Gordon. 2006. "Philip Melanchthon and Martin Bucer." In *A History of Christian Doctrine*, edited by Hubert Cunliffe-Jones, 371–384. Edinburgh: T&T Clark.

Salazar, Philippe-Joseph. 2002. *An African Athens: Rhetoric and the Shaping of Democracy in South Africa*. Mahwah, NJ: Lawrence Erlbaum Associates, Taylor and Francis. https://doi.org/10.4324/9781410602879.

Salzman, Philip Carl. 2008. *Culture and Conflict in the Middle East*. Amherst, NY: Prometheus Books.

Samkange, Stanlake, and Marie T. Samkange. 1980. *Hunhuism or Ubuntuism: A Zimbabwean Indigenous Political Philosophy*. Harare: The Graham Publishing Company.

Sandel, Michael J. 1984. *Political Theory*. New York: Sage.

Santa Ana, Otto, Kevin Hans Waitkuweit, and Mishna Erana Hernandez. 2017. "Blood, Soil, and Tears: Conceptual Metaphor-based Critical Discourse Analysis of the Legal Debate on US Citizenship." *Journal of Language and Politics* 16, no. 2: 149–175. https://doi.org/10.1075/jlp.15038.san.

Sassen, Saskia. 1996. *Losing Control? Sovereignty in an Age of Globalization*. New York: Columbia University Press.

226 BIBLIOGRAPHY

Saussure, Ferdinand Mongin. 2011 [1916]. *Course in General Linguistics*. New York: Columbia University Press.

Scheiber, Noam. 2022. "Amazon Workers Who Won a Union Their Way Open Labor Leaders' Eyes." *The New York Times*. April 7. https://www.nytimes.com/2022/04/07/business/economy/amazon-union-labor.html.

Scheiber, Noam, and Daisuke Wakabayashi. 2019. "Google Hires Firm Known for Anti-Union Efforts." *The New York Times*. November 20. https://www.nytimes.com/2019/11/20/technology/Google-union-consultant.html.

Scheiber, Noam, and Kate Conger. 2020. "The Great Google Revolt." *The New York Times*. February 18. https://www.nytimes.com/interactive/2020/02/18/magazine/google-revolt.html.

Schneider, Nathan. 2018. *Everything for Everyone: The Radical Tradition that is Shaping the Next Economy*. United States: Public Affairs.

Schneider, Nathan. 2021. "Enabling Community-Owned Platforms: A Proposal for a Tech New Deal." In *Regulating Big Tech: Policy Responses to Digital Dominance*, edited by Martin Moore and Damian Tambini, 74–92. Oxford: Oxford University Press.

Scott, George M. 1990. "A Resynthesis of the Primordial and Circumstantial Approaches to Ethnic Group Solidarity: Towards an Explanatory Model." *Ethnic and Racial Studies* 13, no. 2: 147–171. https://doi.org/10.1080/01419870.1990.9993667.

Scott, James C. 1998. *Seeing Like a State*. New Haven: Yale University Press.

Searing, Donald D., Frederick Solt, Pamela Johnston Conover, and Ivor Crewe. 2007. "Public Discussion in the Deliberative System: Does it Make Better Citizens?" *British Journal of Political Science* 37, no. 4: 587–618. https://doi.org/10.1017/S000712340 7000336.

SEC. 2021. "SEC Announces Enforcement Task Force Focused on Climate and ESG Issues." *US Securities & Exchange*. https://www.sec.gov/news/press-release/2021-42.

Sen, Amartya. 1987. *On Ethics and Economics*. Oxford: Blackwell.

Sénac, Réjane. 2017. *Les Non Frères Au Pays de L'égalité*. Paris: Presses de Sciences Po.

Sewell, William H. 1980. *Work and Revolution in France: The Language of Labor from the Old Regime to 1848*. Cambridge: Cambridge University Press.

Shachar, Ayelet. 2009. *The Birthright Lottery: Citizenship and Global Inequality*. Cambridge, MA: Harvard University Press.

Shachar, Ayelet. 2020. *The Shifting Border: Legal Cartographies of Migration and Mobility*. Manchester: Manchester University Press.

Shain, Martin A. 2019. *The Border*. Oxford: Oxford University Press.

Shalev, Eran. 2010. "Written in the Style of Antiquity: Pseudo-Biblicism and the Early American Republic, 1770–1830." *Church History* 79, no. 4: 800–826. https://doi.org/10.1017/S0009640710001034.

Shand, Alexander H. 1990. *Free Market Morality: The Political Economy of the Austrian School*. London: Routledge.

Shehaj, Albana, Adrian J. Shin, and Ronald Inglehart. 2021. "Immigration and Right-Wing Populism: An Origin Story." *Party Politics* 27, no. 2: 282–293. https://doi.org/10.1177/1354068819849888.

Sher, Richard B. 1985. *Church and University in the Scottish Enlightenment: The Moderate Literati of Edinburgh*. Edinburgh: Edinburgh University Press.

Sigmund, Paul E. 2013. *Nicholas of Cusa and Medieval Political Thought* Cambridge, MA: Harvard University Press.

BIBLIOGRAPHY 227

Sikkink, Kathryn. 2011. *The Justice Cascade: How Human Rights Prosecutions Are Changing World Politics.* New York: W.W. Norton and Company.

Simmel, Georg. 1950. *The Sociology of Georg Simmel.* Translated by Kurt Wolff. Glencoe, IL: Free Press.

Simmel, Georg. 1964. "The Metropolis and Mental Life." In *The Sociology of Georg Simmel,* edited by Kurt Wolf, 409–424. New York: Press.

Simon, Julia. 1995. *Mass Enlightenment: Critical Studies in Rousseau and Diderot.* Albany: SUNY Press.

Sindima, Harvey J. 1995. *Africa's Agenda: The Legacy of Liberalism and Colonialism in the Crisis of African Values.* Westport, CT: Praeger.

Sisson, Keith. 2016. "Popes over Princes: Hierocratic Theory." In *A Companion to the Medieval Papacy,* edited by Keith Sisson, and Atria A. Larson, 121–132. New York: Brill. https://doi.org/10.1163/9789004315280_007.

Smelser, Neil J. 1962. *Theory of Collective Behavior.* London: Routledge and Kegan Paul.

Smetana, Suzanne.2021. "ESG and the Biden Presidency." *Harvard Law School Forum on Corporate Governance.* www.corpgov.law.harvard.edu/2021/02/19/esg-and-the-biden-presidency/.

Smith, Adam. 2010a [1759]. *The Theory of Moral Sentiments.* London: Penguin.

Smith, Adam. 2010b [1776]. *The Wealth of Nations: An Inquiry into the Nature and Causes of the Wealth of Nations.* Petersfield, UK: Harriman House Limited.

Smith, Anthony D. 1983. "Nationalism and Classical Social Theory." *The British Journal of Sociology* 34, no. 1: 19–38. https://doi.org/10.2307/590606.

Smith, Anthony D. 1987. *The Ethnic Origins of Nations.* Oxford: Blackwell.

Smith, Anthony D. 2006. "Nation and Covenant: The Contribution of Ancient Israel to Modern Nationalism." In *Proceedings of the British Academy,* edited by Peter J. Marshall, 213–255. Oxford: Oxford University Press. https://doi.org/10.5871/bacad/9780197264249.003.0008.

Smith, Heather J., and Tom R. Tyler. 1997. "Choosing the Right Pond: The Impact of Group Membership on Self-Esteem and Group-Oriented Behavior." *Journal of Experimental Social Psychology* 33, no. 2: 146–170. https://doi.org/10.1006/jesp.1996.1318.

Smith, Helmut Walser. 2020. *Germany: A Nation in Its Time: Before, During, and After Nationalism, 1500-2000.* New York: Liveright.

Smith, Nicholas. 2011. "Blood and Soil: Nature, Native and Nation in the Australian Imaginary." *Journal of Australian Studies* 35, no. 1: 1–18. https://doi.org/10.1080/14443058.2010.541475.

Smith, Rogers M. 2002. "Modern Citizenship." In *Handbook of Citizenship Studies,* edited by Engin F. Isin and Bryan S. Turner, 105–115. London: Sage.

Snell, Daniel C. 2001. *Flight and Freedom in the Ancient Near East.* New York: Brill.

Snell, Daniel C. 2020. *A Companion to the Ancient Near East.* Hoboken: John Wiley & Sons.

Snow, David A. 2004. "Framing Processes, Ideology, and Discursive Fields." In *The Blackwell Companion to Social Movements,* edited by David A. Snow, Sarah Soule, and Hanspeter Kriesi, 380–412. Oxford: Blackwell.

Snow, David A. 2013. "Social Movements." In *The Wiley-Blackwell Encyclopedia of Social and Political Movements,* 1198–1200. Chichester: Wiley and Sons.

Snow, David A., E. Burke Rochford, Steven K. Worden, and Robert D. Benford. 1986. "Frame Alignment Processes, Micromobilization, and Movement Participation." *American Sociological Review* 51: 464–481. https://doi.org/10.2307/2095581.

228 BIBLIOGRAPHY

Sobolewska, Maria, and Robert Ford. 2020. *Brexitland: Identity, Diversity and the Reshaping of British Politics*. Cambridge: Cambridge University Press.

Sohn, Louis B., and Thomas Buergenthal. 1973. *International Protection of Human Rights*. Indianapolis: Bobbs-Merrill.

Somers, Margaret. 1993. "Citizenship and the Place of the Public Sphere." *American Sociological Review* 58: 587–620. https://doi.org/10.2307/2096277.

Somers, Margaret. 1994. "Rights, Relationality, and Membership: Rethinking the Making and Meaning of Citizenship." *Law & Social Inquiry* 19, no. 1: 63–112. https://doi.org/10.1111/j.1747-4469.1994.tb00390.x.

Somers, Margaret. 2008. *Genealogies of Citizenship: Markets, Statelessness, and the Right to Have Rights*. New York: Cambridge University Press.

Somers, Margaret. 2021. "Toward a Predistributive Democracy: Diagnosing Oligarchy, Dedemocratization, and the Deceits of Market Justice." In *Volume 1: Neoliberal Politics and Sociological Perspectives*, edited by Jürgen Mackert, Hannah Wolf, Bryan S. Turner, 56–87. London: Routledge.

Sommer, Bernd. 2008. "Anti-Capitalism in the Name of Ethno-Nationalism: Ideological Shifts on the German Extreme Right." *Patterns of Prejudice* 42, no. 3: 305–316. https://doi.org/10.1080/00313220802204046.

Soysal, Yasemin. 1994. *Limits of Citizenship: Migrants and Postnational Membership in Europe*. Chicago: University of Chicago Press.

Speiser, Stuart M. 1977. *A Piece of the Action: A Plan to Provide Every Family with a $100,000 Stake in the Economy*. New York: Van Nostrand Reinhold Co.

Spinoza, Baruch. 2019 [1670]. *Theological-Political Treatise*. Dumfries & Galloway: Anodos Books.

Spiro, Peter J. 2017. "Stakeholder Theory Won't Save Citizenship." In *Democratic Inclusion*, edited by Rainer Bauböck, 204–224. Manchester: Manchester University Press.

Spiro, Peter J. 2019. "The Equality Paradox of Dual Citizenship." *Journal of Ethnic and Migration Studies* 45, no. 6: 879–896. https://doi.org/10.1080/1369183X.2018.1440485.

Staerklé, Christian, Alain Clémence, and Dario Spini. 2011. "Social Representations: A Normative and Dynamic Intergroup Approach." *Political Psychology* 32, no. 5: 759–768. https://doi.org/10.1111/j.1467-9221.2011.00839.x.

Stalder, Felix. 2018. *The Digital Condition*. Cambridge: Polity.

Staley, Edgcumbe. 1906. *The Guilds of Florence*. London: Methuen.

Stanish, Charles. 2023. "Trust, Demographic Thresholds, and Cooperation in Social Evolution." *The Moral Psychology of Trust*, edited by M. Alfano, D. Collins and I. V. Jovanović, ch. 1. Washington DC: Lexington Books.

Stanley, Joseph Fahey. 2011. "From Medieval Corporatism to Civic Humanism: Merchant and Guild Culture in Fourteenth-and Fifteenth-Century Florence." PhD diss., State University of New York at Binghamton.

Stasavage, David. 2020. *The Decline and Rise of Democracy: A Global History from Antiquity to Today*. Princeton: Princeton University Press.

Steffek, Jens, Claudia Kissling, and Patrizia Nanz, eds. 2007. *Civil Society Participation in European and Global Governance: A Cure for the Democratic Deficit?* New York: Springer.

Stewart, Robert M. 1982. "John Clarke and Francis Hutcheson on Self-Love and Moral Motivation." *Journal of the History of Philosophy* 20, no. 3: 261–277. https://doi.org/10.1353/hph.1982.0037.

Stol, Marten. 2016. *Women in the Ancient Near East*. Berlin: De Gruyter.

BIBLIOGRAPHY 229

Sutcliffe, Adam. 2004. *Judaism and Enlightenment*. Cambridge: Cambridge University Press.

Tajfel, Henri, ed. 1982. *Social Identity and Intergroup Relations*. Cambridge: Cambridge University Press.

Tamanaha, Brian Z. 2004. *On the Rule of Law: History, Politics, Theory*. Cambridge: Cambridge University Press.

Tanasoca, Ana. 2016. "Citizenship for Sale: Neomedieval, Not Just Neoliberal?" *European Journal of Sociology* 57, no. 1: 169–195. https://doi.org/10.1017/S0003975616000059.

Tanzini, Lorenzo. 2018. "Guilds of Notaries and Lawyers in Communal Italy (1200–1500). Institutions, Social Contexts, Policies." In *Social Mobility in Medieval Italy (1100–1500)*, edited by Sandro Carocci, and Isabella Lazzarini, 373–390. Roma: Viella.

Tate, Katherine. 2004 "Political Incorporation and Critical Transformations of Black Public Opinion." *Du Bois Review: Social Science Research on Race* 1, no. 2: 345–359. https://doi.org/10.1017/S1742058X04042079.

Tawney, Richard Henry. 1960 [1926]. *Religion and the Rise of Capitalism*. Piscataway, NJ: Transaction Publishers.

Taylor, Alison. 2018."When CEOs Should Speak Up on Polarizing Issues." *Harvard Business Review*. https://hbr.org/2018/10/when-ceos-should-speak-up-on-polarizing-issues.

Taylor, Alison. 2019. "CEO Activism has Given Way to Employee Activism." *Quartz at Work*. www.qz.com/work/1703005/ceo-activism-has-given-way-to-employee-activism/.

Taylor, Charles. 1994. *Multiculturalism: Examining the Politics of Recognition*. Princeton: Princeton University Press.

Taylor, Robert M., ed. 1987. *The Northwest Ordinance, 1787: A Bicentennial Handbook*. Indianapolis: Indiana Historical Society.

Teichgraeber, Richard. 1981. "Rethinking the Adam Smith Problem." *Journal of British Studies* 20, no. 2: 106–123. https://doi.org/10.1086/385775.

Tempest, Kathryn. 2011. *Cicero: Politics and Persuasion in Ancient Rome*. London: A&C Black.

Teschke, Benno. 2003. *The Myth of 1648: Class, Geopolitics, and the Making of Modern International Relations*. London: Verso.

Tett, Gillian. 2022. "ESG Exposed in a World of Changing Priorities." *Financial Times*. June 2. https://www.ft.com/content/6356cc05-93a5-4f56-9d18-85218bc8bb0c.

Tierney, Brian. 1987. "Religion and Rights: A Medieval Perspective." *Journal of Law and Religion* 5, no. 1: 163–175. https://doi.org/10.2307/1051023.

Tierney, Brian. 1997. *The Idea of Natural Rights*. Atlanta: Scholars Press.

Tierney, Brian. 1998. *Foundations of the Conciliar Theory*. New York: Brill.

Tiku, Nitasha. 2019."Three Years of Misery inside Google, the Happiest Company in Tech," *Wired*. August 13. http://www.wired.com/story/inside-google-three-years-mis ery-happiest-company-tech/.

Tilly, Charles. 1993. "Social Movements as Historically Specific Clusters of Political Performances." *Berkeley Journal of Sociology* 38: 1–30. https://www.jstor.org/stable/41035464.

Tilly, Charles. 2004. *Contention and Democracy in Europe, 1650–2000*. New York: Cambridge University Press.

Tilly, Charles. 2007a. *Democracy*. New York. Cambridge University Press.

230 BIBLIOGRAPHY

Tilly, Charles. 2007b. "Trust Networks in Transnational Migration." *Sociological Forum* 22, no. 1: 3–24. https://doi.org/10.1111/j.1573-7861.2006.00002.x.

Tilly, Charles. 2008. *Contentious Performances*. New York: Cambridge University Press.

Tilly, Charles, and Lesley J. Wood. 2019. "Social Movements Enter the Twenty-First Century." In *Social Movements, 1768–2018*, edited by Charles Tilly, Ernesto Castañeda, and Lesley J. Wood, 99–127. New York: Routledge.

Tocqueville, Alexis. 2000 [1840]. *Democracy in America*. Chicago: University of Chicago Press.

Tomlinson, Jim. 1980. "British Politics and Co-Operatives." *Capital & Class* 4, no. 3: 58–65. https://doi.org/10.1177/030981688001200104.

Tönnies, Ferdinand. 2001 [1887]. *Community and Civil Society*. Cambridge: Cambridge University Press.

Touraine, Alain. 1981. *The Voice and the Eye: An Analysis of Social Movements*. Cambridge: Cambridge University Press.

Treib, Oliver. 2014. "The Voter Says No, but Nobody Listens: Causes and Consequences of the Eurosceptic Vote in the 2014 European Elections." *Journal of European Public Policy* 21, no. 10: 1541–1554. https://doi.org/10.1080/13501763.2014.941534.

Tropp, Linda R., and Thomas F. Pettigrew. 2005. "Relationships Between Intergroup Contact and Prejudice among Minority and Majority Status Groups." *Psychological Science* 16, no. 12: 951–957. https://doi.org/10.1111/j.1467-9280.2005.01643.x.

Tsui, Amy B., and James W. Tollefson. 2017. *Language Policy, Culture, and Identity in Asian Contexts*. London: Routledge.

Tsutsui, Kiyoteru, and Hwa Ji Shin. 2008. "Global Norms, Local Activism, and Social Movement Outcomes: Global Human Rights and Resident Koreans in Japan." *Social Problems* 55, no. 3: 391–418. https://doi.org/10.1525/sp.2008.55.3.391.

Turner, John C., Michael A. Hogg, Penelope J. Oakes, Stephen D. Reicher, and Margaret S. Wetherell, eds. 1987. *Rediscovering the Social Group: A Self-Categorization Theory*. Oxford: Blackwell.

Tyler, Tom R., and Peter Degoey. 1995. "Collective Restraint in Social Dilemmas: Procedural Justice and Social Identification Effects on Support for Authorities." *Journal of Personality and Social Psychology* 69, no. 3: 482–497. https://doi.org/10.1037/0022-3514.69.3.482.

Ullmann, Walter. 2013. *Medieval Papalism*. London: Routledge.

United Nations. 2022. "The World Largest Corporate Initiative." *UN Global Compact*. https://www.unglobalcompact.org/what-is-gc.

United Nations General Assembly.1948. "Universal Declaration of Human Rights." *UN General Assembly* 302, no. 2: 14–25. https://www.un.org/en/about-us/universal-declaration-of-human-rights.

United Nations Human Rights. 2012. "The Corporate Responsibility to Respect Human Rights." https://www.ohchr.org/Documents/Publications/HR.PUB.12.2_En.pdf.

University of South Florida. 2021. "Global Citizens Project Far Exceeds Goal." *USF News*. https://www.usf.edu/news/2021/global-citizens-project-far-exceeds-goal.aspx.

Vallier, Kevin. 2021. *Trust in a Polarized Age*. Oxford: Oxford University Press.

Van de Mieroop, Marc. 2016. *A History of the Ancient Near East, ca. 3000–323 BC*. Malden, MA: John Wiley & Sons.

Van Dijck, Maarten F., Bert De Munck, and Nicholas Terpstra. 2017. "Relocating Civil Society: Theories and Practices of Civil Society between Late Medieval and Modern Society." *Social Science History* 41, no. 1: 1–17. https://doi.org/10.1017/ssh.2016.35.

BIBLIOGRAPHY 231

Van Kessel, Stijn. 2015. *Populist Parties in Europe: Agents of Discontent?* New York: Springer.

Van Oudenhoven, Jan Pieter, Jan Tjeerd Groenewoud, and Miles Hewstone. 1996. "Cooperation, Ethnic Salience and Generalization of Interethnic Attitudes." *European Journal of Social Psychology* 26, no. 4: 649–661. https://doi.org/10.1002/(SICI)1099-0992(199607)26:4<649::AID-EJSP780>3.0.CO;2-T.

Vardi, Liana. 1988. "The Abolition of the Guilds during the French Revolution." *French Historical Studies* 15, no. 4: 704–717. https://doi.org/10.2307/286554.

Veblen, Thorstein. 1994 [1899]. *The Theory of the Leisure Class*. London: Penguin.

Verhoeven, Amaryllis. 1998. "Europe Beyond Westphalia: Can Postnational Thinking Cure Europe's Democracy Deficit?" *Maastricht Journal of European and Comparative Law* 5, no. 4: 369–390. https://doi.org/10.1177/1023263X9800500404.

Vibert, Frank. 2007. *The Rise of the Unelected: Democracy and the New Separation of Powers*. Cambridge: Cambridge University Press.

Vick, Brian E. 2002. *Defining Germany: The 1848 Frankfurt Parliamentarians and National Identity*. Cambridge, MA: Harvard University Press.

Viner, Jacob. 1958. *The Long View and the Short: Studies in Economic Theory and Policy*. Chicago, IL: The Free Press.

Viner, Jacob. 1978. *Religious Thought and Economic Society: Four Chapters of an Unfinished Work by Jacob Viner*. Edited by Jacques Melitz and Donald Winch. Durham, NC: Duke University Press.

Vink, Maarten Peter, and Rainer Bauböck. 2013. "Citizenship Configurations: Analysing the Multiple Purposes of Citizenship Regimes in Europe." *Comparative European Politics* 11, no. 5: 621–648. https://doi.org/10.1057/cep.2013.14.

Viren, Sarah. 2021. "The Native Scholar Who Wasn't." *New York Times*. May 25. https://www.nytimes.com/2021/05/25/magazine/cherokee-native-american-andrea-smith.html.

Viroli, Maurizio. 1992. "The Revolution in the Concept of Politics." *Political Theory* 20, no. 3: 473–495. https://doi.org/10.1177/0090591792020003005.

Vishnia, Rachel Feig. 2012. *State, Society and Popular Leaders in Mid-Republican Rome 241–167 BC*. London: Routledge.

Vitale, Alessandro. 2016. "Myths of Territory and External Borders in the EU's Contemporary Idea and Europe in the Middle Ages." *Acta Universitatis Lodziensis. Folia Geographica Socio-Oeconomica* 26, no. 4: 63–80. http://dx.doi.org/10.18778/1508-1117.26.04.

Vogel, Ezra F. 1965. "From Friendship to Comradeship: The Change in Personal Relations in Communist China." *The China Quarterly* 21: 46–60. https://doi.org/10.1017/S0305741000048463.

Vogel, Ezra F. 1969. *Canton under Communism: Programs and Politics in a Provincial Capital, 1949–1968*. Cambridge, MA: Harvard University Press.

Von Bülow, Marisa. 2010. *Building Transnational Networks: Civil Society and the Politics of Trade in the Americas*. New York: Cambridge University Press.

Von Dassow, Eva. 2011. *Freedom in Ancient Near Eastern Societies*. New York: Oxford University Press.

Von Dassow, Eva. 2018. "Liberty, Bondage and Liberation in the Late Bronze Age." *History of European Ideas* 44, no. 6: 658–684. https://doi.org/10.1080/01916599.2018.1513246.

Von Dassow, Eva. 2023. "Citizens and Non-Citizens in the Age of Hammurabi." In *Citizenship in Antiquity: Civic Communities in the Ancient Mediterranean*, edited by Filonik, Jakub, Christine Plastow, and Rachel Zelnick-Abramovitz, 81–110. London: Routledge.

232 BIBLIOGRAPHY

Wakabayashi, Daisuke, and Katie Benner. 2018. "How Google Protected Andy Rubin, the 'Father of Android.'" *The New York Times*. October 25. https://www.nytimes.com/2018/10/25/technology/google-sexual-harassment-andy-rubin.html?action=click&module=Top+Stories&pgtype=Homepage.

Wakeman Jr., Frederic. 1993. "The Civil Society and Public Sphere Debate: Western Reflections on Chinese Political Culture." *Modern China* 19, no. 2: 108–138.

Waley, Daniel Philip, and Trevor Dean. 2013. *The Italian City Republics*. London: Routledge.

Waller, Richard. 2013. "Ethnicity and Identity." In *The Oxford Handbook of Modern African History*, edited by John Parker and Richard Reid, 94–113. Oxford: Oxford University Press.

Walzer, Michael. 1982. *The Revolution of the Saints: A Study in the Origins of Radical Politics*. Cambridge, MA: Harvard University Press.

Wann, Daniel L., and Frederick G. Grieve. 2005. "Biased Evaluations of In-group and Out-group Spectator Behavior at Sporting Events: The Importance of Team Identification and Threats to Social Identity." *The Journal of Social Psychology* 145, no. 5: 531–546. https://doi.org/10.3200/SOCP.145.5.531-546.

Wanyama, Frederick O. 2008. "The Qualitative and Quantitative Growth of the Cooperative Movement in Kenya." In *Cooperating Out of Poverty: The Renaissance of the African Cooperative Movement*, edited by Patrick Develtere, Ignace Pollet, and Frederick O. Wanayma, 91–127. Geneva: International Labour Office.

Ward, Benjamin. 1958. "The Firm in Illyria: Market Syndicalism." *The American Economic Review* 48, no. 4: 566–589.

Watner, Carl. 2005. "Quod Omnes Tangit: Consent Theory in the Radical Libertarian Tradition in the Middle Ages." *Journal of Libertarian Studies* 19, no. 2: 67–85.

Weber, Eugen. 1976. *Peasants into Frenchmen: The Modernization of Rural France, 1870–1914*. Stanford: Stanford University Press.

Weber, Max. 1966. *The City*. Edited and Translated by Don Martindale and Gertrud Neuwirth. New York: Free Press.

Weber, Max. 2001 [1930]. *The Protestant Ethic and the Spirit of Capitalism*. New York: Routledge.

Weber, Max. 2019 [1922]. *Economy and Society*. Cambridge, MA: Harvard University Press.

Wedgwood, Cicely Veronica. 2005. *The Thirty Years War*. New York: New York Review of Books.

Weil, Patrick. 2008. *How to be French: Nationality in the Making since 1789*. Durham, NC: Duke University Press.

Weil, Patrick. 2012. *The Sovereign Citizen: Denaturalization and the Origins of the American Republic*. Philadelphia: University of Pennsylvania Press.

Weinfeld, Moshe. 1970. "The Covenant of Grant in the Old Testament and in the Ancient Near East." *Journal of the American Oriental Society* 90, no. 2: 184–203. https://doi.org/10.2307/598135.

Weintraub, Jeff. 1997. "The Theory and Politics of Public/Private Distinction." In *Public and Private in Thought and Practice: Perspectives on a Grand Dichotomy*, edited by Jeff Weintraub and Krishan Kumar, 1–42. Chicago: Chicago University Press.

Weller, Robert P. 2019. "Goddess Unbound: Chinese Popular Religion and the Varieties of Boundary." *The Journal of Religion* 99, no. 1: 18–36. https://doi.org/10.1086/700326.

BIBLIOGRAPHY 233

West, Martin. 2018. "Gilgameš and Homer: The Missing Link?" In *Wandering Myths: Transcultural Uses of Myth in the Ancient World*, edited by Lucy Audley-Miller and Beate Dignas, 265–280. Berlin: De Gruyter. https://doi.org/10.1515/9783110421453-011.

Westbrook, Raymond. 2003. *A History of Ancient Near Eastern Law*. New York: Brill.

Westbrook, Raymond. 2015. *Ex Oriente Lex: Near Eastern Influences on Ancient Greek and Roman Law*. Baltimore: Johns Hopkins University Press.

Westenholz, Aagen. 2002. "The Sumerian City-State." In *A Comparative Study of Six City-state Cultures: An Investigation*, edited by Mogen Herman Hansen, 22–42. Copenhagen: Videnskabernes Selskab.

Whyte, Kathleen King, and William Foote Whyte. 1991. *Making Mondragón: The Growth and Dynamics of the Worker Cooperative Complex*. Ithaca: Cornell University Press.

Wicksteed, Philip. H. 2016 [1910]. *The Common Sense of Political Economy*. Sidney: Wentworth.

Wilberforce, William. 2007. *An Appeal to the Religion, Justice, and Humanity of the Inhabitants of the British Empire*. New York: Cosimo Classics.

Williams, Frederick D., ed. 2012. *The Northwest Ordinance: Essays on Its Formulation, Provisions, and Legacy*. East Lansing, MI: Michigan State University Press.

Withol, Diane. 2010. *In and Out of the Marital Bed: Seeing Sex in Late Medieval and Early Modern Art*. New Haven: Yale University Press.

Yack, Bernard. 1999. "The Myth of the Civic Nation." In *Theorizing Nationalism*, edited by Ronald Beiner, 103–118. Albany: SUNY Press.

Yamagishi, Toshio, and Toko Kiyonari. 2000. "The Group as the Container of Generalized Reciprocity." *Social Psychology Quarterly* 63, no. 2: 116–132. https://doi.org/10.2307/2695887.

Yavari, Asadollah, and Zahra Azhar. 2017. "The Origins of Nation and Subjecthood in Ancient Rome: From Gens to Subjecthood, from Citizenship to Nation." *Comparative Law Review* 8, no. 1: 343–360. https://doi.org/10.22059/JCL.2017.62540.

Yoran, Hanan. 2007. "Florentine Civic Humanism and the Emergence of Modern Ideology." *History and Theory* 46, no. 3: 326–344. https://doi.org/10.1111/j.1468-2303.2007.00413.x.

Zachman, Randall C. 2002. "Protestantism in German-speaking Lands to the Present Day." In *The Blackwell Companion to Protestantism*, edited by Alister E. McGrath and Darren C. Marks. Oxford: Blackwell.

Zerubavel. Eviatar. 1991. *The Fine Line*. Chicago: Chicago University Press.

Zizek, Slavoj. 2011. "Shoplifters of the World Unite." *London Review of Books* 19: 8–11.

Zuboff, Shoshana. 2019. *The Age of Surveillance Capitalism: The Fight for a Human Future at the New Frontier of Power*. New York: Public Affairs.

Zuckert, Michael. 2007. "The Fullness of Being: Thomas Aquinas and the Modern Critique of Natural Law." *The Review of Politics* 69, no. 1: 28–47. https://doi.org/10.1017/S0034670507000307.

Index

For the benefit of digital users, indexed terms that span two pages (e.g., 52–53) may, on occasion, appear on only one of those pages

Agamben, Giorgio, 39n.2
American republicanism, 83–85
ancient and classical periods
 chosenness and, 32
 democratic practices and, 38
 demos and *ethnos* distinction and, 31
 development of citizenship in, 26–33
 enslaved persons in, 35
 free bodies in, 35
 genealogy of citizenship and, 26
 Greek model of citizenship in, 26–27, 29–30, 34–38
 Indian model of citizenship in, 32–33
 individual freedom and, 29–30, 32, 34–35
 interest and identity and, 37
 Israel's model of citizenship in, 26–27, 28–29, 31–32
 judicial conception of citizenship in, 36
 kinship to citizenship in, 26–33
 legal rights in, 28
 nationality developed in, 30–32
 Near East model of citizenship in, 27–30, 31–32, 34–35
 overview of, 24–25
 primordialism and, 36–37
 property and, 37–38
 public assemblies and, 28
 public spaces and, 38
 rights and obligations in, 28, 35–36, 38
 Roman model of citizenship in, 26–27, 34–38
 roots of citizenship in, 25–26
 rulemaking and, 34–35
 social community and, 34–35
 territoriality and, 30–33

Anderson, Benedict, 64–65
antisemitism, 9, 77–78, 80, 81, 90
Aquinas, Thomas, 66–67
Aristotle, 28, 113–14
autonomy, 1, 11, 24, 29–30, 58, 102–3

Bachmann, Ingeborg, 185
Bauböck, Rainer, 97, 142, 183n.2
Bentham, Jeremy, 115–16
Bismarck, Otto von, 81, 82
Black, Antony, 5, 42–43, 48–49, 56
Block, Fred, 138
Blut und Boden concept, 81–82, 84
borders and boundaries, 17–19, 54–55, 107, 120–23, 130–32, 140, 141–43
Bose, Satyajit, 20, 155–56
Bosniak, Linda, 23n.6
Bourdieu, Pierre, 96
Brubaker, Rogers, 172, 173
Burckhardt, Jacob, 50–51
Burgess, J. S., 59

Campbell, Archibald, 116–17
canon law reform, 45–48
capitalism, 15, 16–17, 19–20, 55–56, 58, 64, 118–19, 128, 150
Cernekee, Kevin, 163–64
China
 Confucian China, 24–25, 33, 42, 56–57, 59, 60–61
 development of guilds in, 56–57
 guilds in, 42, 56–61
 influence on political authorities in, 59–60
 internal governance of guilds in, 60–61
 kinship and, 56–58

236 INDEX

China (*cont.*)
    nexus between citizenship missing in
        guilds in, 60–61
    outsiders in, 58–59
    territoriality in, 33
citizenship overview, 1–22
    ancient conception of citizenship, 1,
        4–5
    autonomy, 1
    city republics, 5
    classical period, 4–5
    collective action problems, 12–14
    communes, 5
    corporations, 5
    definition of citizenship, 3
    democratic practice diverting from
        citizenship principles, 2–3
    demos and *ethnos* distinction, 6, 12–14
    dual citizenship, 5–6
    grammar and logic of citizenship, 3–4,
        6, 7–9
    guilds, 5
    hinge of history, 4–5
    human condition challenged, 2
    identity, 1–2, 3, 12–14
    interests, 12–14
    kinship, 1–2
    nature and, 2
    paradox of citizenship, 2–3
    paradox of rights, 6, 9–12
    postnational citizenship, 5–6
    primordialism, 2
    promise of human rights and
        citizenship, 5–6
    propositions on citizenship, 6–19
    reviving citizenship, 4
    seams, 6, 17–19
    significance of citizenship, 1
    social embeddedness, 6, 14–17
    twenty-first century guild, 7, 19–22
    unfinished revolution, 5–6
civic education, 30, 117
civic habit, 55–56, 58
Clarke, Samuel, 116–17
classical period. *See* ancient and classical
    periods
Code of Justinian, 112
Code of Ur-Nammu, 28

collective action problems, 6, 12, 109–10,
    126
communism, 93–94, 119, 150, 174–75
Confucian China
    bureaucracy of, 59
    formal citizenship absent from, 60–61
    guilds in, 42, 56–57, 60–61
    kinship in, 24–25
    Qing Dynasty in, 33, 42, 57
    territoriality of, 33
Constantine, 46–47
corporations
    canon law reform sanctioning of, 5, 25,
        45–47, 48
    charters of, 176
    colonization and, 56–57
    digital economy and, 172
    ESG and, 20, 158, 160–61
    guilds and, 57–58, 61–62
    human rights and, 100, 102
    kinship and, 5
    legacy of, 48
    medieval period and, 5, 20, 25, 41–42,
        45–48, 53, 56–58
    modern corporations, 45–46, 48, 53, 56,
        155–56
    overview of, 5, 41–42
    postnationalism and, 106
    regulation of, 20
    twenty-first century guild and, 20–21,
        151–52, 155–57, 172, 173
Cotton, John, 84
Council of Nicaea (325 CE), 46–47

Damore, James, 164
Declaration of Independence, 32, 67–68,
    85
Declaration of the Rights of Man and
    the Citizen (France), 67–68, 76–77,
    94–95
democratic practices, 14, 16, 38, 42–43,
    118–20
demographic reductionism, 8, 139–40,
    186, 191–92
demos and *ethnos* distinction, 6, 12–14, 31,
    62, 110, 187–88, 190–91
diversity, 72, 105, 163–64, 186,
    188, 193

Dong, Guo, 155–56
Douglas, Stephen, 84
Durkheim, Émile, 133
Dutch East India Company, 5, 48, 176

Edward I, 113–14
Elias, Norbert, 7
embeddedness. *See* social
    embeddedness
Enlightenment, The
    American republicanism and, 83–85
    as beginning of modern world, 55–56,
        64, 71, 72–73
    civil rights and, 76–77
    conservative revolution of, 66–71
    constitutional patriotism and, 71–73
    French republicanism and, 75–78
    Germanic response and, 78–83
    human rights and, 87–88
    imagined community and, 64–65
    interest and identity and, 12–13,
        109–10
    international law and, 73–74
    ius sanguinis and, 75, 85
    ius soli and, 75, 85
    kinship and, 65, 70–73, 85
    laws of nature and, 66–71
    migration and, 85
    nationalism and, 64–65, 70, 71–73
    naturalization of categories in, 13,
        69–70, 74–75, 81–82, 85, 118
    natural rights and, 66–71, 76–77
    nature's God and, 66–71
    overview of, 64–65
    Peace of Westphalia and, 73–75
    populism and, 72
    primordialism and, 65, 70, 71, 72–73,
        75, 77–78, 88, 118
    privileging membership and, 73–75
    property and, 87–88
    race and, 77–78
    Romanticism and, 70–71
    self-interest and, 68–69
    subjectivity of, 68–69
    territoriality and, 65
ESG (environmental, social, and corporate
        governance)
    corporations and, 20, 158, 160–61

definition of, 20
examples of, 158–59
expansion of, 22
human rights and, 20, 155–61
increase in, 20
overview of, 20
twenty-first century guild and, 20–22,
    155–56, 174
ethnicity. *See* primordialism
ethnos. See demos and *ethnos* distinction
European Court of Human Rights, 94–95,
    102–3
European Union, 12, 97–98, 101, 103,
    105–6, 159

Ferrante, Elena, 194
Fever Pitch (Hornby), 129
Fewsmith, Joseph, 59, 61
Fichte, Johann Gottlieb, 78–79, 81
first revolution in citizenship. *See* ancient
    and classical periods
Florentine guilds, 50–52, 53, 55
Floyd, George, 91–92
Foucade, Marion, 172, 173
French Absolutism, 112
French republicanism, 75–78
French Revolution, 31–32, 46, 49, 62,
    64–65, 75–76, 77
Friedman, Lawrence, 89, 101
Friedman, Milton, 176

Gamble, Sidney, 59
Geertz, Clifford, 185
gender. *See* primordialism
Georgiev, Georgi, 184n.17
Germanic response to the Enlightenment,
    78–83
Gettysburg Address (1863), 84
Gierke, Otto von, 19–20
Gilman, Russon, 173
Goffman, Erving, 89
Goodwin-White, Jamie, 138–39, 148–
    49n.9, 154
Google case study for twenty-first century
    guild, 161–66
Gordon, Daniel, 75–76
grammar and logic of citizenship
    citizenship-like practices and, 9

238 INDEX

grammar and logic of citizenship (*cont.*)
  civic polity conception of citizenship and, 8
  demographic reductionism and, 8
  formal citizenship practices and, 24
  interest and identity and, 14
  kinship and, 7, 24
  medieval period and, 42
  nationalism and, 7
  overview of, 7–9
  primordialism and, 7–9
  relational process of citizenship and, 7
  seams and, 18–19, 135, 138
  social connectivity and, 8
Greek model of citizenship (ancient), 26–27, 29–30, 34–38
Green, Jeffrey, 173
Gregory VII, 5, 25, 45–46, 47–48
Grosby, Steven, 29, 30, 31
guilds. *See also* medieval period; twenty-first century guild
  Chinese guilds, 42, 56–61
  civic habit and, 55–56, 58
  corporations and, 57–58, 61–62
  European guilds, 48–50
  exclusionary nature of, 43–44
  Florentine guilds, 50–52
  influence on political authorities of, 59–60
  internal governance of, 44, 60–61
  as key instrument of citizenship, 42, 53–54
  limitations of, 44
  overview of, 48–50
  primordialism and, 43–44
  promise and cautionary tale of, 61–62
  republics and, 50–52
  as strike force of political reform, 53–54
  Venetian guilds, 50–52, 55
Gurri, Martin, 105–6, 172–73

Habermas, Jürgen, 55–56, 71–72, 110–11, 123–26
Handlin, Mary, 176
Handlin, Oscar, 176
Hansen, Randall, 92–93
Hegel, G. W. F., 15, 135–36
Henry VIII, 62–63n.2

Hirschman, Albert, 68
Histories, The (Herodotus), 26–27
Hobbes, Thomas, 66, 114, 117
Honneth, Alex, 15, 135–36
human rights
  balance of power and, 89
  as breaking down citizen-alien distinction, 97
  cascading of, 99–101
  corporations and, 100, 102
  cosmopolitan elite and, 106
  Declaration of the Rights of Man and the Citizen, 67–68, 76–77, 94–95
  development of, 87–93
  disenfranchisement and, 105
  diversity and, 105
  Enlightenment and, 87–88
  expansion of rights and, 89
  habitus and, 96
  identity politics and, 91–92, 104–7
  individual autonomy and, 102–3
  international law and, 94–95, 96–97, 99–100
  job performance of, 87–88
  judicialization and, 6, 11–12, 96, 99–101
  migration and, 95–97, 98, 99, 105–6
  misconceptions about, 91–92
  multiculturalism and, 91–92, 99, 104–5
  neoliberalism and, 106
  nexus between governed and governors weakened by, 90–91
  overview of, 87–93
  paradox of citizenship and, 106
  political legitimacy and, 90–91
  politics of rights and, 6, 96, 101, 103
  populism and, 99, 103, 105
  postnationalism and, 91–99, 106
  primordialism and, 87, 93–94, 100, 104–5
  property and, 87–90
  public interest and, 90
  refugee law and, 99, 105–6
  right to claim rights definition of citizenship, 9–10, 60–61, 87, 96
  seams and, 107
  second wave of, 155–61
  territoriality and, 92, 103
  as a tool, 3, 6, 9–10, 87, 193
  transnational citizenship and, 97

twenty-first century guild and, 155–61
two-edge effect of, 91
UDHR and, 94–95
working class and, 105
zoon politikon to *homo legalis* and,
   101–7
Hutcheson, Francis, 116–17

identity. *See* interest and identity
Indian model of citizenship (ancient),
   32–33
ingroup and outgroup thinking, 118–19,
   121–22, 126–27, 140, 141
Innocent X, 73–74
interest and identity
   ancient period and, 37
   borders and boundaries and, 120–23
   capitalism and, 118–19
   civic education and, 117
   collective action problems and, 109–10
   collective identity, 13–14, 31, 189–90,
      191
   collective interest, 37, 125–26, 133–34
   common good and, 116–17
   communism and, 119
   conflict between, 119–20
   creating just civil societies and, 123–26
   definition of identity and, 116–18
   democratic practices and, 14, 118–20
   demos and *ethnos* distinction and, 13,
      110
   Enlightenment and, 12–13, 109–10
   entanglement of, 118–20
   ever-changing community and, 126–28
   felt sense of identity, 13–14, 190
   general will and, 117
   grammar and logic of citizenship and,
      14
   historical and theoretical foundations
      of, 111–16
   identity politics, 13, 87, 90–92, 96,
      104–7, 118, 130, 146–47, 169
   ingroup and outgroup thinking and,
      118–19, 121–22, 126–27
   kinship and, 109
   leitmotifs of, 111–16
   limits of Rawls and Habermas, 123–26
   nationalism and, 13–14, 119

overview of, 12–13, 109–11
political legitimacy and, 113–15, 121
primordialism and, 13–14, 109, 118–20
public sphere and, 117, 124–26
self-interest and, 112–16, 119–20, 123–26
social contract and, 111, 114, 116
social movements and, 121–22
union of minds and, 116
universal norms and, 122
veil of ignorance and, 123–26
welfare state and, 115
international law, 73–74, 94–95, 96–97,
   99–100, 105–6
Isin, Engin, 60–61
Israel's model of citizenship (ancient),
   26–27, 28–29, 31–32
ius sanguinis, 2, 31–32, 75, 83, 85
ius soli, 2, 31–32, 75, 83, 85

Jacobson, David, 184n.17
Jefferson, Thomas, 87–88
Jennings, Ivor, 13
Jerome, St., 46–47, 51
John of Saxony, 116
judicialization, 6, 11–12, 96, 99–101
juridical democracy, 166–71, 175

Karataşlı, Şahan Savaş, 63n.6
Keene, John, 23n.4
Keynes, John Maynard, 19–20, 150–51
kinship
   agency and, 24–25
   ancient period and, 26–33
   celibacy and, 47
   citizenship as break from, 24
   corporations and, 5
   Enlightenment and, 65, 70–73, 85
   fictive kinship, 65, 137
   grammar and logic of citizenship and,
      7, 24
   honor and, 25
   interest and identity and, 109
   medieval period and, 41, 42, 47, 53
   terms of, 29
   territorial kinship, 29, 31–32, 65, 70–71
Kirkpatrick, Jeane, 108n.6
Kocka, Jürgen, 79–80
Kulke, Hermann, 32–33

240 INDEX

Landau, Peter, 45–46
law, international, 73–74, 94–95, 96–97, 99–100, 105–6
Laws of Eshnunna, 28
laws of nature, 66–71
Lebovics, Herman, 77
Le Pen, Marine, 187
Lewis, C. S., 67–68
Lincoln, Abraham, 32, 83–84
Lipit-Ishtar codex, 28
logic of citizenship. *See* grammar and logic of citizenship
Loury, Glen, 16, 144
Lowi, Theodore, 166–70

Maas, Willem, 183n.2
Machiavelli, Nicola, 112, 114, 116
Main Street Employee Ownership Act (2018), 175
Malik, Kenin, 104
Mandeville, Bernard, 114, 117
Marshall, T. H., 23n.6, 156
Mead, George Herbert, 135, 137–38, 139–40
medieval period
    borders and, 54–55
    canon law reform and, 45–48
    Chinese guilds and, 56–60
    civic developments after first millennium and, 45–48
    civic habit and, 55–56
    clerical celibacy and, 47
    community of faith and, 47
    corporations and, 5, 20, 25, 41–42, 45–48, 53, 56–58
    cults and, 46–47
    democratic practices and, 42–43
    European guilds, 48–50
    Florence and, 50–52, 53, 55
    grammar and logic of citizenship and, 42
    hierarchy and inequality challenged during, 51
    Italian cities and, 52–55
    kinship and, 41, 42, 47, 53
    law and, 46
    liberal individualism and, 56

overview of, 41–45, 61–62
    popes over princes conflict in, 46
    primordialism and, 41–42, 43
    promise and cautionary tale of guilds in, 61–62
    republics in, 50–52
    residency requirements in, 53
    Roman and Greek influence on, 52–55
    Venice and, 50–52, 55
    vita activa and, 51–52
Merkel, Angela, 91, 96–97
Messing, Vera, 139
migration, 71, 72, 85, 95–97, 98, 99, 105–6, 140, 155, 160–61, 187
Miller, Andrew, 185
Miller, David, 72, 93, 111
modernity. *See* Enlightenment, The
Moll-Murata, Christine, 58–59, 60–61
Mondragon Corporation, 143–44, 171
Montesquieu, 68–69, 89
More, Thomas, 46
Mosse, George, 78, 80–81
multiculturalism, 91–92, 99, 104–5, 109

nationalism. *See also* postnationalism
    ancient period and, 30–32
    collective identity and, 14
    Enlightenment and, 64–65, 70, 71–73
    ethnic nationalism, 15, 128
    grammar and logic of citizenship and, 7
    imagined communities and, 49, 64–65
    interest and identity and, 13–14, 119
    modern nation-state system, 73–75
    primordialism and, 74–75
    seams and, 130, 145–46
    social embeddedness and, 15
    territoriality and, 31–32
    third revolution and, 188–89
natural law, 66–71
Near East's model of citizenship (ancient), 27–30, 31–32, 34–35
neoliberalism, 105, 106, 156–57, 171, 176
New Right (France), 77–78
Newton, Isaac, 67
Northwest Ordinance (1787), 87–88

INDEX 241

Obama, Barack, 148n.8
Ogilvie, Sheilagh, 43–44, 48–49, 57–58, 176, 178
Oomen, Barbara, 183n.2
Opium War (1839-1841), 57
ordinal citizenship, 172
Orgad, Liav, 183n.2
Ottoman sultanate, 33
outgroup and ingroup thinking, 118–19, 121–22, 126–27, 140, 141

Page, Larry, 161–62, 164–65
paradox of citizenship, 2–3, 106
paradox of rights
  autonomy and, 11
  definition of citizenship and, 9–10
  democratic accountability and, 10–12
  expansion of rights and, 11
  judicialization and, 11
  key test of citizenship and, 9–10
  overview of, 9–12
  primordialism and, 9
  public interest and, 10–11
  rights *per se* vs *inter se*, 10
  as serving and devaluating citizenship, 9–12
  social embeddedness and, 9–10, 12
  tools of citizenship and, 9–10
Peace of Westphalia (1648), 31–32, 41, 73–75
Peng Nansheng, 60
Petrarch, 52
Philip of Hesse, 116
Pichai, Sundar, 164–65
Piketty, Thomas, 11
Plato, 35, 52
Plyer v. Doe (1982), 99
Pocock, J. G. A., 35–36, 101
Polanyi, Karl, 14–15, 135, 138, 171
political legitimacy, 71, 72, 75–76, 77, 82, 90–91, 113–15, 121, 152–53, 168, 178, 194–95
postnationalism. *See also* nationalism
  co-optation of, 106
  corporations and, 106
  human rights and, 91–99, 106
  multiculturalism as synonymous with, 99
  overview of, 5–6

postnational citizenship, 5–6, 91–92, 93, 96, 98, 99, 142, 145, 181–82
  sources of, 96–99
  territoriality and, 92, 95–96
  turn toward, 93–96
Prak, Maarten, 3, 44, 45, 177
primordialism
  ancient period and, 36–37
  definition of, 2
  demographic reductionism and, 8, 139–40, 186, 191–92
  Enlightenment and, 65, 70, 71, 72–73, 75, 77–78, 88, 118
  grammar and logic of citizenship and, 7–9
  guilds and, 43–44
  human rights and, 87, 93–94, 100, 104–5
  interest and identity and, 13–14, 109, 118–20
  medieval period and, 41–42, 43
  nationalism and, 74–75
  paradox of rights and, 9
  relational process of citizenship contrasted with, 7
  seams and, 131–32
  social embeddedness and, 15
  third revolution and, 185–86
property, 37–38, 87–90
Protestant Reformation, 4–5, 26–27, 32, 34, 48, 116
public sphere, 38, 115, 117, 121, 124–26

Qing Dynasty, 33, 42, 57

race. *See* primordialism
Rahman, K., 173
Rawls, John, 110–11, 123–26
Reich, Charles, 88–89
relational basis of citizenship, 7, 14–16, 18–19, 131–33, 134–38, 181, 193–94
Renaissance, 112, 114–15
republicanism, 21, 65, 71, 75–78, 83–85
revolutions in citizenship. *See* ancient and classical periods; Enlightenment, The; medieval period; third revolution
rights, human. *See* human rights

242 INDEX

rights, paradox of. *See* paradox of rights
right to claim rights definition of
     citizenship, 9–10, 60–61, 87, 96
Roman model of citizenship (ancient),
     26–27, 34–38
Rosenberg, Jonathan, 162
Rothermund, Dietmar, 32–33
Rousseau, Jean-Jacques, 39n.12, 67, 75,
     117
Rowe, W. T., 58
Ruffer, Galya, 102, 157–58
Rule of Benedict, 46–47
ruling and being ruled principle, 4–5, 35,
     101

Ságvári, Bence, 139
Santos, Mateus Rennó, 184n.17
scalar conception of citizenship, 18–19, 21,
     97, 135, 142–43, 146
Schmidt, Eric, 162
Schneider, Nathan, 174
Scotson, John, 7
Scott, James, 16–17
seams
   adversarial politics and, 130
   alien-other and, 130–31
   borders and boundaries contrasted
       with, 17–19, 107, 130–32, 140
   civic project and, 143–48
   COVID-19 and, 142–43
   definition of, 132–34
   demographic reductionism and, 139–40
   grammar and logic of citizenship and,
       18–19, 135, 138
   human rights and, 107
   international borders to global seams,
       141–43
   kinetic quality of, 134, 136–37, 140, 143
   moving beyond insiders and outsiders
       in, 134
   multivalent ties and, 138–41
   nationalism and, 130, 145–46
   overview of, 6, 17–19, 129–30
   primordialism and, 131–32
   relational logic of citizenship and,
       134–38
   scalar conception of citizenship and,
       18–19, 135, 142–43, 146

social embeddedness and, 144–45
transnational ties and, 141–43
trust and, 139, 147
twenty-first century guild and, 153
second revolution in citizenship. *See*
     Enlightenment, The; medieval period
sex. *See* primordialism
Shachar, Ayelet, 92
Shin, Hwa Ji, 93
Simmel, Georg, 133
Simpson, Anne, 155–56
Slave Trade Act (1807), 108n.5
Smith, Adam, 68–69, 113, 117
social embeddedness
   capitalism and, 16–17
   definition of, 14–15
   democratic practices and, 16
   disembedment contrasted with, 16–17
   ego and, 15
   nationalism and, 15
   overview of, 6, 14–17
   paradox of rights and, 9–10, 12
   primordiality and, 15
   as recognizable by left and right, 16
   relational basis of citizenship and,
       14–16
   seams and, 144–45
   solidarity and, 16
   twenty-first century guild and, 178
social trust, 72, 74, 90–91, 139, 152–53,
     154–55, 178, 181, 189, 194–95
Somers, Margaret, 8, 16, 138, 144
Spinoza, Baruch, 116
Spiro, Peter, 146
Stanish, Charles, 23n.2
Stasavage, David, 23n.4
suing and being sued principle, 4–5, 36,
     101
Sumerian city-states, 30

Taiping Rebellion (1850-1864), 57
Taylor, Alison, 160, 178–79
territoriality
   ancient period and, 30–33
   autonomy and, 1
   Confucian China and, 33
   Enlightenment and, 65
   human rights and, 92, 103

Italian republics and, 55
migration and, 85
nationalism and, 31–32
Ottoman sultanate and, 33
postnationalism and, 92, 95–96
unbounded territoriality, 33
Tett, Gillian, 22
Thiel, Peter, 164
third revolution in citizenship
adversarial politics and, 185–86
citizenship as collective identity and, 189–91
civic nation and, 187–89
civic polity and, 191–93
demographic reductionism and, 185–86
demos and *ethnos* distinction and, 187–88, 190–91
getting buy-in for, 194–95
integration and, 187
ius civitas and, 193–95
migration and, 187
nationalism and, 188–89
overview of, 5–6, 185–87
primordialism and, 185–86
Thirty Years War, 73–74
Tiku, Nitasha, 161–63, 166
Tocqueville, Alexis, 114–15
Tönnies, Ferdinand, 56, 82–83
transnational citizenship, 97–98, 142
Treaty of Paris (1814), 108n.5
Treaty of Westphalia (1648), 31–32, 41, 73–75
Trump, Donald, 99, 105, 164
Tsutsui, Kiyoteru, 93
twenty-first century guild
accountability and, 21
advantages of, 20–21, 151–54
AI as prompting, 172–73
boards and, 177
charters and, 175–76
civic purpose and, 170, 176–79
corporations and, 20–21, 151–52, 155–57, 172, 173

digital economy as prompting, 172–73
ESG and, 20–22, 155–61, 174
Google case study and, 161–66
human rights and, 155–61
juridical democracy and, 166–71, 175
migration and, 155
as nexus of citizenship, 21
ordinal citizenship and, 172
as overcoming rupture, 21
overview of, 7, 19–22, 150–55
political legitimacy and, 20–21, 168
seams and, 153
social embeddedness and, 178
social trust and, 154–55
special interest politics and, 166–67
stakeholders and, 155, 160, 177
state's role for, 180–83
structure of, 174–79
trade unions and, 175
universities' role for, 179–80

United Nations, 73–74, 94, 159
Universal Declaration of Human Rights (UDHR), 94–95
University of Bologna, 179–80

Van Dijck, Maarten, 55–56
veil of ignorance, 123–26
Venetian guilds, 50–52, 55
virtual citizenship, 102, 157–58
von Dassow, Eva, 27–28

Wakeman, Frederic, 63n.8
Weber, Eugene, 77–78
Weber, Max, 58
Westbrook, Raymond, 28–29
women. *See* primordialism
Work, Robert, 163

Yack, Bernard, 14, 187–89
Yoran, Hanan, 51

zoon politikon to *homo legalis*, 101–7
Zuboff, Shoshanna, 172